'A legendary ... life ... you to discover.'
Jet Li

'I was always a big ... was like a dream come true. His innovative and creative ability was unmatched.'
Chris Tucker

'Jackie reminds me to make every summer count and to think with my heart, he leads by example and lights the way.' Adrien Brody

'Working with Jackie Chan is maybe the most fun I've ever had wo... on movies.' Owen Wilson

'Jackie Chan is one of the great and iconic movie stars of our time.'
Jeffrey Katzenberg

'The legendary action star gets candid telling his life story – in particular, recounting his many brushes with death both on and off screen. You'll be hard-pressed to find a Hollywood memoir with this much blood and (broken) bone. Chan's stories are too fascinating to ignore.'
Entertainment Weekly

'This life story, as told in the star's impossibly colourful memoir *Never Grow Up*, would have Charles Dickens speed-dialling Chan's film agent for movie rights – with tales of Chan's impoverished youth (from age six, enrolled in the abusive China Drama Academy), lost loves, undying ambition fuelled by his insecurity over his upbringing, true bravery and eventual glory.' *USA Today*

'The book is definitively warts (and cracked skulls and broken bones and gallons of blood) and all . . . but Chan also reveals a soulful, thoughtful side – just one you wouldn't want to mess with.' *Kirkus Reviews*

'Undeniably fun . . . winningly upbeat . . . it provides a heck of a lot of entertainment.' *Publishers Weekly*

'With 200-plus films, an honorary Oscar and countless mind-blowing stunts to his credit, the martial arts master reflects here on his remarkable acting career. Chan shares how through the ups and downs, he was able to keep his grace, poise and humility.' *CBS Watch! Magazine*

'Like Chan's best films, his memoir is engaging and entertaining.'
Shelf Awareness

NEVER GROW UP

JACKIE CHAN
with Zhu Mo

TRANSLATED BY JEREMY TIANG

First published in China as *Never Grow Up, Only Get Older*
by Jiangsu Literature and Art Publishing House, 2015
First published in Great Britain by Simon & Schuster UK Ltd, 2018
This paperback edition published by Simon & Schuster UK Ltd, 2019
A CBS COMPANY

1 3 5 7 9 10 8 6 4 2

Simon & Schuster UK Ltd
1st Floor
222 Gray's Inn Road
London WC1X 8HB

www.simonandschuster.co.uk
www.simonandschuster.com.au
www.simonandschuster.co.in

Simon & Schuster Australia, Sydney
Simon & Schuster India, New Delhi

A CIP catalogue record for this book
is available from the British Library.

Paperback ISBN: 978-1-4711-7725-5
eBook ISBN: 978-1-4711-7724-8

Interior design by Davina Mock-Maniscalco
Printed and bound by CPI Group (UK) Ltd, Croydon, CR0 4YY

FSC www.fsc.org MIX Paper from responsible sources FSC® C020471

To my parents

contents

introduction

In 2016, I received an honorary Academy Award for my lifetime achievement in film. After fifty-six years, making over two hundred films, and breaking many bones, I never thought I'd win one, so getting the call was like a dream come true.

At the time, I was filming in Taiwan. My manager, Joe Tam, called and said that the Motion Picture Academy's president, Cheryl Boone Isaacs, would love to talk to me. Cheryl and I got on the phone and she shared the incredible news.

When I say "incredible," it's because I didn't quite believe it. I asked, "Are you sure you want *me*?"

The night of the Governors Awards was pure Hollywood magic. I sat at the award ceremony next to my old friend and costar Arnold

Schwarzenegger. I had no idea what was going to happen, and was surprised by the three presenters who introduced me.

First, Tom Hanks—*Tom Hanks!*—whom I've never worked with but feel like I know well, called me "Chan-Tastic" three times: "Jackie Chan, the man who puts the 'Chan' in 'Chan-Tastic,' because he has worked mostly in martial arts films and action comedies, two genres that have been, for some reason, shall we say, historically underrepresented at the Oscars. A fact that would change if *I* have any pull on the board of governors," he said. "It is especially gratifying to be able to acknowledge Jackie's enormous creativity, his great gift for physical performance, and incredible dedication to his work with this Governors Award tonight.

"Great acting comes in many different forms, but if you're an actor you always know it when you see it. Now, Jackie Chan's films have been incredibly serious, sometimes gruesomely so, as well as incredibly hilarious to the point of delighting millions of peoples around the globe. On one hand, you could say, out of China came another version of John Wayne—the serious films—and out of China came Buster Keaton—the comedic films. How is this possible out of one man? His talents must be truly Chan-Tastic. But Jackie does something that neither of those screen legends was ever able to do. Neither of those great, great artists of the cinema ever put the bloopers on during the closing credits, and those outtakes never showed John Wayne or Buster Keaton fracturing his elbow or tearing his plantar fascia. That's just one of the main reasons why the actors' branch is so pleased to be honoring Jackie the Chan-Tastic Chan."

He's right about the outtakes. Starting with *The Young Master* in

1980, my films have always ended with a postcredits bloopers reel. Along with clips of me messing up my lines or making other mistakes, most of them have to do with stunts gone wrong, so I look ridiculous as I crash to the ground and the crew rushes over.

Then Michelle Yeoh, who is like a little sister to me, talked about our long friendship. "As moviegoers around the world know, Jackie Chan has always been full of surprises," she said. "He surprised me the very first time I met him thirty years ago. I had flown to Hong Kong to shoot a commercial with a superstar called Shing Lung. I hadn't heard of him, but as soon as he walked in I said, 'That's Jackie Chan, that's not Shing Lung.' . . . Of course I recognized him instantly, I knew him by his distinctive loping walk, his giant smile, and by the cloud of infectious exuberance that surrounds him wherever he goes. Jackie is a generous performer. He is as generous to his costars as he is to his audiences. But I would say he's also highly competitive. The problem is, so am I. When we were making *Super Cop*, we went toe to toe. If I did a stunt, then Jackie would have to do an even more amazing one. And I would have to beat that. . . . Jackie pulled me aside and said, 'We have to stop. You roll off the roof of a car, I have to roll off the roof of a building. You jump on the train in a motorcycle, I have to do it in a helicopter. If this keeps up, I'm going to end up dead.'

"But you survived, like always," Michelle continued. "Many show business veterans have received Governors Awards over the years, but tonight, Jackie Chan is the first little boy to win one. His friends and his fans know that Jackie has discovered the secret of eternal youth. He is actually the same as the day I met him. Honest, funny, kind, and, despite the years, still possesses an astonishing physical prowess."

They showed a montage video of some of my scenes, and finally, Chris Tucker, my dear friend and costar on the *Rush Hour* series, came onstage. "The great Jackie Chan . . ." he said. "Working with a living legend was amazing. Every day, I couldn't wait to come on the set to see Jackie Chan. I was late most of the time, but when I got there, Jackie was waiting with his legs crossed, saying, 'Where's Chris Tucker? We are late!' But he didn't complain. He knew I was this young kid who, you know, didn't know his lines, but he went with the flow. Jackie, it was just an honor to work with you and I can't wait to work with you again. . . . You made a lot of people rich, Jackie. A lot of people rich. But honestly, working with Jackie got me global notoriety, too, from the *Rush Hour* movies . . . automatically, working with a global star like Jackie Chan. So I was blessed. I thank you for that, Jackie. . . . I love you, man, you're part of me . . . And congratulations! And I'm so thrilled and honored to be a part of this, to present to you, my good friend, Jackie Chan!"

As I walked up to get the golden statue, I was very touched. Seeing Michelle and Chris, as well as old friends like Sylvester Stallone, in the audience, made me feel like a kid coming home to his family. Later, I found out Joe worked with the Academy to get my pals there to give me such a big surprise.

I gave a little speech, too.

> *I still can't believe I'm standing here. This is a dream. . . . Every year when I watched the Oscars with my dad and mom,*

my dad always said to me, "Son, you've got so many movie awards in the world, when do you get one of these?"

Then I'd just look at my dad—ha ha ha—"Dad, I only make comedy action movies."

Many years later, I came to Hollywood to have meetings with big studio directors. My friend's house—Stallone's house. That was twenty-three years ago. I see [an Oscar] in his house. I touched it, I kissed it, I smelled it. I believe it still has my fingerprints on it. . . . Then I talk to myself, "I really want one." . . .

Finally, this is mine. I want to thank you, Hong Kong, incredible city, my hometown, my 'hood, who made me. China, my country. Proud to be Chinese! Thank you, Hollywood, for all those years, teaching me so many things, and also making me a little bit famous. And I thank you, my family, my wife, Joan, my son, Jaycee, especially, Jackie Chan Stunt Team—this year is the Jackie Chan Stunt Team's forty-year anniversary . . . Thank you from the bottom of my heart. . . . My fans around the world, because of you, I have reason to continue to make movies, jumping in windows, kicking and punching—breaking my bones.

—

We had dinner and there was a party afterwards. As soon as we returned to the hotel, everything was back to normal. The next day, I was right back to work, going to script meetings and discussing new projects.

Michelle said that I'd discovered the secret of youth and that I still had a little boy's heart. I think she had a point there. The way to never grow up is to love what you do. I love movies. Making them keeps me young at heart. Most of the time, I forget how old I am! Whenever I see my son, Jaycee, who is thirty-five, I remember I am sixty-four.

For many, many years, I never thought winning an Oscar was remotely possible. I was famous in Asia but didn't think anyone in America would notice my work. They didn't, actually, until I was in my forties and had made scores of films. So to get the encouragement and recognition from Hollywood—while I'm still young!—was deeply gratifying. And I'm the first Chinese filmmaker in history to receive the award.

The real honor and reward, the one I treasure the most, is getting to live out my childhood dreams in the movies for so long and so well. I intend to keep going.

I've actually set myself a goal of winning another little golden statue. I don't think the Oscars have a rule where you can't win one for acting or directing if you've already won the lifetime honor, right?

Well, my lifetime isn't over yet! At sixty-four, I'm just getting started.

chapter one

CANNONBALL

I was born in Hong Kong on April 7, 1954, the year of the horse. My father named me Chan Kong-Sang, which means "born in Hong Kong."

When I was still in my mom's belly, I was already a naughty child, and liked to move around and kick. There's nothing strange about that, but the weird thing was, my mom carried me for well over the usual nine months. I refused to come out. One day she found herself in unbearable pain, so my dad rushed her to the hospital. She lay there writhing in agony, squirming so much she ended up underneath the bed. After examining her, the doctor said the baby was too big, and this might be a difficult birth. She suggested a cesarean instead.

Now, a cesarean cost several hundred dollars and my parents didn't have that kind of money. The doctor, who had no kids of her own, had a proposal for my dad. If they gave her their baby, not only would she perform the surgery for free, she'd pay them an additional $500. That was a lot of money, and my dad actually considered her offer for a split second. At the time, it was common practice for poor people to give their babies away to be raised by the rich. Not only would the parents get some cash, but they'd guarantee a better life for their children. Fortunately, my parents decided against this option. After all, I was their first child, and maybe their only. My mom was already forty, and might not be able to have another.

My dad signed the consent form for the surgery. Two hours later, I emerged from my mother's belly, weighing in at *twelve pounds*. The doctor and my parents were stunned. My huge size was even reported in the local papers under the headline "Giant Baby." Because I was so hefty, my parents nicknamed me Cannonball. My parents' friends said, "A twelve-pound baby! This kid might end up doing something spectacular!" They even lent my dad some money to pay off his debt to the doctor.

In the 1950s, my parents had fled mainland China for Hong Kong, and found work at the French consulate as a chef and a maid. They were quite lucky for refugees of that era. Even though my parents didn't have much money, we lived in the opulent embassy district Victoria Peak, except we didn't have a magnificent house that faced the street. Our home was run-down, small, and stuck in the back. The folks at the consulate treated us well, but from the very beginning, we existed in two different worlds.

Our home was very clean and very crowded. The three of us were squeezed into a few dozen square feet. My mom polished the furniture that my dad made with his own hands. There wasn't enough room for two beds, so we slept in bunk beds, my parents on the top and me below. I wasn't a good sleeper. I had a screaming fit every night, making such a racket that I woke up the consulate residents. They sometimes came to see if something was wrong, which embarrassed my parents. Some nights, I was so loud, neighbors a few houses away could be heard yelling, "Whose kid is that? Shut up!" When this happened, my mom would bundle me up and take me to the nearby park, where she'd sing to me until I fell asleep. I was a heavy child, and it was exhausting for my mom to carry me around after working hard all day, but she did it anyway.

My dad spent his days busy in the kitchen, and my mom faced piles of laundry. When I was a little older, she would bring me with her while she scrubbed and brushed, ironed and folded. I would crawl around by her feet, almost tripping her. When she wasn't looking, I'd eat scraps of paper or bits of soap, which worried her until she found a solution: If she put me in a full tub of water, I would paddle around happily, amusing myself while she had a bit of peace.

My dad said I looked more like my mom as a child. I was plump, with long hair from birth, small eyes, and a big nose. I'm a bit embarrassed to say that my mom adored me so much, she breastfed me until I was three. She tried to wean me, but I wouldn't let her go. I probably embarrassed her while she was playing mahjong with her friends—a rare break for her—and I would run up to her, lift her blouse, and try to latch on.

Starting when I was four, my dad would wake me at dawn and drag me out of our house to exercise, and then we'd take a cold shower together. He was good with his hands and made the exercise equipment out of scrap materials. Having trained in Hung Gar martial arts, Dad was able to teach me some simple moves, and he'd watch me practice them.

Neighbors would ask me what I wanted to be when I grew up, and I'd say I wanted to be a flying man.

They'd say, "Flying how?"

I'd point at the sky and say, "Flying very high!"

They'd laugh and tell me not to fly yet, that I'd hurt myself. "Wait until you're grown up!"

I knew it was polite to nod, so I did, but I didn't like having to wait for anything. I also wanted to be a cowboy, like in American movies. They seemed so brave and dashing, and I imagined myself being one of them. I pestered my parents for a cowboy outfit, which I proudly wore every chance I could get.

At five, I reluctantly went to school. My parents didn't have a car, so I had to get up early each morning and walk down the hill to the classroom. Before I left, my mom would make me a sumptuous breakfast, then put a sandwich or boxed lunch in my bag. At that age, I had an enormous appetite and loved to eat. I'd start to get hungry on the way down the hill and would finish my lunch before I got to school.

Mom was worried about my safety and put some coins in my bag every day so I could take the bus home rather than walk up the hill at the end of the day. Inevitably, though, I spent the money on noodles, and had no choice but to walk home. If a car passed me, I'd try to thumb a ride, and a lot of good-natured people would give me a lift. I got a ride almost every time, and no one tried to kidnap or hurt me.

Of course, there were the days when my luck was bad and not a single car passed by, so I had to walk all the way home. This took a while. In order to get home faster and keep it secret from Mom that I'd spent the bus fare on food, I took a shortcut up the final slope. I say "shortcut," but it was more like a death trap. I had to scale a sheer rock wall, clinging to branches and outcrops like a monkey, all the way up to our backyard. One time, my dad happened to catch me on the way up, hanging on the lip of the cliff. He scooped me up with one hand, threw me in the garage shed, and locked me in for the rest of the day. That taught me an important lesson: From that day on, I always checked for signs of my father first before I hauled myself over the edge.

The rich kids I went to school with would see me climbing the hill on my way home as they passed by in cars, and they'd shout mean comments at me: "Servant's kid!" "Hey, beggar, if you don't have money for the bus, don't come to school!" After a while, I really couldn't stand the insults anymore. One time on the playground, they said something cruel and I charged at them. We started brawling and rolling around on the ground. I used all the moves my dad taught me, but I was one against many. One of them grabbed my legs; I lost my balance and fell over. My head hit a rock, and everything went black. I lay on the ground, not moving. The kid who knocked me down was an ambassador's son. He ran home to get an adult to help, and everyone else scattered.

Soon, the kid's father appeared, looking anxious. Later on, I found out they were terrified that I'd been badly hurt. After all, this was the embassy district, and one little kid seriously injuring another here could turn into an international incident. If my parents sued them, they'd really be in trouble.

But I wasn't that hurt. I never passed out cold, but I was dizzy and too shaken to stand on my own. The ambassador brought me home, and I drifted off to sleep. When I woke up, I felt achy all over, with a throbbing pain on the back of my head. When I touched it, I found an enormous bump.

My father came home shortly after and said, "Cannonball, the ambassador's son brought a gift for you." He was holding a gigantic box of chocolates. My dad set it down next to me, ruffled my hair—which hurt like crazy—and left.

Chocolates! To a greedy devil like me, it was the best possible present. Even though I was in pain and my head was spinning, I still had my appetite. I ripped open the box and shoved one in my mouth. The sweet taste filled my mouth and helped me feel better about the sting of defeat. So I had another one, and another. Before I knew it, I'd finished the whole box—and started to feel sick. I tried to ignore the churning in my stomach. I certainly wasn't going to throw up anything so yummy.

The door opened again, and my dad came in. Seeing my chocolate-smeared mouth, he said, startled, "You finished the whole box? Don't you know you have to be careful what you eat when you're injured?"

I did *not* know that, in fact. (I was six!) I said, "Oh."

Well, Dad wasn't happy I'd gorged myself, and decided I must have recovered enough from my injury for him to give me a good beating.

I'll always remember that day as the first time I lost a fight. I would face defeat many more times as I grew up, but I didn't know that then. And I'll always associate the bittersweet taste of chocolate with that day.

chapter two

THE BOYFRIEND

To all the other Victoria Peak rich kids, many of them foreign ambassadors' children, I was just a poor Chinese. None of them would play with me. Fortunately, the French consul, my parents' boss, had a daughter about my age who was very beautiful. I'll call her Sophie. We often played together, and she always called me her boyfriend. The word "boyfriend" gave me a sense of responsibility, but to be honest, at that age, I didn't understand what it meant—until someone made fun of Sophie. Then I knew I had to protect her.

As I mentioned, my father was a student of martial arts when he was young, and he continued to practice to stay in shape. He taught me his skills, and my body was naturally powerful. Except for that one fight when I hit my head, I usually won my fights with other kids (and I had many of them). I wasn't a bully, though. I only struck back when someone tried to make trouble for me, or if anyone dared to tease my "girlfriend."

I'd defend her right away. No matter who'd been foolish enough to annoy her or make her cry, no matter whose fault it was, I'd rush over and hit them until they begged for mercy and apologized.

On one of these occasions, my dad happened to catch me beating up one of our neighbors. The kid's face and neck were covered with bruises, and he was wailing loudly. My dad dashed over, grabbed me before I could do any more damage, and helped the other child to his feet. I thought Dad had pulled me off so the other kid could get away. Watching my victim run home howling, I swelled with pride.

Dad? He wasn't as pleased with me as I was.

He dragged me home while I stumbled along, protesting, "But, Dad, I won! I won!"

As soon as we stepped inside out house, Dad took off his belt and gave me a good lashing, then tossed me in the embassy's garbage shed, where I usually ended up when I'd done something wrong. I didn't get it. I'd defended my girlfriend's honor, and I was getting punished?

He said, "I didn't teach you martial arts so you could hurt other people."

I pleaded, "But, Dad, they bullied Sophie first. I had to teach them a lesson."

He glared at me and, without another word, closed the shed door, locked it, and walked away.

I sat down by the bags of trash. Outside, I could hear my mom hurrying over and pleading with my father to let me out. They argued about it for a while, but he wouldn't budge. Then it got quiet again.

I settled in for a long wait. By now, I was very familiar with this cramped space. It wasn't too bad being in there, although my stomach was already rumbling. I was *starving*. If only I had something to eat. I stared at the tiny glimmer of light coming in from the top of the door and thought, *I might as well take a nap*. I wouldn't feel the hunger pangs if I were asleep.

I shut my eyes and thought, *I hate Dad*. I was defending my girlfriend, like a hero. He should praise me, not punish me!

Despite my anger, I drifted off, waking up when I heard someone knocking gently at the door. "Who is it?" I asked.

My mom's voice said, "Cannonball, look up."

Through that gap at the top of the door, she pushed something through. A wrapped package landed on my lap. Before I could get the paper off, I smelled the delicious aroma of an enormous roast-meat sandwich. I thought, *I love Mom!!* It was the best gift I'd ever received in my entire life! I whispered a thank-you and she tiptoed away. I devoured my meal, feeling unbelievably happy.

I was too young to really understand the intricacies of the situation. Later on, I found out why my father had been so angry. The kid I'd beaten up was the child of an embassy official, and Dad was worried that he'd lose his job over the incident. Our family was completely at the mercy of others, and we had to be careful to stay on the good side of our higher-ups. When he finally let me out of the shed, Dad made me go to the kid's house and apologize to him and his whole family. My dad went to hit me again, in front of them. The embassy official was kind enough to stop him and say, "No need for that. Children get into fights. It's no big deal."

This incident didn't make me less willing to fight in Sophie's behalf, but I learned to be cleverer about it. Before striking the first blow, I'd look around and make sure there weren't any adults in sight. Before long, most of the other kids in the neighborhood had either tasted my fists or knew not to mess with me and my friends. After that, I didn't get into as many fights.

chapter three

MY DEEPEST, ONLY REGRET

I hated school from the moment I learned I'd have to go.

One morning, after our usual exercise, Dad said, "Cannonball, soon you'll have to start going to school."

Why?

I knew what school was. I'd seen the rich kids with their schoolbags and prissy uniforms get into their cars every morning to go down the hill, and thought they all looked ridiculous. I could run around our compound and play for as long as I liked. When I was bored, I could help my mom fold the laundry or watch my dad cook or hang out with Sophie, which was always fun.

"I don't want to go to school!" I protested. "I can learn stuff at home!"

It was no use. A few days later, I was pushed out of the house holding a schoolbag and wearing a uniform, just like those kids I hated.

Nan Hua Primary was a very good local school. The teachers were excellent and treated the students with patience and kindness. The students came from good families. The classrooms were nice, too. Everything felt very refined. My mom and dad pulled a lot of strings to get me in there, and as they told me repeatedly, I should have considered myself lucky. At the time, though, I didn't care. As soon as I stepped through the school gate, I was miserable.

Lessons were boring, nothing I cared about.

I didn't understand all the words.

I'd watch the teachers' mouths open and close while my mind wandered off.

Honestly, I would have preferred sitting in the shed, next to the trash bags! Anything would have been better than being stuck in the little desk chair. My favorite class was gym, when we got to go outside for a bit.

The only relief from the monotony of lectures was when I amused myself in class by cutting up. I'd deliberately lean too far back in my chair and fall over, making everyone laugh. I'd make faces at my classmates or use my desk as a drum, making so much noise that the teacher had to stop the lesson to yell at me. When the teachers lost their patience, they made me stand outside in the corridor. One teacher in particular made sure I knew what he thought of me. He glared at me and said, "Mr. Chan, don't think you're anything special."

It didn't matter what he said or did. I was never going to suddenly love school. He sure tried to change my attitude, though. Some of his creative punishments were to make me stand in the corridor holding my chair over my head until he said I could lower it. If the teacher wasn't checking on me, I'd put it down and lean against the wall for a little nap. If I learned anything during this time, it was how to sleep standing up. (This skill came in handy later in life when I'd use that technique to catnap on movie sets.) All the teachers would hang a sign around my neck with my crimes written on it, like "I played the fool in class," or "I lost my textbook," or "I didn't do my homework." Sometimes they just wrote the word "useless"! I couldn't always read the words on the signs, but I understood everything the teachers yelled at me, so I knew what I'd done wrong.

I spent more time in the hallway outside the classroom than inside it, and became notorious in the school. With a reputation to maintain, I kept playing pranks, blowing off my homework, misplacing my books, getting into fights, and being a headache for the teachers and administrators. I shredded my school uniform climbing that rock face to get home and often lost my schoolbag who knows where, which led to a beating from Dad and another afternoon in the garbage shed.

It's no surprise that I was kept back at the end of my first year. My parents were forced to acknowledge that their son might not be academic material. They decided to take me out of that school, which filled my heart with joy. Now I could go back to my carefree life of playing all day!

My happiness was short-lived.

The next year, I was enrolled at Master Yu Jim-Yuen's China Drama Academy, where academics were barely taught. Instead of reading, writing, or math, we learned martial arts, singing, and dancing.

The master said, "Great learning comes from bright morality and affection for the people. To stop here is virtuous. Understanding where to stop brings stability, and with that comes peace. Peace brings with it serenity and clear thinking, with which you can achieve your goals."

Master Yu Jim-Yuen wasn't like the teachers I'd met before who wrote signs and made me hold up a chair. At the China Drama Academy, if you slacked off on your training or failed to memorize the classic Chinese texts you were given, you were caned on your bare behind by the master.

My fellow slacker students and I figured out a system to avoid a lashing. If we hadn't managed to commit something to memory, we'd scare the upstanding classmates into claiming they would say they hadn't done the work either.

Our schoolroom master was named Tung Long-Ying. To this day, I remember how nice his handwriting was—always in a single stroke, very smooth. Of course, none of us could be bothered to learn how to do brush calligraphy, thinking, *What good will it do us?*

Anyway, when the time came to recite texts, he would say, "Chapter Five from *Analects*. Yuen Lou, recite it." Yuen Lou was my name at the academy. We all got new names with "Yuen," after Master Yu Jim-Yuen.

I'd stand and say, "I'm sorry, I didn't learn it."

The master would glare at me and call on my older classmate Sammo Hung, a.k.a. Yuen Lung. "Let's hear *you* recite it," he said.

Sammo would stand and confess that he didn't know the text either. If we *all* said we didn't know it, Master Tung Long-Ying wouldn't bother reporting us to Master Yu Jim-Yuen for punishment. It was one thing to beat one or two kids, but he didn't have the energy to go off on a few dozen.

We grew bolder and bolder. If we knew Master Yu had left the premises to see friends or gamble, we'd do whatever we liked. The boys would fling books around or wrestle, and the girls gossiped loudly. The poor cultural-studies teacher didn't know what to do with us. When our lookout yelled, "The master's back!" we'd jump into our seats and act like we'd been studying hard all along. The academy didn't pay teachers much to put up with brats like us. We chased away eleven cultural-studies teachers in just a few years, and we felt very pleased with ourselves each time.

I have many mixed feelings about my education there, but I do regret not learning to read and write or do math. When I grew up and went to America to make movies, everyone was using credit cards, but I couldn't possibly. At the time, you had to fill out a credit card slip to pay for things, and I didn't know how to write. Every time I signed my name, it looked different. Store clerks would compare the signature on the slip with the one on the card and didn't believe they matched. When your lack of an education makes it impossible to pay for a new shirt, that's when you really feel uncultured. (Currently, I have an unlimited black card in my wallet and could buy a jet plane with it. It's blank without a signature. People trust that I am who I say I am nowadays.)

When I got famous, fans started asking for my signature. I learned how to scribble "Jackie Chan" well enough, but when someone asks me to address it to her name, I have to ask how to spell it. It isn't so bad in America because the alphabet has only twenty-six letters. But it's awkward in China. The written language is far more complex, and when people tell me their names, I can't write them. They'll explain which characters or which radicals to use, and I'll still get stuck. They have to write it out for me to copy, and if it is in cursive, I ask them to separate out each stroke so I can see it properly. It takes a lot of effort and is very embarrassing. I can manage two Chinese autographs in the time it takes to write ten English ones. These occasions always leave me tense and anxious. If I walk into an event, for charity or publicity, and see a pen and paper or a calligraphy brush on the table, I get scared and pretend I have to be somewhere else.

Cultured people are able to write a sentence or two of good wishes on a card or poster. I'd like to do the same, but I don't know how, and that fills me with shame. Whenever I have the chance to speak to young people, I always tell them to study hard. With donations from my fans as well as my own money, I've built numerous Dragon's Heart schools so children in China have a chance to get an education. Whenever I see cultured, poised, and well-brought-up kids from my schools around the world, it makes me so happy for them that they won't struggle like I do. It's gratifying for me to have helped them avoid that pain.

Growing up poor but surrounded by wealth, I thought only about acquiring possessions. Studying meant nothing. As I've gotten older, I couldn't care less about material things, and learning is everything. If I have one thing I wish I'd done differently in life, one regret, it's that I wish I had applied myself at school and studied more.

The director Feng Xiaogang once said to me, "Jackie, if you'd worked harder at school, you wouldn't be Jackie Chan now. You should be grateful that you *didn't* apply yourself."

That might be true, but I really wish I possessed more knowledge. I often misuse words when I'm talking, which leads to many misunderstandings.

Bruce Lee was an educated man and even studied philosophy. As a result, his words were always very deep. He once said, "Water has no shape, so you can't catch hold of it, or hit it, or hurt it in any way. You, too, should be as mobile and formless as water. When you pour water in a cup, it becomes the cup. Pour it in a bottle, and it becomes the bottle. Pour it in a teapot, and it becomes the teapot. Water can drip, and it can crash. Be like water, my friend." Only someone with a good education could have made that excellent speech.

I could *never* come up with something that meaningful.

I often refer to myself as an oaf, but for many years now, I've learned as much as I can, and I keep trying to correct my mistakes and better myself. I hope young people will make the most of their potential and hit the books, or they might regret slacking off, like I do.

chapter four

A DECADE OF DARKNESS

Going from a rich-kid school like Nan Hua Primary to the rigorous, disciplined China Drama Academy (CDA) was a complete 180. Many people have asked me how that came to happen.

Around the time I was held back at my first school (held back, expelled, whatever), my father got offered an excellent new job as the chef at the American consulate in Australia, with a much bigger salary. It was a great opportunity for him, but it meant he'd have to leave Hong Kong and live apart from my mom and me for a while. He wouldn't be around to keep an eye on me, and if I was already so mischievous that I was kicked out of elementary school, he started worrying about what kind of future I'd have.

My dad's friends had heard about Master Yu Jim-Yuen's China Drama Academy. They suggested a tough environment like the master's would change my unruly nature; plus, I would learn skills—martial arts, singing, dancing, and acting—that would make me employable one day doing Peking opera, which many of the drama academy students performed.

The hitch was, the CDA was a boarding school. Sending me there would mean they'd never see me. I was seven years old. It might sound cruel to send a child that age to boarding school, but given their circumstances, my parents had to consider the option.

One morning, my dad announced that instead of our usual morning routine, he was going to take me out to play. I was thrilled! I changed into my cowboy outfit, grabbed a toy gun, and romped outside. All morning, Dad didn't scold me once. When I asked for a sweet-bean-paste bun, he bought it for me right away. It was unthinkable.

I should have known.

We arrived at the CDA, and he took me inside. I saw the courtyard full of boys and girls in white shirts and black trousers. They were standing in rows, practicing kicks, and looked very impressive. I thought, *This place is cool!* After wandering around for a few hours, I fed on the energy and excitement, and didn't want to leave. When Dad said, "How would you feel about going to school here?" I was thrilled by the idea.

The master informed my father that he would have to sign a contract to commit me for three, five, seven, or ten years. Dad asked me how long I wanted to stay, and I said, "Forever!"

My parents were uneasy about the idea, and Mom was hurt that I was so excited to go, but they agreed to send me to the CDA for the full ten years and signed on the dotted line. I was now my master's "property" and would live within the walls of the CDA for the next decade. My master could have beaten me to death in that time and gotten away with it.

In that moment, my childhood came to an end.

By the time I understood what had happened, it was too late. My impulsive decision led to my decade of darkness, though it was in those ten years that I became Jackie Chan.

My daily routine at the CDA:

Wake up at 5:00 a.m. for breakfast.

Practice kung fu until noon.

Lunch.

Practice until dinner at 5:00 p.m.

Dinner.

Practice until bedtime at 11:00 p.m.

Do it again the next day.

For ten years, I got only six hours of sleep, night after night. Like all the other boys, I slept on a rolled-out mat in a corner. The carpet on the floor hadn't been cleaned for years and was filthy. We ate, slept, pissed, and had nightmares there, and it was covered in spilled food and my master's phlegm. It had accumulated so much crud, the carpet was three times heavier than when it was new.

My father moved to Australia, and Mom stayed behind to help me with the transition. She visited me once a week, bringing my favorite candy and snacks, which I shared with my friends at the academy. She also brought a big bucket of hot water. She'd borrow a tub from my master and give me a bath. Water was scarce in Hong Kong then, so we got to shower only twice a week at first (later on, it was just once). My mom would weep while she bathed me because she could see all the welts, cuts, and scars on my body from the canings and beatings. I told her, "It's fine, I'm used to it," which made her cry even more.

After a few of her visits, everyone started making fun of me for getting baths from my mom, and they called me spoiled.

The next time I saw her, I threw a tantrum, saying, "Don't hug me like I'm a little kid, and stop bringing me bathwater! I'm grown-up now!"

She didn't say anything, just nodded. Looking back now, I see how selfish and stupid that outburst was. My mom boiled the water at the consulate, carried it down the hill, walked for a half hour to the funicular tram station, paid the precious ten-cent fare, walked for another half hour to the Star Ferry terminal, paid another ten cents for the boat to Kowloon, then walked from the station to Mirador Mansion, hurrying all the way while carrying a forty-pound bucket of hot water. All that, just to give her son a tepid bath.

I'd been at the CDA for two years when my father returned to Hong Kong from Australia to pack up their things. Mom was going with him when he returned to Canberra. He and Mom came to see me at the academy, not to pick me up and take me with them, but to say good-bye. No more candy and baths from Mom. No more visits at all. Before leaving the academy that day, Dad treated my master and classmates to a gourmet meal. I was allowed to see them off at the airport. Dad gave me a cassette tape player; Mom's parting gift was a bag of fruit. As I watched them walk away to their gate, I started crying and didn't stop until their plane took off. I was really alone. They would be thousands of miles away on another continent. I was nine.

After their departure, I cried beneath the covers every night for a week until I began to accept reality and distance myself emotionally from them. It wasn't easy to pull away. They sent me a new cassette tape each week, and I'd sneak off to the back staircase to listen to their voices. When I heard them say, "Our boy, we miss you so much," I'd started sobbing again. When I got a bit older, they included money in their packages. By then, I'd stopped listening to the tapes. They said the same things every week—that they missed me and hoped I was well—and the sentiment just made me sad. Whenever I saw the other kids' parents visit or watched them pack up to leave for a weekend at home, I would feel miserable.

What made the separation worse was the day-to-day slog of life at the CDA, the constant training, the corporal punishments. No breaks at all, not even if you were sick. In fact, sickness wasn't allowed. In my ten years there, I got sick only once. It sounds unbelievable now, but I was too scared to fall ill.

It happened when I was nine, I believe. One day after lunch, I started vomiting and felt weak all over. Nanny Fong, our white-haired caretaker, said, "Your head is burning up! Quick, get to bed, I'll bring you some medicine." Did this mean I could skip training? Surely I'd have to rest for at least two days. The very thought filled me with joy, as sick as I was. I lay down in the corner and listened to the others doing pull-ups and practicing flying kicks.

Then my master saw me lying on the floor and said, "What's wrong?"

I said, "I'm . . . so . . . sick . . ." I might have exaggerated a bit.

"He has a fever," confirmed Nanny Fong.

"A fever? All right, then. Fine. Everyone stop training. Stop!" said my master.

The others came to a sudden halt. He turned back to me. "You. Get up and do one hundred left leg thrusts."

I gaped at him. *Really? But I'm burning up!*

You didn't defy the master, though. I got up and did it. Then he made me do one hundred right leg thrusts, followed by one hundred left flying kicks, then one hundred right flying kicks. My whole body ached. After I finished, he said, "Do you feel better?"

If I didn't say yes, he'd make me train harder. So, immediately, I cried, "Yes, much better!"

From then on, every single kid in the school didn't dare get sick.

Everyone at the academy had the same goal: to start performing onstage as soon as possible. Shows of children singing, dancing, miming, and doing acrobatics onstage—the Peking opera style—were still popular back then, so there were many opportunities. It was our greatest dream to appear in a production. It was what we'd been training to do.

One day, our master arranged for our first public show. Everyone got excited, especially when he announced that he would pick the best among us for solo parts. Many of us had trouble sleeping that night, all of us hoping that we'd be chosen.

The next morning, we all got up very early and waited for him to announce his selections. He read out our names one by one: "Yuen Lung, Yuen Tai, Yuen Wah, Yuen Mo, Yuen Kwai, Yuen Biao . . ." As I mentioned, all our CDA stage names started with "Yuen." I was Yuen Lou, and Sammo Hung was Yuen Lung. As my fans know, Sammo and I made many movies together and are very close still. I am godfather to one of his sons. But back then, we didn't always get along well. Yuen Lung was older, and he bullied the younger students quite a bit, but we didn't retaliate because we were supposed to respect seniority above everything else. Even today, so many years later, I still respect him as my elder. No matter how much we fought each other, though, if we faced an outsider, the unbreakable bonds of brotherhood tightened between us. As the saying goes, "Fighting within these walls disappears at an outside threat."

The master had read six names. Only one left. A rustle went through the crowd. Who would it be? He cleared his throat and made us all hush. "And finally, Yuen Lou!" I jumped to my feet and did a forward spring to stand in front of everyone.

"The seven of you, bow to your schoolmates!" We bent deeply at the waist. Our getting to perform main parts meant everyone else would be reduced to background performers, or else stuck operating the curtains, stage-managing the props, putting on our makeup, and other backstage jobs. Although everyone else was jealous, the collective sense of honor exceeded everything. There was a burst of warm applause and cheers from the audience. Everyone was proud of us. The Lucky Seven, as we became known, were born. What no one could have anticipated was that we would go on to make such a stir in the movie industry.

Everyone on that team had his own special abilities. Yuen Biao could master the most difficult acrobatic stunts, including walking on his hands as easily as on his feet. Yuen Wah could do the highest backflips. Yuen Tai had a huge amount of energy. Yuen Biao and Yuen Mo excelled in all sorts of martial arts moves. Yuen Kwai was great at face painting. The oldest of us, Yuen Lung, was handsome and the best boxer in the school. Although I didn't shine in any one area, I was a good all-rounder, and there was one thing I could do better than anyone else: I could run fast. That's because I had to run away from Yuen Lung all the time! We were assigned roles that played to our strengths, so Yuen Lung was always the emperor or general, while Yuen Biao's scrawny physique made him perfect for comedic parts. When we did the classic *Journey to the West*, Yuen Lung was the Monkey God, Yuen Biao played Sandy, and I was Pigsy. As part of the Lucky Seven, I became known as the Little Foreigner because I'd grown up at the French consulate on a diet of milk and bread. I was stronger and better nourished than the others. I also had the nickname Two Portions because that's how much I ate.

Before Yuen Biao joined the academy, I was the youngest kid in the school and everyone picked on me. Then he showed up and he became the target. From his first day, he seemed fragile and wouldn't stop crying after saying good-bye to his parents. I felt sorry for him. I went over to introduce myself and comfort him a little. After lunch, he watched us practice, and we urged him to join in. He turned out to have a fair bit of talent and could turn professional-looking somersaults. Our master praised him and in the same breath criticized Yuen Lung and Yuen Tai in comparison, which didn't help Yuen Biao.

The unwritten rule in our school was that the big would bully the small, and the small would obey the big. I often stepped forward to protect Yuen Biao. We were powerless against the aggression of our older schoolmates, but we developed good escape skills. Once, Yuen Lung borrowed money from Yuen Biao. Then we were on a bus, and Yuen Biao didn't have money for the fare, so he asked for the money back. Yuen Lung refused. When I spoke up for Yuen Biao, I got hit but didn't dare strike back. I just ran away, with Yuen Biao right behind me. At that time, Yuen Lung wasn't fat, but he was starting to put on weight and he couldn't possibly catch us as we raced off the bus and vaulted over the railing. Back at school, we got beaten anyway, of course.

Once, Yuen Kwai and I got into a fight over who knows what, and everyone formed a circle around us to watch. My scissor kicks were known to be very powerful, but just as we started to mix it up, someone yelled, "No scissor kicks!" If someone called it out, you just couldn't do it. We traded blows until our master showed up suddenly. We were all startled and started running.

He screamed, “Stop!”

We all froze. Yuen Kwai and I were still breathing hard, glaring at each other with hatred. Our master said, “You like to fight? Fine, everyone else get out of the way. You two stand there and duke it out.” We stared at him, stupefied. “Fight!” he roared, and we had no choice but to start up again.

If you don’t already know, fighting is *exhausting*. After thirty or forty seconds, you can barely go on. I didn’t know then about finding my footing or controlling my breath. All I could do was jab until my fist hit flesh. In a minute, we were both on the floor, completely out of energy.

“Not fighting anymore?” asked our master.

“We can’t go on.”

“You can’t? Very good. Kneel, facing each other, and slap each other.” We had no choice but to do as he said, slapping once with the left hand, then the right, until our arms were out of strength. To start with, we hit as hard as we could, but soon we weakened. Our faces were puffy, and we were bleeding from the mouth and crying from pain and exhaustion. Seeing that we were completely spent, our master made us lie flat on the ground and caned us each ten times. Those ten blows resounded through the room. We almost fainted. Even worse, he kicked us out of the Lucky Seven. We regretted ever getting into that fight.

From then on, there were no fights. If people really had to hit each other, they made sure our master didn’t see it.

When we were a bit older, in our teens with years of opera performances under our belts, we started going around to film studios in search of odd jobs. Our main form of transport was a double-decker bus. A school manager was in charge of making sure we were seated properly on the right bus. He was supposed to pay for our tickets—at ten cents apiece per way, it would have been three or four dollars for all of us round-trip—but then he'd tell the driver, "Family member, Tsui Luk, 1033." His son was a bus driver, and as a relative he was entitled to travel for free. Just uttering that magic phrase, he didn't have to pay for any of us. He'd give us our twenty cents and wave good-bye as the bus pulled away.

We were supposed to save half the money for the ride back, but we'd buy snacks with all of it, and when we got on the bus to return, we'd say to the driver with a straight face, "Family member, Tsui Luk, 1033," and ride at no charge.

One day, there were too many of us pulling this trick and the conductor got suspicious. He started swearing at us, "I don't believe Tsui Luk has more than ten goddamn children." He insisted on our buying tickets. There was a bit of a tussle, and his bag of change and tickets tipped over. I remember we were going down Prince Edward Road at the time, and the conductor shouted to the driver not to stop but to go straight to the police station so he could have us all charged. We yanked the door open and jumped out, several of us hitting the ground in a roll and then popping upright, completely unhurt, standing arms akimbo and chests out. I guess that was our first offstage stunt performance.

One time, Sammo broke his leg while training, then fainted

from the pain. He had to go to the hospital and recovered there for a long time. Before the accident, he was in great shape, but his grandpa brought noodles in thick gravy to the hospital every day, and he swelled up like a balloon. His leg got better, but he never lost the extra weight. He was so round, our master stopped letting him perform. Dejected, Sammo packed his bags and left the academy. Before leaving, he gave the rest of us a warning: "The time of opera is almost over. The future is in movies! When I get famous, you can all come and find me there."

Hey, no arguments from us! We were trying to get movie work! When we did, we got paid $65 per day on set. Our master kept $60, leaving us with $5 as pocket money. It didn't seem fair, but no one questioned it until after Yuen Lung left the school. Then the next oldest student, Yuen Tai, said to the rest of us, "We ought to keep more money. Five dollars is too little. Our master is keeping too much."

This struck a chord, and after some heated discussion, we decided to go and speak to him together, with Yuen Tai taking the lead. After years under the master's tyranny, we approached him with our hearts in our throats, but to our surprise and relief, our master didn't blow his top. He slowly turned his back and said, "You're all grown-up now. You're ready to fly." When we heard these words, we all cried with joy. When our share rose to $35, we thought it was a great victory!

He's right! I thought. *I am grown-up now.* I was making $35 for a full day's work when I could get it—*if* I could get it—and I thought I was doing great.

Boy, did I have a lot to learn.

chapter five

FIRST LOVE

Fifteen is the age when many of us first experience romantic feelings, and I was no exception.

When I reached that year, I'd been hanging out with a gang of boys since I was a little kid, sharing the experience of harsh training for hours a day under our master's watchful eye. We considered ourselves lucky if we got through a day without a beating. I didn't have the time or energy to think about girls. There were girls at the school, but I'd known them for so long, I thought of them as my sisters, nothing more.

Now and then, I'd overhear my classmates whispering about girls and relationships. I'd think about Sophie, the daughter of the French ambassador, the "girlfriend" I'd gotten into so many fights for. I had this idea that girls should be either playmates like her or caregivers like my mother. I also hoped I'd be able to take care of a girl myself someday when I grew up, just like heroes in the movies.

In the '60s, Teochew opera had been thriving in Hong Kong for a few decades. But in recent years, the shows had to be adapted to local audiences' tastes by incorporating martial arts. This style of opera was known as xung gong hay. It grew popular very quickly, and in no time, its fame spread as far as Southeast Asia. Every Hungry Ghost month—a summer festival season in many Asian countries—my classmates and I were invited to give this type of performance. Posters would go up, and they'd set up a stage on the sidewalk to do the show right there on the street.

When I was fifteen, we were invited to perform in Thailand. There, I fell in love with the ingenue of the troupe. I'll call her Chang.

Chang, also from Hong Kong, was an older woman—one full year older than me. I acted opposite her each day, and we got to know each other while we danced. It hit me like a bolt: *I like her!* This revelation triggered as much anxiety as happiness. Did she like me back? I had no idea. I hoped she did, and I plotted ways to spend more time with her.

The Thai gig ended, and we returned to Hong Kong. It was a return to the joyless existence of sweat and hard work as I fell back into the routine of training at school and making the rounds at movie studios for day jobs. But once Chang and I were back on familiar ground, we started dating seriously. I didn't know anything about relationships then. All I cared about was figuring out how to be with her as much as possible.

My master was very strict about our staying focused on work, so I had to pretend to go on the 6:00 a.m. bus to the studios, but would sneak off to Kowloon Park instead to meet Chang. She couldn't leave her house until ten, so I'd sit alone for four hours, waiting, practicing kung fu. People in the park who were doing tai chi would stop and watch me. This appealed to the performer in me, and it helped pass the time.

And then, she'd arrive! When I saw her coming, my heart quickened. We were just two kids, sitting side by side on a park bench. I would put my arm around her shoulders, and would leave it there until it went numb and I had to awkwardly lift it up with my other hand to remove it. At noon, we'd go buy some food, but for the most part, we stayed on that bench, at that park, for as long as we both dared. Late at night, she'd go home, and I'd turn up at the academy, acting like I'd just finished work. I had to take cash out of my allowance (my parents still sent me some money each month) to hand over to the master, pretending it was my day's wages.

Two years passed like this.

The truth of Yuen Lung's parting words became more and more apparent as we were booked fewer opera performances each season. This affected Chang as well. One by one, the CDA students left the school and threw themselves into the movie industry, the world of the future. Eventually, it was my turn to say good-bye to my master.

This was a special day. My dad came from Australia. He chatted with my master while I packed my things, stuffing all those years of possessions into one small suitcase. I put on three pairs of jeans, because it was a school tradition that anyone leaving the academy had to endure ten lashes of the cane.

I knelt on a stool and held out the cane and said, "Master, I'm leaving."

He came over and ruffled my hair. "No need for that."

I let out a breath. "Thank you, Master." I picked up my suitcase and said, "Good-bye, Master." Then I bowed and left with my father.

As I walked away, I turned and gazed at the school gate, and felt a whisper of fear. My life there had been harsh, but it was the only home I'd known for ten years. My dad hailed a taxi. I got in, still anxious. But when the car turned onto Jordan Road and I couldn't see the building anymore, I shouted, "Finally! I'm out of there!"

I was seventeen years old and suddenly free. My dad wanted me to move to Australia and live with them, but I wanted to stay in Hong Kong and try to break into the film industry. I'd studied kung fu for ten years, and at the studios, I could display my skills. Plus, of course, Chang was here. I didn't tell him about her, though.

Seeing how determined I was, my dad bought me a small apartment in San Po Kong for about $40,000 Hong Kong dollars, about $5,000 USD. It seems like a tiny amount now, but that amount was what my parents had saved in tips and wages over ten years at their grueling jobs.

At that moment, I understood why my parents had chosen to leave me for Australia. In Hong Kong, they didn't have the ability to earn much money, having nothing to sell but their labor. I'd worked hard for ten years, and so had they. Everything they earned, they gave to me, to provide me with a place to live.

Many years later, my dad moved back to Hong Kong and lived in that small condo. I asked him many times to move into the big house I'd bought him, which was in a better neighborhood, but he said no each time. I resorted to lying to him, saying I'd sold the condo and he *had* to move into the house. For the rest of his life, he believed me. In truth, I still own that place. I've kept it as a reminder of everything my parents did for me.

Before that condo, I'd never had a room of my own. As a kid, I slept in bunk beds with my parents. At the school, we'd slept on mats next to each other. Now I had a space that was just for me. The apartment was cramped and run-down, but I was delighted with it. Right away, I went out to get materials to make myself some basic furniture, like my father had made for our home way back when. It was an adjustment, going from the bustle of student life to being all alone. I had to get used to solitude, and honestly, I never did. Even today, I like to have a lot of people around me and hate to eat alone.

The best part of having that apartment: Now Chang could come here instead of meeting me in the park. She came by every morning at ten, and we played house, tidying up, doing laundry, making meals. I'd go off to try to pick up work as a stuntman at film studios, and she would hang out at my place until she had to go back home.

In my quest for work, I went to the Shaw Brothers Studio, along with everyone else. Shaw was the biggest film company at the time, and it had both a TV complex and soundstages for film. Many of us waited there for our shot. Many people vied for a few roles, the sort of part where they show your body but not your face, an extra who got kicked or stabbed or beaten. Sometimes, a producer might ask you to do some heavy lifting, moving equipment and so on. It didn't matter what it was. If there was any work to be done on set, we were all happy to do it.

I often skipped going to Shaw, though, so I could be with Chang. If I got a job, I'd come home from work and make her laugh about the funny things that happened on set. Our days were incomparably wonderful . . .

. . . Until the day her father found out about us. We bumped into him when we were out together, and I remember thinking, *The cat's out of the bag now.* We'd kept our secret for years, but now we had to fess up about it. He asked what I did for a living, and he was not happy to hear that I was a stuntman. In no uncertain terms, he demanded that she leave me. There was no room for negotiation. He said right to my face, "A martial artist will never amount to anything. Don't you dare touch my daughter."

It was humiliating. His words were harsher than any pain or suffering I'd endured on set. The blow to my self-esteem felt much worse than being beaten by my master. I almost burst into tears right then and there.

Chang said she wouldn't leave me, but her parents put a lot of pressure on her. She tried to keep it from me, but we'd be sitting together, talking, and then she'd suddenly burst into tears. I could see how upset she was about this conflict. Her parents or her boyfriend? She was very young—we both were. How could anyone that age choose? I didn't make it easy for her. I'd say, "Let's just elope to Australia! Go home and get your passport, and we'll leave right away."

She couldn't do that to her parents, of course.

I remember smashing up a chair in frustration and trying to calm myself down to think. Maybe I hadn't amounted to anything or accomplished very much yet, but from then on, I knew there was only one path I could take: straight up. I had something to prove—to Chang, to her parents, and to myself.

I threw myself into work and said yes to every opportunity, even if it meant traveling and being away from Hong Kong. I started to get regular jobs from a few film units, and they took me to more locations. I bonded with the other guys and started hanging out more with them, in places that exposed me to new temptations. I'm not talking about other girls. I was just young and, having been sheltered for so long, was discovering how much fun there was to be had in the outside world! I'm naturally fun-loving, but at the academy, I hadn't had any time for things like bowling (which became a real passion of mine), visiting underground gambling dens (something else I got a little too excited about for a while), and just hanging out with my friends in clubs and restaurants.

I liked this new wide world and wanted to be in it as much as possible. In my mind, Chang started to become the person who kept me away from it. I still loved her, but I found myself making excuses to avoid her. It was always "I'm busy" or "I've booked a job," but actually I was off to the pool hall to meet my crew. I'd have brought her along, too, but she didn't like these sorts of places. Compared to gambling, staying at home with her was boring, and I'd resent her for making me do it. The idea of her waiting at home for me made me feel guilty, and I associated that feeling with her, too.

I was a terrible boyfriend. When I think of how I behaved back then, I'm ashamed of myself. If I saw a light in the condo window when I was walking up my block, I'd turn around and head back to have more fun with my friends. I acted like a rebellious child, or a wild horse throwing off its reins. Sometimes, we'd be out for a stroll, and I'd pick a fight with her over nothing so I had an excuse to run off and have more fun.

As I slowly became more established in the movie business, I spent even less time with her, but she stuck with me. She was a well-known opera performer, and many rich men went after her, but she turned them all down. She once told me, "If you don't marry me, then no one will."

Her words (or was it a warning?) turned out to be true. The more famous I got, the farther I drifted from Chang, and we eventually broke up. Within a few years, I would meet Joan Lin, the woman who became my wife, and we had a son. When Chang heard about the birth of Jaycee, she cut off contact with me completely. She refused to see me, but she did visit my parents, who had always been fond of her. Whenever they visited from Australia, she'd spend a day with them. It was just as well; I was too busy working to keep my parents company anyway. Chang also stayed in touch with some of my friends, and they kept me posted on her life.

Early on in our relationship, I told her that when I could finally afford a car, she'd be the first person I took for a ride. We'd already split up when I bought my first car, but I called again and again, wanting to tell her I'd done it, and that I wanted to keep my promise. She would not take my call. I'd also promised to buy her a nice watch and tried to send her one, but she wouldn't accept that either.

When I heard she'd opened a boutique, I sent my colleagues to go buy clothes there and bring me the receipts so I could reimburse them. I sent people out every day to her boutique. She must have found the sudden surge in business strange. After a few months of this, one of my secret shoppers came back and told me there was a "Clearance Sale" sign on the door. Was she closing down? He went back to investigate and reported that she said her heart wasn't in it anymore. The business was hard and gobbled up every single day, so she decided to sell off her remaining stock and close her doors. Naturally, I sent another person to clean her out, buy every last piece on the racks, including the racks! Then I learned that she decided to close the shop because she knew all her customers were people I'd sent.

More guilt! Through mutual friends, I passed her the message that I'd like to buy her a house, or some other gift, but she said no. Even my wife invited Chang, through friends, to have dinner with us, but she never accepted.

She moved away, and I haven't seen her for decades. Chang's a great girl, with integrity. She never did marry. To this day, I still miss her. I hope we will see each other again someday.

chapter six

NUMBER NINE

When I was just starting out as a stuntman, life was hard and my future was uncertain, to say the least. My days were a cycle of training, waiting for work, shooting a film, getting beaten up. Some days, I'd ride the bus to the studio and get my makeup on, but I'd wind up empty-handed anyway. If the lead actor or actress was unavailable for whatever reason and the movie was on hold that day, the extras wouldn't get paid. I'd come all that way for nothing. It was unfair. Eventually, all the martial artists got together to fight for our rights, and we reached an agreement with the studio to receive a flat fee of $30 for half a day's work even if no film was shot. If the cameras were rolling, we would get the whole $65.

It was a grind, but this period of my life did have its moments. In 1973, I was an extra in the film *Enter the Dragon*, starring Bruce Lee.

In one scene, he bashed me in the head with a stick, striking me much harder than he meant to and knocking me to the ground. It hurt, but I was honored to have been hit by Bruce Lee! Afterwards, he apologized effusively, told me I was doing a great job and that I was very brave. It was an incredible moment for a young kung fu artist, and one I will never forget.

Behind the Scenes by Zhu Mo

Hello, I'm Zhu Mo, a longtime friend of Jackie's. I've done publicity for Jackie's movies for years. In 2012, I accompanied him on humanitarian trips to Myanmar and Thailand.

On these trips, I became closer to Jackie, who I call "Big Brother," and his crew. He treats them like his family. Everyone spends almost all their waking hours together, talking about work, eating, drinking coffee, or just chatting. He has friends all around the world, and no matter where he goes, he'll always be with a big group of people.

Whenever he's in the mood, he'll start telling his astonishing, terrifying, hilarious, or touching stories, and we listened with our mouths open. He is such a consummate actor that these tales often turn into performances, and become utterly spellbinding. Even as I listened raptly, I started to think I should really capture these fascinating stories to share with others.

Soon after, Jackie paid for his entire production

team to take a trip to Singapore. While there, I brought up the idea of writing a book of his endless supply of stories about the movies. He said, "Sure, give it a try."

From that moment on, and for the next three years, I started following him around and collecting Jackie Chan stories to create this book.

One story I always loved was about Jackie's commitment to playing dead.

For a long time, Jackie only got to play background roles where his face wasn't shown, or as a bad guy who got smacked in the face, or someone in a crowd who gets kicked by the hero. He observed how things were done and learned about the process, like how the director would call the set to action by saying the sequence, "Camera . . . rolling . . . start . . . action."

They often needed people to play corpses on set. Of course, dead bodies don't move and the actors had to be completely still. Many performers were inexperienced, and held their breath from the moment the director said, "Camera." They'd be gasping by the time the scene actually began, their chests with knives and swords sticking out heaving up and down, driving the directors mad. Jackie learned to take his deep breath on the word "Start," so he was able to remain still for the entire take. Afterwards, the director would point at Jackie and announce, "That guy's pretty good at being dead!"

One time, at some studio or other, a director wanted two warriors to fight in the rain, with a whole lot of dead bodies in the background, all stuck full of knives. It was a cold day, and the actors were all soaked, so many of them couldn't hold their breath long enough; plus, they were shivering, so the blades were shaking all over the place. The director yelled, "Cut, cut, cut! You can't move, you're all dead, remember?" Then he pointed at Jackie and said to his assistant, "That guy is the best corpse, make sure we get him in tomorrow as well!"

Jackie was now in demand as the best corpse in kung fu. The others would make fun of him for being so earnest about playing dead. They thought it was hilarious. At the end of the day, he was just a kid making a few dollars a day. He may have seemed overeager, but that same attitude is what got him to where he is today.

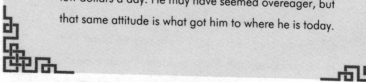

The neighborhood where we gathered to catch the bus was a red-light district, full of nightclubs. We were a bunch of red-blooded boys, and passing through the area every day was a thrill. Rather than trudge back home every night, only to have the hassle of returning first thing in the morning, some of us found it more convenient to go to a nightclub where we could shower and hang out with the girls who worked there until morning.

A night in a club wasn't free, of course.

Even though I made next to nothing, I spent all my wages on drinking, gambling, and girls. We all did. We enjoyed simple pleasures every day and didn't think about the future. Although no one said so out loud, we all knew that, if something went wrong, we wouldn't live to see the sun rise the next day. We had a short-term mentality, which meant recklessly spending our money and our youth, because tomorrow might never come.

I remember the first time I went to a club. I was shy but acted like a big man anyway. The girl who served me—I knew her as Number Nine—was beautiful, with a sweet personality. On my second visit, I simply asked, "Is Number Nine here?" And that's how it was every time after that. Whenever I showed up, everyone in the club would call out, "Hey, Number Nine, your boyfriend's here."

This nightclub was pretty run-down, but it was the best I could afford. Every night, Number Nine and I would squeeze into her dingy little cubicle, the low ceiling right above us. The room wasn't soundproof either, and we could hear pretty much everything around us, clear as crystal. There were times when I'd notice people trying to peep through the cracks in the door at us. Yet this little cubicle seemed like paradise to me.

Each morning, Number Nine would wake me up with a light tap on my shoulder to rouse me for work. I'd get up right away, have a shower, then go wait for the bus with my fellow martial artists. At this time, I was living day by day, with no real plans for the future. I had friends, but my family was far away. Work was grueling. The red-light district was an oasis of warmth in my otherwise cold existence.

One afternoon, we finished work early, and a group of us went out to a Hong Kong–style café to eat. A short while later, the actor Leung Siu-Lung came in. I waved hello to him, and the girl he walked in with waved back. I thought this was odd that a strange girl would seem so happy to see me and went back to my food. The girl kept staring at me, and some of the other guys even teased me about it. I wasn't sure what was going on. Why was she looking at me? I was too embarrassed to look back at her.

That night, I went to see Number Nine as usual. As soon as she saw me, she said, "Why did you ignore me at the restaurant today?"

That was her? I was stunned. I realized that I'd never seen her in full daylight before. Every time we'd met, it'd been at the club, in dim lighting, with her in heavy makeup. In the afternoon sun, when she was plainly dressed, her face scrubbed, I had no idea who she was. In fact, I didn't really know anything about her. Not her real name, her age, where she came from. I only knew she was Number Nine.

That was it. I decided that this was no way to live, and no way to treat a woman. I needed to focus on my goal, to be a martial artist. Not just that, a lung fu martial artist. I had to stop going to nightclubs and get serious about my career.

Lung fu martial artists were second only to the fight director on the action team. "Lung fu" means "dragon tiger," and the name alone is enough to give you a chill. They were highly skilled stuntpeople, and every lesser martial artist longed to become one. They were also an indispensable part of the team and had some degree of job security.

From that day on, I put all my energy and strength into my work.

chapter seven

MY BIG BREAKS

When I was a nobody, I often got cursed at on set. Once, I was supposed to stand next to the female lead. My hair was long at the time, and when I hit my mark, I unconsciously flicked my hair. The director yelled cut and came over to scream at me, cursing my family back eight generations. I was stunned and ran off in tears. All the other martial artists laughed at me for crying. My shame turned into rage. I grabbed a wooden prop knife and was about to rush over to hack at the director. "You can scold me, but why did you have to bring my mom into this?"

Sammo Hung, who was working on this picture, grabbed me. "Are you crazy? Don't do that!" The next day, I quit. After that experience, I would never use foul language at anyone on my set, and I make sure no one else on my team does either.

I was in a pitiful position, but I carried on and learned what I could. At the studio, I'd take note of how people used their equipment. Sometimes I even wrote things down on a scrap of paper I kept in my pocket.

The fight director on this film seemed to me to be the coolest person on set. He showed up in a beautiful sports car that roared through the gates, and I stared at it hungrily. One day, he passed by me, then reversed. He glanced at me and asked, "Aren't you on our team?"

I said I was, and he told me to get in. I opened the door, sat in the seat with my legs outside, brushed off my trousers and feet. As he drove toward our location, I kept perfectly still, not moving at all. When we arrived, I got out and bowed to him and said with utmost politeness, "Thank you, director." After that, he gave me a lift every day. We talked, and I learned a lot from him. I was cast in all his subsequent films and later became his assistant. It was just a little gesture, but I got his attention, and he must have decided I was sensible.

I became known as the first to arrive on set and the last to leave. My attitude was enthusiastic and committed, with the intention of making a good impression on everyone. I got into the habit of volunteering to do the most difficult or dangerous jobs, and told the directors that I wouldn't need extra pay for it. After I pulled off whatever stunt it was, I put on a "No big deal" expression and never let on about how much pain I was in.

Meanwhile, Sammo had done well at a big studio, Golden Harvest, and got a contract as a movement director. Yuen Biao and I followed him there, hoping to pick up some work. Through the Sammo connection, we established ourselves at that studio.

I was working as an extra on a movie there. For a fight sequence, the director wanted the male lead to vault a high balcony railing, fall with his back to the ground, flip in midair, and land steadily before continuing his fight. The director was notoriously unprofessional and frequently abused his power by ordering the fight crew, a.k.a. the body-not-face people, to do unsafe stunts. This was one of those occasions. While the male lead sat off set sipping a cup of tea, the main director ordered the fight director to find someone else to do the sequence—without wearing a wire. What's more, he didn't want to soften the fall with cardboard boxes or mats so that the scene could be captured in a single take.

The fight director, an older man we all respected, was not happy. "There's no way we can do this without a wire. I won't let my guys take that risk," he said. Not only was he famous, he treated his team well. When we went out drinking, he always told us, "If the day comes when you get to be fight directors, too, don't make your artists do anything they don't want to, or something they can't do."

The main director refused to accept this. "The scene will look fake with a wire," he said. "Do what I'm paying you to do!"

Before the fight director could respond, I stepped forward. "Excuse me, I'll give it a try."

My volunteering immediately enraged the fight director. "What's the matter with you?" he asked. "Are you tired of living?"

I completely understood how he felt. My coming forward contradicted him and made him look bad in front of everyone else. The action sequences were his responsibility, and he'd said he couldn't do it. And then I said I could.

I pulled him to the side. "I know you're right, but hear me out," I said. "If I pull this off, it's because you taught me well. If I fail, the director will come off like an idiot. I don't want to be a nobody forever. I need to prove myself! Even if I fail, at least I tried!"

All he could do was nod. He knew he couldn't stop me. He turned back to the director and said, "This young man wants to try it, so let him. But I and the rest of my guys are quitting. Being a good director doesn't make you a good person. We rely on our real abilities and our health to make a living, and you have no right to look down on us and treat us like we're expendable." After his speech, he turned back to me. "Make your body as light as possible, start rolling as soon as you hit the ground, and make sure you don't land on your head or back. Remember this!"

The makeup artist touched up my face, and the wardrobe person came over with some new clothes. Slowly, I went up to the balcony and looked down at the crowd below. I murmured to myself, "You have to prove you can do this!"

From below, the director shouted, "Action!" and we were rolling.

The bad guy on the balcony launched a flying kick at me, and I flipped right over the railing, face-first! Flying through the air, my back arched, I spun around to face-up, and somehow managed to land unsteadily on my feet. I thought, *Yes! Success!*

Everyone was screaming and cheering for me, and I heard my colleagues shouting my name. The fight director ran over and slapped me on the back. "You're amazing! You're going to become a lung fu martial artist."

Wild joy filled my heart, but I had to calm myself down. To everyone's shock and horror, I said, "I want to try it again, and this time I'm going to nail the landing!"

And you know what? I did.

One jump changed my life. It brought me a lot of attention, sealed my reputation, and allowed me to become an extremely young lung fu martial artist. From then on, I could imagine a future for myself, of fun and excitement, and maybe fame and fortune, too.

Not too long after I became a lung fu martial artist, I got a phone call from a famous kung fu movie producer's assistant. Good news! "He needs a male lead for his new film, the sort who knows how to fight. I recommended you, and he's willing to meet you," said the assistant. I couldn't contain my excitement. After so many corpse jobs, I had a shot at a leading role? My face would be on camera? I was so overjoyed at the prospect that I didn't pay much attention to what came next. "They can't pay you much. I don't know what the number is . . ." she said.

"I don't care," I said. "I'm in!"

When I arrived on set, though, I realized how low-budget this production was. As a CDA student, I'd appeared in some crappy films that were shot, beginning to end, in three days. And as a professional martial artist, I'd taken tumbles at a bunch of studios. I'd developed a keen sense of when a film was going to be good and when it was just hack work.

The film was released in the USA with the interesting title *Master with Cracked Fingers*; the original Chinese title was *The Cub Tiger from Kwang Tung*. When I heard the title, I wasn't sure if I was playing a human or a tiger. Joking aside, it was my first leading role (and I did play a human). The story was about a war between rival gangs. I played a man seeking to avenge his father. There was no script or fight director, the sets were dreadful, and the equipment was the opposite of state-of-the-art. We often ran into overtime. The whole production was amateurish and confusing.

As the male lead, I was directed to strike bizarre poses and do my action sequences in front of the camera. One by one, the crew dropped out over the course of filming until there was no one left. Then the director and producer vanished, too. Not one person on that film got paid. I remember on our last day of filming, we lined up to receive our daily wage and no one came to give it to us. I felt responsible as the lead to support the stuntmen, having been one for so long. I paid them with my own money, of which, as I've made clear, there was very little. By the end of filming my first starring role, I was flat broke.

I had to make more money. The way to do that was to take the next step up and become a fight director. I'd always wanted to direct, in part because of something my father once said. He was dressed in all white, preparing dinner. Since morning, I'd watched him chopping meat and preparing vegetables. Standing by the window, with the setting sun on him, he said, "Son, I'm sixty years old, but I can still cook, and that's how I make a living. You're young now. Will you still be able to do martial arts when you're sixty?"

That question left a deep impression on me.

I might not be able to fight when I was sixty, but I could direct fights. Plus, the fight directors were in charge of hiring and drew a bigger salary. At the time, I thought being a fight director was as high as I could hope to go. If Sammo Hung could do it, so could I!

But until I got the big job, it was back to kicking and flipping. One day, I landed hard on the floor after a stunt and had to stop work for the day. Everyone packed up and went home, but I stuck around. I was still too sore and exhausted to walk back to the bus. Someone came over to say hello to me, and even though I wasn't in a sociable mood, I said hi back. I'm glad I was friendly; this mystery person then told me who he was and what he wanted. He worked for a production company, and he needed a fight director for a new movie.

"Our budget isn't large, and we can't afford an established fight director. That's why we want to work with a newcomer. Lots of people have told me you're extremely talented, so I've come to see if you'd be interested in signing with us," he said.

Another low- or no-pay job? I didn't care! This was my chance to be a director. Wasn't it the opportunity I was dreaming about?

I blurted, "Where do I sign?"

The man looked taken aback, as if he hadn't expected me to agree just like that. We arranged to meet the next day to talk over the details.

Early the following morning, I went to his office to meet the producers in person, and we soon had the contract signed. I asked if I could hire some assistants, and they said yes, so I immediately hired two classmates, Yuen Biao and Corey Yuen, a.k.a. Yuen Kwai, to join the production. To get them to work for peanuts, I bragged about how amazing the film was going to be and talked up our glorious future. I couldn't believe my luck. Finally, I would get to experience how it felt to be the guy in charge, the one calling the shots.

You can probably guess what happened next. When I arrived on set, I realized in two seconds that it was another disorganized amateur production. The place was in chaos, with people quarreling all over the set. The producers interfered with the cinematographer's setup while the director grumbled at the art department. The set decoration was abysmal. Yuen Biao didn't complain (he was younger and wouldn't dare), but Corey groused, "This isn't the way you described it *at all*." I was deeply embarrassed. What had I gotten us into?

Sure enough, the film was another turkey, an utter failure. Even though Yuen Biao, Corey, and I gave it our all, there was no overcoming the problem with the production, or the script. I played two different characters, which is hilarious now that I think about it. In the end, it earned only tens of thousands at the box office.

Still, this outfit hired me to work on their next film, also as a fight director. And this time, the movie was . . . just as much of a flop as the last one! The film company had hoped to change their fortunes with me, and now they were mired in debt and could barely pay everyone's wages.

It was around this time that Bruce Lee, the most famous and influential martial arts star in the world, died at the age of thirty-two from an allergic reaction to pain medication. With his passing, kung fu films grew much less popular in Hong Kong. It was as if audiences were grieving for Lee, and refused to watch action films without him in them. Even though many film executives attempted to create "the next Bruce Lee," no one succeeded. Before long, the local market started churning out rom-coms and comedies, and anyone associated with martial arts was toast.

I'd only had a taste of being a fight director, and then every opportunity dried up. My career was stuck in the doldrums. Except for the apartment my dad had bought me, I had nothing at all. It was suddenly difficult to live alone in Hong Kong. I stopped contacting my colleagues at the studio and tried to brainwash myself into thinking that there were plenty of other things I could do besides being in movies.

What do you do when you are at rock bottom and need emotional support? You call your mom. I phoned my parents in Australia, who immediately urged me to come see them. They had the status of permanent residents there and hoped to convince me to join them. With nothing going on in Hong Kong, I bought a discount plane ticket to Australia.

chapter eight

WELCOME TO AUSTRALIA

Although I'd traveled in Asia, I'd never been abroad before. This would be my first overseas trip.

I walked onto the plane, put my bag in the overhead bin, and kept my precious bowling ball on my lap. At that point, I didn't know if I was ever going to return to Hong Kong, and I had to bring my ball with me. On board, they passed out a form, which instantly gave me anxiety. I didn't know any English, so a friendly male flight attendant had to help me. I didn't understand any of the announcements, so I didn't dare to sleep. When the plane descended a few hours later, I thought, *The flight was a lot shorter than I expected.* The airport we landed in was very backwards. I disembarked with everyone else, not knowing where I was or what I ought to do, but I sensed that this place wasn't Australia.

The nice flight attendant saw me standing there, confused, and explained that I had an overnight layover in Indonesia, and my trip to Australia would resume the next day. He helped me make a reservation in a shabby hotel (the most I could afford) and got me in a taxi. He warned me not to go out at night because of the anti-Chinese sentiment in Indonesia at the time.

In the tiny hotel room, I was afraid I'd lose my passport, so I lifted up a table and hid it underneath. My cash was strapped to my body, and I didn't think of removing it. Sitting alone in my room, I felt lonely and bored. Then there was a knock at the door. It was the flight attendant who'd been so helpful. I eagerly invited him in, but quickly realized that he wasn't interested in just hanging out and chatting. My first clue? He asked if he could touch my muscles! And then he asked for a kiss. He'd been very kind, but I asked him to leave.

Alone again and exhausted, I fell asleep. The next day, I woke around six and managed to get a taxi to return to the airport. When I got there, I realized I'd forgotten my passport under the table! Luckily, I knew the English word and yelled "Passport!" at the driver. He took me to a phone booth by the side of the road, and I called the hotel to ask them if they could send someone to the terminal with it. Amazingly, they agreed. The driver told me I had to tip the delivery man and he took $50 Australian dollars from me. Then he said I had to pay the cab fare, too, and grabbed $100 Australian dollars out of my hand and sped away. I didn't think anything of it at the time, but later, I realized I'd been ripped off.

Back on the plane, I was seated next to a very fat man. He inconsiderately monopolized the armrests on both sides, so I was squeezed into a corner. When we landed, I was relieved to see all the English signs. I couldn't read them, but I knew I was finally in Australia. I happily lined up to get my luggage and ran out the airport doors, expecting to find my parents waiting for me with open arms. But they were nowhere to be found.

I went to the taxi stand. I had to get to Canberra, which I remembered because it sounded like "camera," one of the few English words I knew. I kept saying to myself, "Camera, camera, camera." I found a taxi and put my luggage in the trunk, then gave my address to the driver. He said a whole lot of things in English and repeated them until I got the gist: "You're in a place called Sydney, and Canberra is very far away." Then he mimed flying, and said it was at least another hour away *on a plane*.

I almost collapsed.

I got my luggage out of the trunk and was suddenly very scared. I had no idea what to do. If I had to get another flight, where would I buy the ticket? How would I change planes? And where should I go? I didn't know anything at all.

I went back into the airport and spotted the fat man from before. I followed him closely and watched as he went to another counter and put his luggage on a scale, then said something to the person behind the desk, who took the bags from him. I thought, *If I give them my luggage and they accept it, then I've got it right.* So I did the same thing, and sure enough, they took it. Then they gave me a boarding pass and told me what time to come back. I was in a fog and didn't understand what they were saying to me. They gave me back my documents and a whole stack of tickets.

The whole time the counter clerk was talking, I kept my eyes on the fat man and decided to follow him. He went window-shopping, so I did, too. He had breakfast at a restaurant, and I waited for him at the door for more than an hour before he emerged. I kept going. He sat down by a gate, and I did, too. He went through to the minibus, and I did, too. On the bus, the fat man handed over a ticket. I had no idea where mine was, so I handed over the whole stack. As it turned out, a bus ticket was in the pile with my boarding pass. Finally, I was back on the plane—the right one, by total luck and circumstance.

And so, after many twists, turns, and transfers, I arrived at the Canberra airport. It was nearly deserted. All you could see was the runway, forest, and desert. I exited the building and noticed a white-haired man in the distance. When I got closer, I recognized my father. In the few years since we'd last seen each other, his hair had gone completely white.

I walked over to him, and a tiny woman started hugging me. I looked at her and realized it was my mother. The last time I'd seen her, some twelve years ago, we were the same height. I'd gotten so much taller since then.

Seeing them both, thinking of all the trouble I'd had getting here, I burst into tears.

I was finally back with my parents. I was so glad to be with family, safe in their love and protection. It was like I could finally breathe again.

That feeling didn't last long, though.

In Canberra, I had nothing to do all day and was totally dependent on them. I felt like a parasite. I didn't want to learn English and hated the food. Most importantly, I missed the film studio.

After a few months, I realized that Australia was *their* home, but it wasn't mine. I loved them, but not my life with them. I lied to my parents and said a big work opportunity had popped up in Hong Kong and that I needed to go back. They might have seen through the lie, but they didn't ask too many questions. My dad just said, "We'll always be here for you. If things don't go well in Hong Kong, come back."

chapter nine

AUSTRALIA, ROUND TWO

When I opened my Hong Kong apartment door, I got a real shock. After being empty for only several months, the place was a mess. Dust and cobwebs were everywhere, furniture was ruined.

I had to regroup and start over. First, I cleaned up my apartment. Next, I phoned Sammo and asked him to help me find a job. He came through for me, and I was hired on a Golden Harvest production. The kung fu movie scene had changed so much in such a short time. When I returned to the studio, the others treated me like I was completely new to this.

The film was called *Hand of Death*. Sammo was the fight director, and I was his assistant. I also played a supporting role. The director was named John Woo.

I said to Sammo, "Who's John Woo? I've never heard of him."

"He's new," he replied.

Nowadays, John Woo is world-famous, having directed dozens of hit movies, but in the mid-'70s, he was still green—but so was I.

Many directors handed over the fight sequences to the fight director entirely while they took a nap or left for the day, but not John. He watched every sequence we came up with closely, and talked about how they should be broken down into small shots, how each action should be completed. He was nice to everyone on set, unlike older directors I'd worked with before who threw violent tantrums. When we took a break, he told me a lot about directing, even though I had no idea then that I would soon become a director myself. All in all, I greatly admire him. We met in Hollywood many years later and reminisced about *Hand of Death*. The two of us had a few good laughs about it. It was touching to talk to him again and reflect on how far we'd both come.

It wasn't a *bad* film, but it didn't do well. The industry was still limping after Bruce Lee's death. I hoped I'd be about to get more work through Sammo, but he delivered some depressing news. "The studio has had to cancel a lot of projects," he said. I understood what he was trying to tell me, even if this was a hard truth to accept. "Never mind finding work for *you*, I might not be able to hang on to my own job."

I slumped in my chair. Hanging on the studio walls were photographs of their movies, a time line of the glorious past of action films. Did they have a future at all? I had no idea what would happen next in the industry. It was clear that there was no path going forward for me. Even if I did get work as a hired body, I'd earn no more than $50 a day. What kind of life was that?

Utterly defeated, I thought of visiting my parents again.

I'd been back in Hong Kong for only a short while and had hoped to make a name for myself before returning. Instead, I might have to beat a shameful retreat from Hong Kong and slip back into Australia in disgrace. I felt awful. My money was almost gone, and soon, even buying food might become difficult. I'd trained at the drama academy from a young age, and all I knew was kung fu. All I had was my ability to do martial arts. Was I really going to leave it all behind *again*? I didn't seem to have a choice.

On the way home, I gazed at the skyscrapers and bright city lights on either side of the street, and felt like they had nothing at all to do with me. After all this time, and dozens of movies, I was still a loser.

The agony really hit home when I counted my savings and realized I didn't even have enough cash for a plane ticket!

An angel appeared in the form of my first girlfriend, Chang. She'd heard about my troubles and stuffed $20,000 Hong Kong dollars into my hand. It was a huge sum, and I tried to refuse it, but she insisted it was just a loan, and I could pay her back when I started earning again. I took the money, feeling awful about it. Before leaving, I went to a watch shop and spent a few thousand on fancy watches for Mom and Dad, plus a few gifts for the manager of my little condo. I said a silent good-bye to Hong Kong. (Now maybe you understand why I felt so terrible about what a bad boyfriend I was to Chang, and why I was so desperate to repay her kindness to me after I became wealthy.)

My return trip to Australia was much smoother than the first. When I gave Mom the watch, it brought tears to her eyes. This was my first present to her. Dad fetched a piece of cloth and wouldn't stop polishing his watch. I knew they were both very happy to see me and be a family again.

This time, I vowed to make a serious attempt to build a life for myself in Canberra. I took an evening language class. The teacher asked for my name, and I said, "Chan Kong-Sang."

She said, "That name won't do. We'll call you Steven."

At the American consulate where my parents worked, everyone called me Paul, including the many GIs who lived there. I think it was because my parents called me Cannonball, which is "Ah Pau" in Cantonese, and sounds sort of like "Paul." I had no idea that Paul was an actual English name. And so I was Paul at home and Steven in class.

The teacher spoke so fast that I had no hope of keeping up, so I stopped going. My next attempt at building a life was to get a job. A driver for a Taiwanese expatriate organization got me a position pouring cement. When I arrived at the work site, the supervisor asked me my name and the Taiwanese driver said, "His name is Jack." Actually, Jack was *his* name. From that day on, at the job, I was Jack. My English was slowly improving, and I could already tell that "Jack Chan" didn't have much rhythm to it. My solution was to add a *y*, and I became Jacky.

I got up at five every day and stood by the roadside to hitch a ride to the construction site. Once there, I mixed cement in freezing winds and learned how to use a wheelbarrow. Even though my kung fu training made it possible for me to work fast, I was always exhausted at the end of the day. I watched the more experienced workers building walls, and was filled with admiration. I tried to learn from them.

During this time, my life was very disciplined and joyless. I would lie awake at night and think about the dreams I used to have. My heart ached with frustration about how things had turned out. I thought, *Get another job and your days will be so packed, you won't think about this stuff.* Also, if I had more money, I might be able to stir up some fun. So I took a second job at Lotus Restaurant, owned by my father's friend.

My new routine: bricks and mortar during the day, home for a shower at 4:30, then off to the restaurant at five. I made about $800 Australian dollars a month. On my way home from the construction site, I walked through a grove of trees. Knowing that my mom would be waiting for me at the house, I always stopped in that grove to brush the dirt from my body and reset my attitude. No matter how tired or depressed I felt, I walked in the door laughing and whistling, and gave my mom a big hug. When she asked if I was tired, I'd answer with a firm "No" so she'd be convinced I was fine.

My primary task at the restaurant was to prepare and wash the vegetables. When I finished that, I'd help the others with their duties until we stopped taking orders at 10:00 p.m. When there was nothing further to do in the kitchen, I'd walk around the dining room to bus tables, ask if the customers wanted coffee, tea, or ice cream, and do whatever else needed doing.

The more I helped out, the more people liked me, and so they taught me how to do their jobs. Soon, I knew all about working at a restaurant. I gradually rose through the ranks to become the sous-chef. The Lotus was popular, especially on the weekends, when there'd always be a thick stack of order slips. I had to prep the ingredients and seasonings, then quickly hand them to the two chefs. I didn't speak English and couldn't understand the menu, but the slips only ever had one word or two on them, so "egg foo young" became just "egg," or "Yeung Chow fried rice" would just be "rice." I managed to get things done by guessing correctly.

A tiny scoop of ice cream with a couple of lychee nuts went for $2.50 Australian dollars, but cost the restaurant just pennies. I couldn't help thinking, *God, that's a hefty markup!* When no one was paying attention, I'd put out extra-large servings of ice cream. When the boss spotted me doing it, he gave me a warning to stick with the rules.

To this day, I never order fried rice in a restaurant unless I know the chef and trust she'll make it for me fresh. What Chinese restaurants do is take a pile of leftover ingredients, fry them up, and put them in the fridge for a week and add rice as needed. Sometimes, I tell the waiter, "Leave out the beans, the shrimp, and the pork." That way, I know they can't use week-old leftovers in my rice.

I made many friends while I was working in Australia. My co-workers at the restaurant liked to tease me, saying a lot of women came there because they liked me. I enjoyed the kitchen banter, and when I really got going, everyone would forget to do their work. My boss, To Yuet-Cheung, once said to me, "Jacky, do me a favor, stop telling so many jokes. Save them for after work."

I was so busy during those days, I'd fall asleep as soon as my head hit the pillow. My dad said it made him happy to see me like this, but my mom knew better. I was learning and I had friends, but I wasn't happy. Those old dreams of mine would not get out of my head.

"Child, what you're doing now isn't what you want to be doing," she said to me one day. "It's not what you ought to be doing either." She knew me well, and her insightful words were spot-on, and spoken so kindly that they made me crumble.

"I've spent so many years mastering kung fu, and it's useless. I have nothing, I don't know what I'm doing," I confessed.

She hugged me and tried to comfort me, but couldn't really help. No one could, or so I thought.

I'd tried to put kung fu out of my mind and forget about the movies, but people in the action-films scene in Hong Kong hadn't forgotten about me.

I got a telegram from the producer Willie Chan, the general manager of Lo Wei Motion Picture Company. He was preparing for his next feature, *New Fist of Fury*, and wanted to offer me a contract. Initially, I thought he wanted me as a stuntman, and I was about to reply that I was now living so far away that there was no point. But the next sentence in the telegram left me stunned. "We want you to play the lead role," it said. My fee would be $3,000 Hong Kong dollars, or $350 USD.

After a few seconds, I decided to accept this job, even though it would still leave my future uncertain. That fee wasn't enough to live on. And what if the movie flopped? I'd be right back where I was before. But I had to follow what was in my heart. This would be my last shot. I just had to take it.

Before I left, my boss at the restaurant gave me a leather wallet with $10 in it. He said he hoped I'd earn lots of money and come back with a full wallet.

When I said good-bye to my parents—again—they didn't try to stop me. Mom was proud of me, I think, for following my dreams. Dad gave me a deadline. "If you don't make it within two years, you will move to Australia for good." I was twenty years old.

I agreed. Two more years. That would be it.

chapter ten

BECOMING THE DRAGON

Even though the pay was terrible, *New Fist of Fury* would still be my first experience working with the top tier of the industry. Director Lo Wei had single-handedly molded Bruce Lee's career. He'd created masterpieces like *Fist of Fury* and *The Big Boss*. Of course I was excited to work with him!

The feeling wasn't entirely mutual. Lo Wei complained that my nose was too big and that I wasn't handsome enough, but he put those fears aside. He wanted *New Fist of Fury* to be a major work that would herald the arrival of a new kung fu star. He even re-created the team from *Fist of Fury*, getting many of the original actors to reprise their parts. The story would be completely different, though. Listening to his impressive pitch, my heart was thumping like a drum. Could the star of the future they were pinning their hopes on really be me?

Sitting there in Lo Wei's office, I signed the first artist contract of my life. It was for two years, with a monthly salary of $3,000, plus an additional $3,000 per film. I was obligated to appear in every movie Lo Wei made and to accept any role I was given.

Looking back, it was a stingy contract, but at the time, it seemed fair. I finally had a stable job with a regular income.

Now that I was an official studio player, my new boss wanted to tinker with my appearance. He approved of my body, but that was about it. Just about everything else needed fixing, including my crooked teeth and small eyes. He suggested plastic surgery, but luckily, I made good excuses to avoid that. If I were recovering from surgery, I couldn't do fight scenes for a while, and wasn't that why they wanted me in the first place?

Lo Wei also wanted to change something else about me: my name.

When I was little, my parents called me Cannonball or Shandong Cannon. My dad's nickname was Old Shandong, so I sometimes got called Little Shandong. My actual name was Chen Gangsheng in Mandarin, or Chan Kong-Sang in Cantonese. When I entered the drama academy, my master named me Yuen Lou. Then, when Sammo Hung left, I took over his name, Yuen Lung. So Chan Yuen Lung became my first stage name, as an actor and fight director. In Australia, I'd been Steven, Paul, Jack, and Jacky. How many names could one person have?

They insisted that, for a new beginning, I needed another new name. Lo Wei went to the author Pan Liudai, who was very well-known at the time, and asked her to help think up some possible choices. Her son, Kam Chiang, was an actor, too, and I'd worked with him. When I went to her home, she'd written out lots of names containing "lung," which means dragon, and asked which one I wanted. She said, "Your original name Yuen Lung is no good, because 'yuen' sounds like 'circle,' which means 'over,' like 'full circle.' The Little Dragon was Bruce Lee, and he's dead. 'Big Dragon' doesn't sound like a good name. What do you think?"

I picked a name that meant "Literary Dragon," because I thought that would make me seem more cultured, but she thought the word "literary" was too small for me. I suggested Chi Lung, after General Chow Chi-Lung from *Romance of the Three Kingdoms*, but she said that was too small, too, and that I should be more ambitious and choose a big name. I leaned toward Shing Lung, or "becoming the dragon," but how could I think I was worthy of such a name?

I said, "Cloud Dragon?"

She rejected that, too. "You'll never get anywhere in the clouds; your head and tail will always be hidden as you dart in and out, forever in a fog."

I said, "But I like Cloud Dragon."

"Why don't I just choose for you? You should be Shing Lung."

Becoming the dragon. "No way, that's too much for me."

She insisted. "None of the others are right for you. This is your name now. Becoming the Dragon!"

I only agreed because I didn't think the name mattered as much as she did. Making money was far more important, and Lo Wei appeared to have cracked that code. He certainly came off as rich. Sometimes I joined him when he went shopping. He'd take his time browsing, and I'd sit in a corner, waiting. Every single item in these places looked so expensive that I didn't dare touch anything. Once, after sitting for a while, I got bored, stood up, and went to look at the clothes. Something caught my eye, and I asked the salesgirl, "Could I have a look at that?"

She scoffed, "It costs a lot; you can't afford it." Her face showed nothing but disdain.

I retreated to my seat, feeling utterly defeated. Yes, it was very expensive, I knew that, but couldn't I even have a look at it?

Lo Wei was still shopping, so I couldn't storm off indignantly at the rude treatment. All I could do was sit there glaring at the salesgirl and finding her more and more hateful. She was polishing this and tidying that, glancing at me from time to time. Maybe she didn't mean anything by it, but I was convinced she was looking down on me.

When Lo Wei finally appeared, she hurried to greet him, cooing, "How are you, Mr. Director?" She fawned over him obsequiously. Ugh, she was vile.

I arrived on set very early for the first day of shooting and found everyone freaking out because the fight director had quit the job at the last minute. I offered my services, and they agreed right away. Ironically, my pay for fight direction was three times what I was earning as the male lead. After all, I had a lot of experience in this line of work but was still fairly new as an actor.

New Fist of Fury was not a happy shoot.

Lo Wei wanted to turn me into Bruce Lee the Second. I played a cold-blooded, rage-filled, inhuman killer who sought revenge only. Nothing about this role spoke to me, and so my performance was stiff and unconvincing. Privately, I complained to Willie Chan, "I'm not suited for this role. The director wants me to be the next Bruce Lee, but that's not the direction I want to go in."

There were early signs it wasn't going well. I heard some whispered criticism of me on set, comments like "Becoming the Dragon? More like Becoming a Corpse! Becoming a Worm!"

While the sound mixing for *New Fist of Fury* was taking place, I decided to slip in and watch. I snuck into a control booth next to the one with the voice actors so I could hear them working, but they had no idea I was there. Everyone was working late into the night. When my face appeared on-screen, the performers started talking about me. "What on earth was Lo Wei thinking? Big nose and tiny eyes. How does he have the nerve to call himself Shing Lung with a face like that? What a waste of money." Tears started flowing down my cheeks. I snuck out of there, completely destroyed.

When the box office figures came out, they were dismal.

Looking at those numbers, I almost bought a ticket back to Australia right away. I was so stressed-out, I started sweeping Lo Wei's office and picking up the trash, reverting to habits I'd formed at the drama academy.

Luckily, I was under contract, so Lo Wei found another role for me right away, in *Shaolin Wooden Men*, directed by Chen Chi-Hwa, a young guy I quickly got to know and worked well with. I learned a lot from him, too, though this film turned out only so-so.

In the months that followed, I worked with the superstar Jimmy Wang on *Killer Meteors*, then played the leads in *To Kill with Intrigue*, *Snake and Crane Arts of Shaolin*, *Half a Loaf of Kung Fu*, *Spiritual Kung Fu*, and *Dragon Fist*.

I would sneak into the dubbing booth for each movie to hear what they said about me. Each time, they made biting remarks, and I sat there weeping as I listened. But I understood. Dubbing means watching each scene over and over, and if someone already didn't like me, having to look at my face dozens of times was going to make them even more annoyed. As time went on, I got used to the criticism. They said the same few things anyway. Sometimes, while they were trashing me repeatedly, I fell asleep in the next booth.

These movies had some things in common: They all told a story of revenge, and all of them either flopped or were never released. My reputation was, fairly and squarely, box office poison.

You're probably thinking, *How many times can this guy fail before he has a success?* Believe me, I was thinking the same thing every minute of every day.

I'd already been to hell and back as a martial artist, fight director, and actor, and I still hadn't made a name for myself. I was having a rough time under contract with Lo Wei, starring in film after film I didn't want to make. I could clearly see the problems with them, but no one wanted to listen to what I had to say. I wasn't allowed to challenge the producers and directors or helm any films myself.

Then, one day, the independent film producer Mr. Ng See-Yuen came to see me, and said he wanted to borrow me from Lo Wei to make a new movie.

As far as I was concerned, working with a new producer could be a chance to break out of the Lo Wei formula and get a fresh start.

"If you had your choice, what sort of movie would you make?" he asked frankly.

I didn't answer right away. Every producer in the past had told me that my opinion was worthless and that I should just listen quietly to my elders.

After a pause, I said, "Mr. Ng, right now everyone's trying to turn me into the next Bruce Lee, and I've been forced to go along with it. But it will never work. He's a legend, and no one could ever surpass him. So why don't we go down an entirely different path?"

I could tell that Mr. Ng agreed with me. I stood up to help explain what I meant with movement and expressions. "Bruce Lee always kicked high, but I keep my legs low to the ground. Bruce Lee would scream and roar while fighting in order to demonstrate his power and rage, but I prefer to cry out and pull faces, to show how much pain I'm in. Bruce Lee is superhuman in the audience's eyes, but I just want to be a regular guy. I want to play ordinary, flawed people who sometimes despair. They aren't heroes; there are things they can't do."

When my little performance was done, Mr. Ng came over and shook my hand. "You're absolutely right! That's the sort of film we'll make."

In that spirit, I entered into a collaboration with Ng See-Yuen.

In quick succession, we made *Snake in the Eagle's Shadow* and *Drunken Master*. Both these films were hugely successful, and even surpassed Bruce Lee's numbers.

Just like that, I was no longer box office poison.

After all those years of failure, seemingly overnight, I was a hit.

chapter eleven

OVERNIGHT SUCCESS

Between 1978 and 1979, I had three massively successful films in a row: *Snake in the Eagle's Shadow*, *Drunken Master*, and *The Fearless Hyena*. People stopped me on the street to ask me to sign autographs and take photos with them. Wherever I went, people would throw drunken-master punches at me, and gossip magazines had paparazzi tailing me every day. Finally, I knew what it felt like to be a star. The real sign that things had changed for me: The chatter in the dubbing booth was completely different. Now, everyone was gushing praise: "That kid's not bad at all. He can even act with his hands."

After fifteen years of hard training, I was an overnight success.

At the time, I'd been earning $3,000 per movie, living in a small condo in Hong Kong. My pictures were making millions. When my contract was up, Lo Wei made me an offer.

Behind the Scenes by Zhu Mo

One day, when he was still with Lo Wei, Jackie noticed the janitor looking depressed. He asked what was wrong, and the janitor said he was old and wanted to retire back home. He'd asked the studio for some money as a retirement fund after all his years of service, but they'd said no. Jackie had known the man for about a year. They ran into each other at the studio every day and would chat for a bit. Sometimes, the old man would tell him a joke or two, and they bonded over shared laughter. Jackie couldn't stand to see him so dejected, and knew that the studio would never come through for him.

After a moment, Jackie said, "I have three thousand in my bank account. You can have all of it." The old man was shocked and refused to take it several times. Jackie insisted and finally, the janitor accepted.

After making three hits in a row, Jackie was now a bona fide Hong Kong star. These films topped the box office, and he became a hot property, fought over by every studio. Of course, Lo Wei hoped to renew his contract, and offered to raise his per-picture fee to $50,000, but if Jackie broke his contract, he'd owe the studio $100,000. A loyal person, Jackie agreed to the terms.

Lo Wei gave him a contract, but the terms weren't filled in. Still, he directed Jackie to the dotted line to sign. "I've just come back from abroad and haven't had time to prepare a proper contract, just sign here and I'll put everything else in later, then give you a copy," Lo Wei told him. Jackie didn't think about it too much, but duly signed. He believed that his senior in the business, the man who'd helped get him this far, wouldn't cheat him.

What happened next was astonishing. Golden Harvest, a rival studio, offered Jackie a contract for $1 million per film, then upped it to $2.4 million, and then $4.8 million. These sums were beyond his wildest dreams. But to accept Golden Harvest's offer, he'd have to break his existing contract with Lo Wei. That would be a betrayal, though, and Jackie hated to do that. Still, Golden Harvest was offering more money than he'd ever thought he'd make in his life. It was a difficult choice.

Many friends advised him that actors are usually popular for only a short while, and he had to make his money while he could. What was he waiting for?! After much consideration, he finally decided to sign with Golden Harvest.

When he heard about this, Lo Wei threatened to sue Jackie for breaking his contract. This was expected, but now he said the number they'd agree to was not $100,000, but $10 million!

Lo Wei had filled in the blank contract with different terms. This was a major blow to Jackie. Besides the emotional pain of being cheated and lied to, he was stuck. Even if he were to sign up with Golden Harvest, he'd never be able to come up with $10 million for Lo Wei.

Just as Jackie was at his wit's end, the old janitor came to see him. He said that he'd also done some filing at the studio and could testify that Lo Wei personally ordered him to alter the co ntract. All these documents were handwritten back then, and the old man had been in charge of this one. Lo Wei had instructed him to add a stroke on top of one of the characters, turning it from ten 十 to a thousand 千.

The old man said, "Don't worry, if he sues you, I'm prepared to tell the court what really happened."

Whether this is a case of foolish people having foolish luck or of virtue being rewarded, the matter of $10 million in damages went away just like that. And because of this whole incident, Jackie was able to sign a contract with Golden Harvest, starting a new era of Jackie Chan films.

It was a very moving experience returning to Golden Harvest. Before this, I'd been a hired body in countless films there, and I associated the studio with old friends. When I'd first showed up at Golden Harvest as a kid, I'd risked my life for pennies, quietly waiting to make my mark. I hadn't expected that day to come so soon.

My manager, Willie Chan, liked the deal and my prospects at Golden Harvest. He thought they'd be able to build my career to last, that studio heads Leonard Ho and Raymond Chow were trustworthy partners who'd be good to work with. For their part, Mr. Ho and Mr. Chow promised to find me a bigger market beyond Hong Kong and Southeast Asia. They hoped to make me an international star, the biggest Chinese icon in the world after Bruce Lee.

Leonard Ho and Raymond Chow had set up this company together. Their personalities complemented each other well, and the division of work between them was clear. Mr. Chow was responsible for expanding the business, while Mr. Ho took care of making the actual movies. They'd met while working at Shaw Brothers, and were already a perfect double act. It was their collaboration that filled Golden Harvest with new possibility, and me with confidence about working with them.

At our initial meeting, after a bit of small talk, Mr. Ho said to me, "Today I'm here to listen to you. I want to find out what you think." At the time, I hardly knew what I thought. I was still struck by my sudden, dreamlike fame and couldn't see beyond that. But I had to say something so he'd think I was insightful. I stammered for a bit, and then started to feel my stomach hurt.

Willie Chan noticed how awkward this was getting and hastily stepped in. "Jackie's last few movies have been very successful, and we're grateful for your recognition. Actually, we'd love to hear what you most appreciate about his movies, and what Golden Harvest would like to see in his future films. That might be more helpful for our collaboration," he said, putting the ball back in their court.

"Before becoming a star, Jackie was already well known in the martial arts world. That's when I started to pay attention. I do feel, however, that his films until now haven't begun to tap his potential, and I really hope to help him find and consolidate a style that truly belongs to him," said Mr. Ho. "For instance, he's already blending action with comedy. We could take this as our starting point and try to give audiences something fresh with every film as we discover what the true Jackie Chan style is."

These words really touched me. It was like he'd spoken what was on my mind.

"We started this company to make money, of course," he continued, "but I guarantee that as long as you're making films for Golden Harvest, I'll never interfere with your budgets and accounting. You have complete freedom to shoot and produce each picture as you see fit. I won't go through your numbers or limit your production schedule. You just make movies and leave the money side of things to us."

I was shocked. This was beyond my wildest dreams. Golden Harvest sounded like paradise.

"One more thing," said Mr. Chow. "Your name."

This again? To break into the English-speaking markets, he thought I should have an English name. He suggested I make one tiny change to Jacky Chan, switching to the feminine spelling "Jackie." It scanned better on a movie poster. I agreed, and Jackie Chan was born.

This meeting was the beginning of a very long partnership. Although Raymond Chow was the big boss and I saw him frequently, Leonard Ho and I discussed the nitty-gritty of film production. From the outside, we seemed like very different people. He was always dressed in a respectable, well-tailored suit, tastefully accessorized with impeccable ties and watches. You could tell from my wardrobe that I was nouveau riche. Still, the difference in our styles didn't prevent us from getting along well from our first meeting, and better with each passing year. Eventually, he recognized me as his godchild, and I treated him with as much respect as if he'd been my own father.

The first movie I made after joining Golden Harvest was *The Young Master*. I did my very best to make a good film, to repay the trust my two bosses had put in me, and to show the industry that my success wasn't just down to luck. For one scene, I shot more than fifty takes, because I had to kick my fan into the air and catch it with one hand, and I wanted this move to be perfect. Every take cost money, but, true to their word, they never gave me grief about how much the movie cost to make.

And that scene? It was beautiful.

chapter twelve

THE GHOST OF BRUCE LEE

The Golden Harvest offices were built on top of a graveyard, and it seemed that everyone who worked there had spooky ghost stories to tell. After Bruce Lee died during the filming of *Enter the Dragon* in 1973, no one at Golden Harvest dared to go into his dressing room.

When I got there, it'd been sitting empty for six years. I thought, *If no one wants it, then I might as well take it.* They changed the name on the door from "Bruce Lee" to "Jackie Chan."

At the time, I often stayed late at the studio, editing films. If I was too tired to go home, I'd just sleep in my office. Everyone acted like I was taking my life into my hands to do so because it was haunted. I said, "Fine, I'd like to see a ghost."

One night, I was on the edge of sleep when I heard a tapping noise outside. I thought, *It's just a door creaking*. A while later, there was a shuffling on the stairs. I thought, *It's just mice*. Then the sound of something bigger, moving faster. A cat chasing the mice? There was a logical explanation for everything, nothing to be scared of. (Right?)

Then, outside my door, I heard a sharp *tok-tok-tok*. Someone was clearly knocking on the door. Now I was at a loss. What was happening? "Who's there?" I asked. No answer.

I had to take a look! If it was the ghost of Bruce Lee or anyone else, I wanted to have a chat with it.

To keep my courage up, I shouted "Hey!" as loudly as I could while pulling the door open. I looked outside and, much to my amazement, I saw . . . a dog. He was as surprised as I was by my shouting. He barked at me and then ran off.

The corridor was concrete, and the only warm spot was the little square of carpet in front of my door. The dog had been lying there, and when he scratched himself, he bumped against the door. That was the thumping noise I'd heard.

Lesson learned: You have to check everything for yourself. If I hadn't opened the door and just let my imagination run wild, I'd have told everyone that this place really was haunted by Bruce Lee! Now that I'd solved the Case of the Itchy Dog, I was able to sleep there from that night on, no fear, no problem.

Now that I was finally making the films I wanted to make, I also got to set the tone at the studio. My aim was to repay others with kindness.

Not only did I need to respect other people's professional abilities, but I also had to make sure my own professionalism and work attitude served them. While filming and in the recording studio—with the same dubbing artists who'd mocked me—I was clear and decisive about what I wanted. I'd supervise the background noises, too, like hawkers shouting, "Get yer steamed buns, bean paste!" or the soft rustling of clothes during fight scenes, footsteps, music, background din. I was a perfectionist with sound and movement—and then I'd buy everyone dinner. You give respect, you get respect. They were all very happy to be working with me.

I continued to serve as fight director on my films, too, and gathered together a group of professionals who became known as the Jackie Chan Stunt Team. Out of all the stunt teams in Hong Kong, mine was the first to have specially designed uniforms. I just liked seeing everyone looking sharp, and thought it'd be cool if they all dressed alike. I bought them all open-necked short-sleeved shirts, embroidered with the initials "JC" in white, black, and yellow, and sent them to an excellent tailor to be fit perfectly. When we all stepped out together in our shirts, we looked very stylish.

How did it feel to go from being flat broke to being a millionaire, practically overnight? To go from being an uneducated loser to being a famous star?

It was fantastic!

My first impulse was to go out and buy everything I'd ever wanted within the space of a week.

Remember that snooty salesgirl who turned up her nose at me when I was shopping with Lo Wei? I returned to that shop with my stunt team flanking me on all sides like bodyguards. I found that salesgirl, pointed at the displays of shirts, and said, "This, and this, and this, and this. I want to try them all on." In those days, shirts came wrapped in plastic and cardboard and were stuck full of little pins. She had to unwrap every single one. I undid the buttons and slid them on for a second, then discarded them like garbage. She must have brought me dozens.

Next, I tried on shoes and pants, leaving another big pile on the floor, and another round of pointing at things with a clipped "This, not that. This, not that. Wrap them up and send them to my hotel." As I turned to leave, she looked like she was about to collapse.

The manager scurried over and said, "Sir, I'm sorry, she doesn't remember what you said."

I replied, "I was very clear; didn't she understand me? I want all the ones on this side, but not the ones on that side. Every item should be packaged like new, with every last pin, and they should all be sealed." And with that, I walked out.

I still have all those shirts, tossed in some corner of my house. I never wore them. It was all about getting my revenge on that saleswoman. You know how long it must have taken her to fold all those shirts? It thrilled me to think of it.

You can see how spiteful and immature I was. Now I know that my revenge on this hapless girl was about ignorance and ego. I'd never treat someone like that now.

For a while there, as I adjusted to my fame, I had a big chip on my shoulder. When I was a lowly martial artist, I'd often walk by the Peninsula Hotel and gaze in the window and feel small, like I didn't deserve to set one foot in there. After fame found me, I met Hong

Kong entertainment mogul Sir Run Run Shaw there for afternoon tea. I was finally getting in the door, literally and metaphorically. Followed by eight members of my team, I strolled in dressed in jeans and a tank top so everyone would see that Jackie Chan had arrived.

A waiter came over and said, "I'm sorry, sir, we don't allow tank tops here."

I said, "Oh? No tank tops? Then bring me a shirt." They fetched one and I put it on, not even doing up the buttons, and sat down to tea with Sir Run Run.

The next day, I had another meeting there. This time, I wore a shirt . . . with a pair of shorts. I strutted in, and once again, the waiter came over and said, "I'm sorry, sir, we don't allow shorts here."

I replied, "Fine, get me some pants." They brought out trousers, and I stepped into them right there in the coffee shop, not bothering to zip them up. Lots of people were gawking and pointing, and I felt like a king. All the rich people were respectably dressed, but I wasn't going to play their game. And they'd have to deal with me anyway.

One day, I took $500,000 *in cash* and brought my entire stunt team to Albert Yeung's watch emporium. With my crew of twenty waiting outside, I strutted in and said, "Show me your top ten watches. Are these the most expensive? With the most diamonds? Good, I'll take seven of them. No need to wrap them, I'll wear them out. And I'll pay cash!" And with that, I turned and walked out. Seven watches, one for every day of the week. When I met martial arts friends from the old days for a meal, I made sure to roll up my sleeves so they were on full display.

I drove drunk all the time. In the morning, I'd crash my Porsche, then in the evening I'd total a Mercedes-Benz. All day long, I went around in a haze.

At the time, paparazzi constantly rushed at me, cameras ready. I made my stunt team cover my license plates with their shirts, and even threatened to punch the photographers once for every shot they took of me. I really was quite a nasty jerk.

Back then, the Hong Kong film scene had many action teams—Team Lau, Team Hung, Team Yuen. Naturally, I wanted my team to be the richest and most admired. So I'd give them money to buy expensive cars, and we'd go out in a huge entourage of sixteen cars—seventeen, including mine!

I started to carry large amounts of cash at all times. After you live in poverty, cash gives you a sense of security. I spent a fortune on meals and drinks for my friends. I like having lots of people around me, and every meal was with a big gang. My son, Jaycee, once said to his friends that he can't remember a single meal where it was just him, his mom, and me. This hasn't changed since my younger days. Around ten years ago, I spent $16 million in one year paying for other people's meals. Friends from all over the world would come to visit me in Hong Kong, and I'd want them to experience the best food and wine; then we'd go to karaoke bars and nightclubs. If I really wanted to show them a good time, it'd cost me $50,000 a day. I gave out extravagant gifts, too: watches, cars, custom-made leather jackets, cases of expensive wine. I loved being in the position to show my feelings for people by giving them things.

One year, I made up my mind to save some money. No more big

meals out. Every night, I didn't know what to do with myself, so I'd return to the studio and sit there editing films, finding stuff to do, until I thought enough time had passed. Then I'd look at my watch, and it would still be early. That year was painful. At the end of it, I did the math and worked out I'd saved $8 million on meals. So I asked myself, *What's the point? Why torture yourself like that?* That was the last time I tried to curb my spending.

Going out and drinking every night did start to erode my professionalism. I went through a phase that was known as "one before lunch, one after lunch."

If I was called to the studio at seven in the morning, I'd arrive at noon. Everyone would be waiting for me. I'd show up in dark glasses, looking listless. Why the dark glasses? To hide the fact that my face was puffy from a night of drinking.

As the star and director of my movies, I was called "the little boss." As soon as I graced the set with my presence, I'd say, "Okay, let's shoot a scene." I'd just woken up, and my face was still puffy, so we couldn't do close-ups, only wide shots. At 12:30, the scene would be finished, and we'd break for lunch.

After lunch, I'd need a nap in Bruce Lee's dressing room, with or without his ghost. I'd wake up around four or five. We'd set up, shoot one scene, strike, and wrap for the day. And I'd think of which wide shot to shoot the next morning.

Hence "one before lunch, one after lunch."

When we filmed in the hills, if I wanted a nap, they'd have to set up a tent for me to keep out the light, and everyone would stay far away so as not to disturb me. They'd even rig an electric fan to give me some breeze.

One day, I was hungover, doing my "one before lunch" shot, when our producer, Leonard Ho, showed up for a site visit. I got flustered, thinking I was about to get chewed out by my boss, so I pretended I wasn't feeling well. I looked terrible anyway. He said, "Hello," and I doubled over in pretend pain and then fell to the ground with a thump.

Leonard shouted, "Quick, send him to the hospital! Bring the car round!"

They got me into the car, and as soon as I was in, I opened my eyes and whispered to the driver, "Is Leonard still there?"

They told me he'd gone, so I took the car to the hospital, washed my face, and returned to the studio.

I behaved terribly back then. A hundred people were waiting for me to show up, and I arrived in that state and wasted so much time. I needed a serious ego check, and I would get it in the early '80s, the first time I went to America.

chapter thirteen

WELCOME TO HOLLYWOOD

My bosses at Golden Harvest decided that the time was ripe to introduce me to Hollywood. To make me more independent and force me to work on my English, they put me on the plane to America alone, without a translator or companion.

A man named David picked me up at the airport. As soon as he saw me, he started dancing around, striking drunken-master poses. This cheered me up after the long and lonely flight. Really excited, he started telling me about the movie Golden Harvest had set up for me in America. "They've reunited the team from *Enter the Dragon*," he said. "It's a great lineup, and the script is awesome, too. I think you'll be a big star over here in no time!"

Oh, no. After that string of failures in the '70s trying to turn me into the next Bruce Lee, I was not too thrilled about walking in his footsteps again.

The person in charge of this project was Golden Harvest's international manager, Andre Morgan. He'd worked with Raymond Chow for twelve years and spoke such fluent Cantonese that I was taken aback. At that point, I knew almost no English. Andre assured me that this film, titled *The Big Brawl*, was going to be huge and that it would showcase my kung fu skills to American audiences. The budget was $4 million USD, a shockingly large amount compared to my Hong Kong budgets. Andre also wanted me to do press interviews and go on TV to raise my profile here.

I quickly learned that an American film shoot was completely different from what I was used to in Hong Kong. The American way was very rigid. The director, Robert Clouse, who'd worked with Bruce Lee on *Enter the Dragon*, stuck strictly to the shot list for every scene, and had fixed ideas about where the camera should go and how the actors should be positioned. There was nothing wrong with this way of doing things, but it didn't suit me.

In Hong Kong, we fooled around on set to try out different approaches. We would change the dialogue on the spot. That was not allowed in America. My English was so bad anyway that I had to focus all my attention on getting my lines right and forgot to make facial expressions. I would stammer through my speeches, looking wooden.

With action sequences, I was used to creating my own complex, beautiful movements, but this director insisted on sticking to the script and wouldn't give me room to improvise. Repeatedly, I tried to suggest different sequences to him, but he replied, "No, we'll shoot it as written" every time.

Scenes that should have been filled with breathtaking action just had me walking back and forth. "No one's going to pay money to watch Jackie Chan taking a stroll," I told him, to no avail.

During the filming, I went out for an Italian dinner with a couple of friends. At the time, I was fond of going around in a vest, showing off my muscled bare arms, thinking I looked pretty cool. We were drinking a bunch of beers, and eventually, I had to go to the bathroom. I stood up and started walking over there, but swerved and went straight into the door. Bam! When I woke up, I was on a sofa by the restaurant entrance. One of my friends had his foot in the automatic door, while the other was fanning vigorously, trying to get me some air. I saw their lips move but didn't hear a word they said.

My manager rushed to phone the studio and let them know what had happened. The head of Golden Harvest wanted me to go for a full-body examination right away.

I was brought to the hospital, and they wanted to give me shots and take my blood. I've always been more afraid of needles than anything else. Snakes, cockroaches, and mice don't bother me, but as soon as I see a syringe and imagine it plunging into my flesh, pumping liquid in or taking blood out, I feel terrified! A few years earlier, while shooting *Drunken Master* in Hong Kong, I'd fallen and hit the corner of my eye. At the hospital, the doctor said I needed stitches. When I refused, he stuck a giant Band-Aid over the wound, after which I went straight back to the set and continued filming. Halfway through, I started bleeding again. Ng See-Yuen, the director, brought me back to the hospital. The doctor said I really needed stitches. I asked if there was another way. He said yes, they could widen the wound and electronically cauterize every single broken capillary. I said fine, let's do that. The doctor said it would hurt far more than stitches, and I replied that I didn't care. Each jolt of electricity made me shake, but it was still better than having a needle sticking into me.

Despite this terror of needles, I let them draw my blood at the American hospital. When the results came in, the doctor asked me in English, "How old are you?" I said I was twenty-two. He informed me that I had the cholesterol of a thirty-eight-year-old.

Next, he asked what I normally ate, and I said, "A hamburger for breakfast, a hamburger for lunch, and a hamburger for dinner." I hadn't been in America long, and my English wasn't good enough to say more than "burger," "fries," "Coke," or "pizza" in a restaurant. So I ate fast food and drank soda three meals a day.

When the doctor heard this, he warned me, "You can't go on like this. You have to eat other foods. You have the sort of physique that could survive on water, but if you keep eating this stuff, your health will suffer." That's when I cut those things out of my life. Since then, I haven't had fast food or a carbonated drink more than five times.

After we wrapped *The Big Brawl*, the studio booked me another film right away. Andre was delighted. "It's called *The Cannonball Run*. Tons of Hollywood stars are lined up to appear in this with you. It's not an action film, so you can focus on the acting." The name alone gave me a good feeling. "Cannonball" was my childhood nickname, after all. I hoped this film wouldn't be as rigidly directed as *The Big Brawl*.

I played a Japanese race car driver, which I wasn't comfortable with, but it was too late to change so I had to make the most of it. The Hollywood stars in the film—Burt Reynolds, Sammy Davis Jr., Farrah Fawcett, Dom DeLuise, Dean Martin, Roger Moore—would say hello politely when they saw me, but that was it. No recognition of who I was or acknowledgment of what I'd done.

That was when I realized I wasn't actually a major star. As the Chinese saying goes, "There is always a taller mountain." I might be big in Hong Kong, but in Hollywood, I was nobody. When I returned to Hong Kong after this shoot, I told every famous person I knew, "You should visit the States to learn what a megastar actually is." I thought I was impressive with my $4.8 million Hong Kong paycheck, about $600,000 USD. American stars made $5 million USD per movie. I had big dreams about making that kind of money (and I would far exceed it later in life), but at the moment, on that set, it seemed very far off, if it was possible at all.

Sammy Davis Jr. did make a point of talking to me. He said, "I've just come back from Japan. I know you're famous over there."

"I'm from Hong Kong, not Japan," I said.

"Oh, right, you're a Hong Konger. *Sayonara!*" He spoke Japanese to me every time we met, and I didn't bother correcting him.

He wasn't the only one. Most everyone assumed I was Japanese, and I couldn't make them understand that I wasn't. I didn't have too many lines; my role was to pull silly faces to get laughs. Days would go by without my having to talk at all. I started to feel more and more depressed on set, and finally stopped speaking to anyone. I just sat in a corner, sulking.

During that entire time in Hollywood, when I turned up at events in a suit, people would ask, "Where are you from?"

"Hong Kong."

"Oh, Hong Kong, is that a part of Japan?"

"No, Hong Kong is Hong Kong, and Japan is Japan."

Many of the people I met had no idea where Hong Kong was, or that all Asian countries didn't have the same culture. I got the idea to reinforce that I was Chinese by wearing traditional Chinese clothes, which ultimately became part of my brand. It not only helped establish my nationality in America, it set me apart, too. I'd never have to worry about turning up somewhere dressed identically to anyone else. I would always be unique.

In a lot of old photos of me, I'm wearing traditional Chinese *women's* clothes. I preferred them. The colors, pale pink and blue, were more vivid, which I liked, and they had unusual designs. Wearing women's clothes also set me apart from other men. I was always thinking of how to differentiate myself from everyone else. The English word is "outstanding." I learned in America that most successful artists developed a signature style. Once you've found a special look and make it your own, you leave an impression on your audience and no one will ever forget you. The idea of creating a look for myself—and also my movies—became very important to me. If you know a movie is mine right away from the look alone, then I've succeeded.

The Big Brawl, released in 1980, was a flop. I bought a ticket and watched it in the theater. I didn't have to worry about being recognized because no one was there. A few Chinese showed up, but Americans simply weren't interested. Although I knew the shoot had been lackluster, it was still painful to see the empty auditorium.

The studio wanted me to do publicity to support the film, and they lined up lots of interviews for me. My colleagues had warned me that you needed to be psychologically prepared to face American reporters, but I thought they were making a big deal out of nothing. After everything I'd suffered when I was younger, and everything I'd been through, how bad could a press conference be?

"How is your name pronounced?"

"Are you Bruce Lee's disciple?"

"Can you break a brick with your bare hands?"

"Can you show us some karate?"

"Let's see some kung fu!"

When all these questions came flying at me, I didn't know how to cope with them. I was famous all over Asia, and people treated me with respect. But here, I was supposed to be a performing monkey? For one TV interview, I flew all the way to New York. The host's questions were terrible, and my English was worse, so I hardly said a word. In the end, they just cut my segment.

That night, I lay on my hotel room bed and cried. This was much worse than I'd expected. Why did I give up a perfectly good Asian market to come to this place where no one liked me?

I spoke to a few experts about what went wrong with *The Big Brawl* (apart from the script, the direction, and my acting), and they told me that American audiences didn't believe there was any force in my kicks and fists.

"You were fighting with the same guy for ten minutes," one said. "You kicked him eight or nine times and he's still standing. In Bruce Lee movies, his leg shot out, and the guy went flying!"

That would have been much easier to film, a punch here, a kick there, but that is not how a Jackie Chan film works. I couldn't make something like that, nor would I want to.

The Cannonball Run was released in 1981. My name and the name of Michael Hui, my Chinese costar, were both prominently featured in the Asian posters to ensure sales. In America, Burt Reynolds got top billing. The film did well in Japan and America but did badly in Hong Kong. My fans did not want to see me playing a Japanese character, nor were they happy that I'd been relegated to comic relief, the butt of jokes for a bunch of Americans.

After my first venture in Hollywood, I returned to Hong Kong with my tail between my legs. But as you know by now, I don't take defeat lightly. After a few years, I was ready to try again.

chapter fourteen

THE FLING

A few days ago, I had dinner with a friend. He mentioned, quite smugly, that he had a Hasselblad camera. Just like that, I was transported to an evening many years ago when Teresa Teng, the Taiwanese singer, and I were standing on a beach in Los Angeles, watching the sun slowly drop beneath the horizon. She said, "That's so beautiful, we should take a picture." We'd just bought a Hasselblad camera, so we quickly whipped it out and loaded it. The mechanism was complicated, and by the time I'd managed to get the film in, the sun had set. The two of us stood by the sea, laughing.

I often wonder about her, and if we would have wound up together if things had played out differently between us. But life doesn't work like that. You don't get to do over parts or go back and change your path. Your life is decided by your character and the decisions you make in the moment.

Teresa and I met by chance while I was filming *The Big Brawl*. Life was hard when I first got to America. I was learning English during the day, and at night I'd sit in my hotel room watching TV. Now and then, I'd practice roller-skating for the movie. Once, I took some Hong Kong friends to Disneyland. We walked along, chatting merrily. Then I heard someone speaking Mandarin and giggling with her friends. When I looked over, who should I see walking toward me but the famous Teresa Teng in a big group of men and women? This was unexpected.

"What are you doing here?" I asked.

She was startled to see me, too. We didn't know each other well—we might've been introduced once or twice back home—and we were both there with friends, so we just said "Hi" and "Bye," and went our separate ways without exchanging phone numbers.

A few days later, I was in Westwood to see a film, when I bumped into her again. I was entering the cinema as she was leaving it, and we laughed about the coincidence. We stood there chatting. She was on her own that day, and so was I. I was going to this movie to improve my English, and it was probably the same for her. In the course of the conversation, we realized we lived close together—just three blocks apart. That time, we exchanged numbers.

This really was fate. We'd never run into each other back home, but it happened in America twice. I asked her out and we started spending time together. Her mom was visiting at the time and would sometimes make me soup. Teresa knew I was working hard to master roller-skating, so when she told me she wanted to learn, I was happy to teach her.

Some days, I roller-skated to her place. She was just starting out, so I needed to hold on to her arm. Just imagine, Jackie Chan and Teresa Teng roller-skating down a sidewalk in Los Angeles. No one recognized us, of course. (In Hong Kong, it would have made headlines.)

I wasn't so thrilled with how the movie was going, but with her, I was happy. We had a wonderful time together practicing our English, walking along the beach, taking photographs, feasting on crabs or getting dinner in Chinatown. I'd pick her up in my car, and we'd get lost driving around Los Angeles, seeing the sights. I wouldn't say we were dating per se. But being with her was the only time I felt joy. Perhaps it was the same for her.

Unfortunately, I was due to start filming in San Antonio, and she had to return to Taiwan. I told her that when I was done with my shoot, I'd look her up.

The Big Brawl did badly, as I've said. I returned to Hong Kong in despair, wanting to regroup and make another film to restore my image. I quickly put a creative team together and we went to Korea, where we spent three months working on the script. At the time, there were many Hong Kongese–Korean coproductions. Ours was the largest team Korea had ever seen. We had twelve electricians and sixteen carpenters. The preparations must have taken four or five months in total, but, sadly, we had to quit only two days into the shoot. The film was set in the summer, but by now it was winter, and no one could withstand the freezing temperatures. On day three, everyone was turning blue, and I said, "Okay, that's enough. Back at the hotel." We all trudged over there and huddled around the heaters. We'd already spent about $2 million, a lot of money at the time.

I phoned our producer, Leonard Ho, and told him what had happened. After asking if anyone had frostbite, he simply said, "Cancel filming." That was truly heartwarming. The team returned to Hong Kong, and I started changing the script and thinking about where to film instead. I heard myself say, "What about Taiwan?"

I told myself this was for the film, that Taiwan had the landscapes we needed and would be a perfect place to shoot. Looking back now, I know that I also secretly wanted to see Teresa Teng.

While location scouting in Taiwan, Teresa and I had quiet meals together. I went to one of her concerts, too. Sitting in a special box above the auditorium, I saw her looking up and knew she was gazing at me. The crowd clapped and shouted their hearts out for her, and I thought, *That's my girlfriend.* No one knew we were together. I made sure to leave before the end of the concert. If we'd been photographed together, it would have been explosive news in Taiwan.

Although I loved spending time with her and was in awe of her talent, I knew there were problems. Right from the beginning, our personalities were very different, and we were unable to meet each other halfway. Or, to put it another way, she was too good for me.

She was always polite and soft-spoken, while I was a clumsy oaf.

She was elegant, and I wore a vest with as many gold chains around my neck as I could get. She enjoyed time alone, while I liked excitement and having tons of people around me. Wherever I went, I wanted people to take my coat and pull out chairs for me, but she liked to be low-key.

One day, she phoned me and asked if we could have dinner. I said, "We have dinner every day."

She said, "I meant alone."

We went to a French restaurant where she'd booked us a private room. Back then, I didn't know how to make sense of the menu or order wine. The waiter handed everything to me, and I just stared at it. Teresa took the menu and sorted it out, ordering with some English and French words mixed in.

It made me feel like an uneducated fool and I threw a little tantrum. She suggested I have my steak cooked medium and I said, "No, I want it well-done." She ordered red wine; I insisted on having beer. She raised her wineglass and sniffed delicately, while I guzzled my drink. She asked how it tasted, and I said, "Terrible." When our soup arrived, she dipped her spoon elegantly into her bowl, while I picked up my bowl and drank straight from it. Our steaks came, and before she'd even taken her first bite, I'd finished mine. This was one of those restaurants where they wouldn't bring the next course until the previous one was done. So as not to keep me waiting, she had to say she was finished with her steak, too. By the end of the meal, I was absolutely stuffed, and she was still starving.

A French dinner usually takes two or three hours, but we were done after thirty minutes. As we walked out, I said, "Never bring me to this sort of restaurant again. I have a meeting to go to." I turned on my heel and left.

I behaved so badly because of my deep insecurities. Ever since I was a little boy, I'd been looked down on by rich kids. Then I'd had a grueling decade at the CDA and started work at the lowest level of society. What I hated more than anything was when those in power were dismissive toward those without. Any whiff of snobbishness or superiority set me on edge. This attitude affected my relationship with Teresa. But it wasn't her fault. She'd done nothing wrong, and I was horribly unfair to her.

One day I was in a script meeting, when she phoned to say she was leaving Taiwan for a while and would like to see me. I invited her to the studio. She showed up in an evening dress and high heels, probably having just finished performing. I thought she looked stunning. All the other guys were dumbstruck.

I don't know what madness came over me. It was like I wanted to look cool in front of the others.

I said one word: "Sit."

She sat by herself in a corner, and we went on with our script meeting. For more than an hour, I didn't say another word to her. Then she stood up and said, "Jackie, I'm leaving."

I said, "Fine."

She walked out the door. The guy next to me, Fung Hark-On, said, "Jackie, shouldn't you go after her?"

I said, "Yeah, I guess," still trying to look cool. But I ran for the elevators. The double doors had already closed. I went back inside and looked out the window. Eight stories below, she got in a Cadillac and drove off.

Like nothing had happened, I went back to my script meeting. A short while later, the phone rang. I answered it and heard her voice.

"Jackie, it looks like you don't need me, so you should just hang out with your guys," she said, and hung up.

The next day, she called again and said she'd left something for me at the hotel reception desk. I went back after work and picked up the package from the concierge. It was a cassette tape of her singing "Return My Love to Me." Some lyrics: "I was never in your heart, return my love to me."

The film I was making in Taiwan was called *Dragon Lord*. It was an exhausting shoot, and many people got injured. The hospital was full of our crew. All I thought about each day was getting the job done, and it felt like my brain was cracking from stress. There was no room left for love. Her giving me that tape was it for us. I didn't reach out, and she was gone.

A few months later, she gave a concert in Hong Kong. My agent met Teresa for a drink after the show. She told him, "You know what? I hate him."

My agent repeated what she said, and that was when I realized how awful I'd been. I'd hurt her thoughtlessly, carelessly.

The next time I saw her was at an award ceremony organized by the businessman Peter Lam. He called to ask if I'd present Teresa Teng with her prize. My instinct was to say no, because I knew she probably still hated me. I asked, "Does she know I might be presenting?"

"Yes!" he said.

"Really? In that case, I'd be happy to," I said. It would be my chance to apologize and try to make up for the ignorance of the past.

That night, she was supposed to sing a song first. I hid backstage, and halfway through her performance, during a musical interlude, I walked out with the trophy. When she turned and saw me, she didn't whoop with joy. Not by a long shot. She practically ran off the stage, and I had to chase her. She wouldn't stop and refused to take the award from me. I kept after her, and in the end she took it, but she wouldn't shake my hand or thank me. She just stormed off.

Peter Lam admitted afterward that he hadn't told her about my presenting the award. He thought it would be a pleasant surprise because he knew we'd once been close.

If there'd been anything left between us, it was truly destroyed now.

I saw her again a few years later at the entrance to the Shangri-La Hotel. She was getting into an elevator as I was leaving one. Another coincidence. We stared at each other; then she smiled and so did I. We didn't speak. She was with her friends, and I was with mine. I kept smiling until the elevator doors had closed on her. It was a moment. Maybe she'd forgiven me a little.

In May 1995, my assistant Dorothy took a cell phone call from America. The caller said, "It's Miss Teng. I want to speak to Jackie."

Dorothy said, "Jackie's not here now; he'll be back in a few days." Dorothy passed the message to me and I intended to call Teresa back, but I got distracted and forgot.

To my shock, a few days later, I heard that Teresa was dead.

She'd had a severe allergy attack at a hotel in Thailand. She was only forty-two. I was completely stunned. In an instant, all my memories with her flashed through my mind, and my tears wouldn't stop falling. Ever since, whenever anyone's left me a message, I always call back right away.

Because of my filming schedule, I was unable to attend her funeral.

In 2002, I released an album in China that included me singing a duet with her on her song "I Only Care About You." I hope my message was somehow able to pass through space and time, bringing my eternal apologies to her.

chapter fifteen

FREE FALL

Back in Hong Kong after my disappointing 1980 American misadventure, I was ready to use what I had learned in Hollywood about myself, my style, and my goals for action films.

The movies I made with Ng See-Yuen were a new direction for martial arts films, but now that I'd signed with a new studio, I wanted to go in a more original direction. No longer would I lean on the tropes of the eccentric master and lazy disciple, nor would the narrative revolve around training. I wanted my scenes to be clean and simple, but with production values comparable to mainstream films. On this point, I would be very different from older kung fu films like Bruce Lee's or the Shaw Brothers'. In 1980, I made *The Young Master*, the story of a man who is kicked out of his school and goes off on his own mission to find his lost brother. It was a great success. The film served as a marker, an end point. I was saying good-bye to the past and moving on to a new stage of my career.

Edward Tang—my longtime collaborator and the screenwriter I work with to this day—started taking inspiration from Hollywood movies, namely Steven Spielberg's *Raiders of the Lost Ark*. He wanted to make a film full of gunfights and stunt-filled combat sequences, which led to us creating a script then called *Battle on the High Seas*.

Set in the early twentieth century, the story was about a gang of pirates destroying a Hong Kong naval fleet. I played the naval police chief, Ma Yu-Lung, who'd transferred to a land unit but continued to track down and capture pirates.

There were two other major roles: an upright cop and a local small-time swindler. They brought color and humor to an otherwise tense story. When Edward and I discussed the script, it was clear that the only two people who could do justice to these parts were my old schoolmates Sammo Hung and Yuen Biao. We were all veterans of the movie industry and skilled action performers, and we knew each other very well. A single look or gesture, and we knew exactly what one another was thinking. Our unbeatable chemistry made the shoot go smoothly, and we had a great time. We were so close on that shoot, we even showered together.

For an important stunt sequence in the film, my character would be chased through the streets, climb a flagpole, and jump onto a clock tower, then fall facedown onto the ground. After much discussion, we decided there was no way to fake it. The only way to get this scene would be to shoot it for real, and I'd have to do the stunt myself.

The production team started working out how they could slow down my fifteen-meter free fall so I wouldn't actually plummet to my death. The solution was to go through a couple of cloth awnings. *That's it?* I thought. *Nothing between me and the ground but scraps of fabric? Well, okay.*

After we'd planned the shots, Yuen Biao looked at me doubtfully. "Are you sure this will work?"

Looking confident, if not feeling it, I replied, "No problem. Let's give it a go."

The crew made a sandbag that weighed the same as me and flung it off the clock tower. It ripped through both awnings and hit the ground, splitting apart, sand splattering everywhere. I could only stare at it, stupefied.

"One test doesn't mean anything, let's tighten the awnings and try again," I said. The second sandbag was more fortunate and landed intact.

At the time, in Hong Kong, shooting anything on location meant turning a public space into a movie set. We were filming in a parking lot and caused a major disruption for the people who lived and worked nearby. I've always believed that a slow approach produces the best work, so we needed to occupy it for several months. This meant many people weren't able to leave their cars in their usual spots and had to park a distance away, causing traffic problems in the neighborhood. Luckily everyone was very understanding, and no one complained. Instead, many people showed up to watch us.

As we were preparing to film this particular scene, we found out someone had leaked the news that I'd be doing the clock-tower plunge in person rather than using a body double. Suddenly, everyone from office workers to street hawkers and passersby rushed over to have a look. At lunchtime, even more people showed up, bowls in hand, to gawk while they ate.

Standing at the top of the tower, looking down at all the people, I lost my nerve. "I'm not jumping today," I announced. Disappointed, the crowd dispersed.

In fact, for the next few days, my heart started pounding fast whenever we set up to shoot this scene. I'd look up at the tower, work out how far I had to fall with only some flimsy bits of cloth in the way. If I landed a little too far forward, my head would split open. A little too far back, and my legs would snap. How on earth would I do this? I would try to steel myself and think, *Just grit your teeth and do it!* But each time I stood on the edge, I pictured that split sandbag and instinctively stepped back.

On our first try, I climbed to the top of the tower, and my stunt team slowly helped me out the window until I was clinging to the minute hand of the clock. Before the cameras even started rolling, my entire body weight hung from that metal rod and my hands started to throb. I yelled for my team, and they pulled me back inside.

On our second attempt, I got into position, but had to be pulled back in again. Raymond Chow and Leonard Ho were at the set that day. When they climbed the tower and saw how dangerous the stunt was, they urged me to reconsider. "If you don't want to jump, then don't," said Leonard. "We can use a stunt double."

"Stunt doubles are human, and they'll be scared, too," I said. "I can do it."

For six days running, I found a different excuse to avoid shooting that scene. One day, I'd say the overhead light didn't work. The next, the sky was too cloudy. The day after that, the sunset wasn't right. I was the director, and no matter what I said, the lighting and cinematography units had to agree with me. We didn't shoot a single frame for six days.

On day seven, the sunlight was perfect, and I climbed the clock tower once again, my heart thumping. Sammo Hung was watching from below. Seeing me hesitate again, he yelled, "How long are you going to wait? There's nowhere to park—I have to walk here every day. Are you doing this scene or not?"

I shouted back, "Why don't you be the director? Shoot this one for me!"

Sammo said, "Sure, I'll do it!" And with that, he grabbed the camera and called to the crew, "Get ready!"

I told my stunt team to leave the area so I didn't have them to pull me back in. I was determined to hang from the minute hand until I ran out of strength, and then just let go.

From below, I heard four cameras starting to roll and Sammo shouting, "Are you ready? Everyone's waiting for you!"

I grabbed onto the minute hand. If you watch that scene now, you'll see that I'm clinging on for dear life until I can't hold on any longer. There was no acting involved—it was all real. When I heard "Rolling, action," I waited until my hands ran out of energy, throbbing with pain, before loosening my grip. *Here we go.*

My body went into free fall.

I hit the first piece of cloth, ripping it apart.

I tore through the second awning.

With a crash, I landed on the ground.

There wasn't enough time for me to turn in midair to slow down and reduce the impact, so I just went smack on the pavement and my neck twisted sharply. But I didn't die.

After icing my injury for a while, I told everyone I was ready to go again. "What? Are you crazy?" asked Sammo. He and Yuen Biao thought I'd lost my mind. The shot we had lasted only four seconds, and wouldn't make enough of an impact. I wanted the sequence to take up ten seconds of screen time and be presented from multiple angles. They didn't bother trying to talk me out of it. We set up for take number two.

On the second try, the fall went the same way. When I hit the ground, my brain fogged up. I'd crashed hard twice in quick succession. I really was crazy. Yuen Biao was in this scene, too. He rushed over and helped me to my feet, murmuring in my ear, "Quick, stand up. You have to say your lines now, otherwise there'll have been no point jumping!" Hearing his voice, I somehow managed to struggle upright and mumble a few sentences. Yuen Biao and the other actors dragged me off and the scene was wrapped.

The film was released with the title *Project A*, and it was a huge success. My two comrades and I had boldly broken new ground and found a new direction for kung fu films. As far as I'm concerned, the most important thing about this 1983 film was that it forged the key element of my cinematic reputation: I always perform my own stunts, no matter how dangerous, and never use a body double. To this day, I'm known for it, and it separates me from everyone else. When audiences see my films, they know it's me taking the risks and endangering my life. In the beginning, people would shriek and think I was a madman, but now they're used to it.

As we were preparing to film *Wheels on Meals*, Sammo had a bright idea. "I want to bring a crew to Spain and film there," he said. "It's too much trouble in Hong Kong: You have to get permits for everything and they won't let us film where we want to. The movie won't look good if we don't have enough backdrops! We need to try somewhere else."

I agreed with him. We would have foreign settings and we could use foreign actors, which would make the film feel more international and exotic, and increase our chances of being distributed abroad. The strategy worked. *Wheels on Meals* did well globally. Despite having far smaller budgets than Hollywood and lacking special effects and worldwide distribution channels, we were making inroads with just our fighting spirit and our willingness to take such huge risks.

In fact, since *Dragon Lord*, not one insurance company has been willing to cover a Jackie Chan film. We're blacklisted all over the world. And proud of it!

Slowly but surely, we were coming to define what makes a Jackie Chan film. The plots and settings were different, but there are key characteristics.

1. **Common men.** In every film, I get beaten up badly. I have no image to protect and don't mind looking hideous on-screen. I play everyday men with problems and imperfections—not the sort to start a fight, but, when backed into a corner, they'll battle to survive.

2. **Improvisation, especially in the fight sequences.** Important scenes get two words of script direction, such as "big fight" or "small fight." Fight scenes in American films were short and existed just to show how powerful the lead actor was. In my films, fights are drawn out from beginning to end, and these scenes are precisely what the audience wants to see. Later on, my American scripts replaced fight descriptions with a simple line: "Let Jackie Chan design this."

3. **Stunts!** Other films use different shots and quick cuts to show the action, but in a Jackie Chan film, if there's anything dangerous or exciting, I'll do it myself in a single unbroken take.

4. **Starting with action.** Not that plot is unimportant, but we build ours around thrilling action.

5. **Exotic settings.** My films are set all over the world. I want to visit every interesting spot on this planet and capture it on film.

6. **Positive values.** I'll never express anything vulgar, mean, cruel, or negative.

This formula has been in place since the mid-'80s, and it's still working for me thirty years later! Why? It's unique to me. As I've told my team over the years, I don't want to copy anyone or be like anyone else. There's only one me, and I'm it.

The problem with having this reputation is that I had no choice but to push my body and courage to new heights with each new movie. People say that every bone in my body has been broken at least once, which is an exaggeration. But only slightly. From my hair to the tips of my toes, every inch of my body has been wounded. I'm sure that's the experience of every stuntperson, though, and not just me.

My ankle joint pops out of its socket all the time, even when I'm just walking around, and I'll have to pop it back in. My leg sometimes gets dislocated when I'm showering. For that one, I need my assistant to help me click it back in. I've been delaying shoulder surgery for three years now—I'm supposed to have a couple of screws put into it—so I can't lift heavy objects. The cartilage in my kneecaps has been worn away, so I can't go running.

When I was younger, I was always getting carried away and dragging other people into my life-risking schemes. If "making of" documentaries were popular back then and someone had filmed what we did, you'd think we weren't human. Looking back, it's a miracle we weren't all killed. But everyone just went for it. We always had a stretcher on set and a car waiting with its doors open so anyone who got injured could be driven straight to the hospital.

During a particularly difficult action sequence in *Police Story*, the first martial artist jumped in, broke his hand, and was driven away. The second got hit on the head and was carried away. Seeing the rest of the team start to shuffle nervously about who'd go next, I cursed, got changed, and did the stunt myself. With a crash, I made the leap . . . and *also* got taken to the hospital, blood streaming from my mouth. I've always said that I'd never ask anyone on my team to do something I wouldn't do myself!

I can't keep count of the injuries I've accumulated over the decades. There might be some mistakes in the following list:

- **Head.** I got hit so hard during *Hand of Death* that I passed out. The worst injury was filming *Armour of God* when I needed brain surgery. (More on that later.)
- **Ear.** The *Armour of God* incident resulted in permanent hearing loss in my left ear.
- **Eyes.** When my brow ridge shattered during *Drunken Master*, I almost lost an eye.
- **Nose.** I broke my nose on *To Kill with Intrigue* and seriously injured it in *Dragon Fist*.
- **Philtrum (upper lip).** It got torn so badly during *Police Story 4*, you could see my teeth through it. I superglued

it back together and went on filming. By nightfall, it had almost healed.

- **Cheekbone.** I broke it filming *Police Story 3: Super Cop*.
- **Teeth.** In *Snake in the Eagle's Shadow*, a tooth was kicked out of my mouth.
- **Jaw.** After *Dragon Lord*, my jaw was so messed up, I couldn't speak for a long time.
- **Throat.** I got strangled during *The Young Master*.
- **Neck.** The most serious injuries were from falling off that clock tower in *Project A* and jumping off a building in *Mr. Nice Guy*.
- **Shoulder.** It was dislocated during *City Hunter*.
- **Hands.** They were burned during *Police Story*. I damaged my hand and finger bones in *The Protector*, and my whole hand got twisted around during *Project A*.
- **Arm.** Stabbed in *Snake in the Eagle's Shadow*, with blood everywhere, all captured on film.
- **Chest.** I had a bad sternum injury during *The Young Master*, and when I fell off a cliff during *Armour of God II: Operation Condor*.

- **Back.** So many injuries. I almost snapped my spine between the seventh and eighth vertebrae during *Police Story* and hurt it again when a wire snapped and I fell to the ground while filming *Chinese Zodiac*.

- **Pelvis.** Dislocated during *Police Story*.

- **Thigh.** Hit by a car during *Crime Story*.

- **Knees.** So many! The most serious injury was during *City Hunter*.

- **Ankles.** I broke my ankle making *Rumble in the Bronx*. My whole leg got twisted round, but I went on filming in a plaster cast. When I was bored, I would pull a sock over the cast and draw a running shoe on it.

- **Foot.** While filming *Who Am I?*, I was playing with a Swiss Army Knife, tossed it in the air, and then dropped it. I don't know what I was thinking, but I tried to catch it with my foot and stabbed myself. When I took off my shoe, it was a bloody mess. I wrapped a bandage around it and went on filming.

Nowadays, I don't take those kind of risks, or ask my stunt teams to. Even if a stunt is one-tenth as dangerous as what we got up to back in the day, we'll plan and calculate and set up fail-safes before we let anyone attempt it. I don't want young stuntmen going down the road I did, suffering so much and making their families worry. Used to be, with my team's reputation, we couldn't always recruit new people. Now we have the safest, most advanced equipment. Every wheel, every piece of rope, every buckle, is perfectly secure, and we make sure everyone is fully trained to use it. Not only do we guarantee everyone's safety, we try to keep them as comfortable as possible.

In 2013, *Chinese Zodiac* won two awards for fight direction. Onstage, I said I wanted to share my award with all the stuntpeople across the world. They risk their lives behind the scenes every day. I am lucky to have had a chance to be known and appreciated for my work. When I get injured, the whole world knows about it. Many stuntpeople break bones and even die, and no one knows or cares. I wish movie audiences understood, acknowledged, and applauded their contribution to film. How about Oscars for the Best Action Film, Best Movement Director, Best Male and Female Action Actors? The performers who risk their lives for your entertainment deserve a turn in the spotlight.

chapter sixteen

THE GRITTY

As a kid, I wanted to be a policeman, a boxer, a hired thug, an FBI officer, and a secret agent.

As a director, I hired a screenwriter to write out the dreams of my youth, making them come true, one by one. I got to be a cop, a soldier, a spy, all of them—except one. I'm still trying to get a movie about a firefighter made. The one role I can't really play is the hot leading man. I'm not the physical type to have women falling all over me, and I certainly don't have that much confidence in myself. My natural casting is a normal guy, i.e., one who isn't draped with babes.

As an actor, I've been able to experience lives I'd otherwise never have. I know how lucky I am to work in this profession.

There is a dark side to the entertainment business, though, especially in Hong Kong.

My dad's advice to me was always "Don't touch gambling, don't touch drugs, and don't touch secret societies."

Back in the '70s and '80s, Hong Kong and Taiwan's secret societies were hard to avoid. They were rampant. These gangs did all the same things criminal organizations do in America, and they were often intertwined with the entertainment world, with protection and loan-sharking. Try as we might, we simply couldn't avoid them.

One day, a few of us were out for a steak dinner, when a kid suddenly kicked the door open and came in. His hands were stuffed into a small bag he had slung around his neck. We looked up at him, and he stared back. Something felt wrong.

The person next to me said, "Stop! What are you doing?"

"Nothing."

"Fuck! Take it out, don't scare us, show us your hands and tell us what you're doing."

The kid quickly left. It turned out he'd meant to go into the next room but had kicked in the wrong door. The rest of that dinner was fraught with anxiety, and I couldn't finish my steak. The kid probably had a hand grenade in his bag. That's the best weapon for when you're outnumbered.

Another time, I was working as the fight director on a film and staying at the Lincoln Plaza Hotel. We were almost done for the day. It was very warm, and I was standing outside. Two people came over and asked, "Who's the fight director?"

I said, "I am. What's up?"

One said, "All we've got on us is a flat spike. What do you think?"

A "flat spike" is a ring with three sharp prongs attached. It's worn on the thumb and used as a weapon. It's not life-threatening because they wrap it in cloth so only a couple of centimeters of the spikes poke out, but it will shred your flesh in a way that won't heal for a long time.

Seeing the weapon, I said, "Um, I'll go get the producer." I went into the office and asked, "Who are these people?"

A lot of our studio crew had underworld connections, so everyone came out to have a look. The gangsters saw a crowd approaching and quickly fled. I'm not sure why they were there. A shakedown? To get a part in the movie?

The next day, I was in my dressing room very early in the morning. Normally when I was at the studio, my door stayed open. Even if I wanted privacy and shut it, people knew they just had to knock and I'd open it. Someone knocked at the door, and I assumed I was wanted on the set. It seemed a bit early, though, so I looked through the peephole. All I could see were two forty-two-inch katana swords! They were wielded by the two men who'd shown me the flat spike. I took a hasty step back, feeling numb all over. The gangsters were outside my door, with lethal weapons. I started shaking. I stared at the shadows of their legs in the crack of the doorframe, dreading what was to come next.

What should I do? I told myself, *Don't panic! Remain calm!* I retreated to the inner room and remembered the two fancy knives I'd bought as a gift for my father. They weren't wrapped yet. I strapped on my martial arts protective gear, two of each item so my arms were well protected, and grabbed the knives.

I told myself, *Don't be scared. You have knives.*

As a martial artist, I knew it was easy to injure yourself using two blades at once, accidentally cutting your left arm when you swing in that direction, so I just kept reminding myself, *I have two knives, I have two knives.*

Well armed, I wasn't afraid anymore. I tiptoed back to the door, planning to start hacking as soon as it opened. But when I peeked through the hole again, no one was there. They'd left. I put down my knives and picked up the phone. I dialed the set and, taking the receiver under a pillow to muffle the noise, I whispered, "Something's happening; come quick."

After hanging up, I stepped back and waited for the shadows to reappear. At this point, I hoped they *would* come back so I could hack them to bits. I felt like running out and chasing after them.

After twenty minutes, another knock. I looked out and saw two members of my team. I opened the door for them. They were wearing suits and walking funny when they came in, like there was something wrong with their legs.

I asked, "What's up with your legs?"

They had katana swords, too, but didn't want to carry them around openly, so they'd stuffed them down their trouser legs. I told them what had happened earlier, and they told me not to worry, that they'd already checked the area and hadn't seen any suspicious characters.

Together, the three of us went downstairs to the set. On the ground floor of the building, the lobby was full of armed people, my whole team, the lighting guys, the assistants. One of my guys said, "Look, Jackie, everyone's on your side and ready to go!"

Later on, we found out that those two men had been lying in wait for me. I'd embarrassed them at the studio earlier when I dismissed them, and they came back for their revenge. Good thing I didn't open the door right away as usual or I would have been chopped to death. We went on with the shoot, but after that, the studio assigned two armed men to stand guard on the premises.

Apart from being threatened by gang members, I've also had to be wary of scams and grifters, people who knew I was rich and plotted to separate me from my money.

One time, after we wrapped for the day, a local producer warmly invited me to his home for a party. But when I arrived, the place was empty. He said, "Oh, it's not a big gathering. A few of us are playing pai gow."

As I've mentioned, I have been known to gamble. When I was just out of the academy, I gambled a lot—and lost a lot. I'd seen all kinds of scams, so I was always suspicious and on the lookout for cheats.

Following my host into the inner room, I saw a group of people gambling and knew that I was their intended mark. I said, "How about this? Let's go get dinner, and then we can play afterwards."

They said, "All right," and put down their cards right away. When I saw that, I had confirmation that my suspicions were right.

Real players wouldn't do that. If you were in the middle of a hand and someone said, "Let's go get dinner," you'd finish the hand. You wouldn't put your cards down in the middle of one. But that's what these people did, and I almost laughed, thinking, *You haven't planned this very well, have you?*

I had dinner with them, making sure I had a couple of drinks during the meal. Afterwards, I said, "Oh, boy. I don't feel so good after those drinks. I should go home. I'll gamble with you another day. How about tomorrow?" The next day, I boarded a plane and flew off.

Quite a few years later, I saw this producer again. He said, "Jackie, I'm sorry, we were all in it that time to scam you."

This crew had, apparently, suckered a lot of rich people out of millions. Once those wealthy marks were on the hook for a fortune, they were forced to drag other celebrities into it. It was like a pyramid scheme for scamming.

Once, friends in Taiwan took me out to dinner, and as soon as we sat down, they started introducing me to other people who came to the table. Another warning sign. Afterwards, we went for a stroll that led us to an underground gambling den, where they would play as a pack to make me lose. As soon as we entered, they gave me $500,000 New Taiwan dollars in gambling chips to tempt me to stay. I'd lose all that, and far more, if they had their way. I said, "I'll come back another day, I feel a bit strange from the alcohol," and dodged another bullet.

This same group tried to lure me in again. I must have downed a dozen glasses of whiskey, full to the brim, toasting every one of these people at dinner . . . and then I threw up all over the floor, and they had to bring me back to the hotel. Heh, that was a good one.

It was tricky to navigate through the underworld dangers back then. I'm glad I got into the business young and learned about all these scams when I didn't have much money to lose.

chapter seventeen

THE LOVE OF MY LIFE

Back in the day, there was a magazine in Hong Kong called *Cineart*. I got a phone call from the editor, Annie Wong, who said she wanted me to look at some photos she'd taken. I went to meet her at Worldwide Gardens in Sha Tin. When I walked in, two young women were sitting there. One was Annie Wong, and the other was Joan Lin.

Joan was a Taiwanese movie actress, an award-winner who'd starred in megahits with her partners Charlie Chin, Chin Han, and Brigitte Lin (a.k.a. "Two Chins, Two Lins," as they were known). I was very good friends with Charlie Chin, so I knew exactly who she was and liked her from that first meeting.

The next time I was in Taiwan, I phoned her and said, "You told me you'd take me out to dinner if I was ever in town."

She said, "Great. What do you want to eat?"

As usual, I was with my entourage, and she'd brought along her little sister. Although she'd wanted it to be her treat, I had so many people with me, I insisted on paying. She didn't object, but then she started ordering for everyone.

Long ago, I told the guys on my stunt team that I didn't like eating fish. They took that as a directive, and when we went out to dinner, they'd tell everyone, "Don't order fish. Jackie doesn't like fish." If they saw anyone eating seafood, they'd say, "Take that somewhere else!" I enjoyed being leader of the pack, and got used to thinking of myself as a non–fish eater.

When Joan started ordering, my gang chorused, "No! Jackie doesn't eat fish!"

She asked, "Why not? The fish here is delicious."

That was that. We had fish, and, man, were my guys happy (I guess they'd missed it!). We had a great time, and the food was soon all gone. Joan didn't talk much during the meal, but the strange thing was, my team had a great impression of her afterwards. They kept saying to me, "Jackie, she's so beautiful, and such a nice person."

"Yeah, she wants me," I said, or something obnoxious like that. Very mature.

I asked her out several more times. As I got to know her, I slowly realized she was different from the other women I'd spent time with. She was even-tempered and approachable, not at all like a star. She dressed plainly and didn't like expensive clothes or jewelry. I behaved like an oaf as usual, but it didn't bother her. I never felt uncomfortable with her. Not once did she correct my pronunciation, grammar, or manners. When we ate out, she was happy to go to less fancy places and eat the same food as me. She was happy to hang out with my friends and watch us drinking and playing cards in some dive bar. No matter what I said, it always made her laugh.

All of this made me feel free to be myself. She appreciated me as a person, not because I was a movie star. I never asked her why she liked me, but that question was frequently on my mind. Still, she wasn't pushing me away.

One day, we were having dinner, when she mentioned she was in the middle of filming a movie and had an action scene the next day. She'd never done much action before and hoped I would give her some pointers about staying safe. The next day, the entire Jackie Chan Stunt Team turned up on Joan Lin's set to give her some pointers.

That was how I pursued girls: I overwhelmed them.

I was filming in Hong Kong while she was filming in Taiwan, but I'd drop by her set whenever I could, bringing her something to eat. I also asked her to come visit me on my set. It was obvious to everyone that we cared about each other. Gossip about our relationship started appearing in various newspapers, and a lot of fans weren't pleased with our being a couple. She was a beloved actress with a respectable image, while I was a vulgar kung fu guy who was unworthy of her. A Japanese paper claimed we'd already gotten married, and two of my ardent fans killed themselves because of it. This was getting serious. I worried that these lies would lead to one of us—or more fans—getting hurt. If the media had been as all-powerful then as it is today, we probably would have split up long ago.

Then, in 1981, Joan told me she was pregnant. I said right away, "I want to keep the baby." I might have seemed calm, but I was freaking out on the inside and didn't know what to do, though not because I didn't really want to have this child. If false rumors of our marriage caused fans to kill themselves, God knew what a pregnancy would do. I asked Leonard Ho for advice, and he suggested moving Joan to America and having the baby there in relative secrecy.

It seemed like a viable strategy. I asked her what she thought, and she agreed to go. She was at the height of her fame, but she turned down all the movie roles she was being offered and moved to California. I was busy filming, so I couldn't go with her. Instead, I sent my manager to make the trip with her and get her settled. Then my manager returned, and she was all by herself, with no one to take care of her.

I worked through her whole pregnancy and didn't visit her in America once. I made it over there only when the baby was about to be born. My manager suggested we get married first, so we found a pastor and went to a rooftop coffee shop in Los Angeles. It was lunchtime, and the place was packed. We got a private room, but it was still very noisy, and we could hear all the conversations going on outside. It was hardly the wedding of anyone's fantasies, but we didn't have that luxury.

The pastor said, "Do you?"

We said, "We do," and we were hitched.

She was admitted to the hospital that night. I kept her company for many hours, but the baby was taking his time to come out. I was groggy from jet lag, so I asked a friend to stay with her while I went to get some sleep.

At our place, though, I couldn't fall asleep. Too many thoughts were running through my head. For one thing, what should we name the baby?

Finally, my chance to choose a name without input from movie producers or foremen on a construction site!

You need a powerful name in this life. What would be best? I'd given this a lot of thought. My ideas included doubling my name—Chan Chan—or calling him Dot Chan, but instead of the word "Dot," his name would just be an actual dot. Or, similarly, he could be J Chan, so if his schoolteacher punished him by making him write his name over and over, at least it wouldn't take him long.

I talked it over with my manager, and he said none of those were proper names and we wouldn't be able to register them. My father came up with the name Jo-Ming, or "ancestral brightness." As for his English name, we thought of Peter, David, and so on, but none of those sounded right. Then I had a brain wave and came up with naming him my initials! J.C., or what about Jaycee? I liked that! Jaycee.

Just as I lit on that idea, my friend called from the hospital to say my son had been born! I rushed over to meet him for the first time.

Most babies are ugly when they're born, and Jaycee was no exception. But I didn't much care what he looked like. I wanted to make sure he was healthy. Then I checked if he was "double-boned." Most people are single-boned, but I was always told I was double-boned—that is, my bones were larger than normal people's. Martial artists need thick bones. I took one look and saw that my son was double-boned, too, which pleased me to no end. Only then did it sink in that this baby was my child, and then nothing else mattered. I started crying. My manager cried, too, and said, "I never thought Jackie Chan would have a child of his own." The implication was that I was still a child myself—which was true in spirit. We laughed through our tears.

Joan was worn-out but overjoyed to finally hold our son and become a mother. I stayed with my new family for as long as I could, but unfortunately I had to go back to Hong Kong to carry on filming—a whole production was waiting for me. I left a close friend to stay and help Joan in any way possible.

As happy as I was that Joan and Jaycee were both fine and that I was a father, I have to admit that some doubts popped into my head. For whatever reason, I started to think about some of the stories I'd heard from my friends over the years about times they'd been tricked, hurt, and lied to by women. One of my martial artist friends came home after a movie shoot to find his entire house cleaned out by his girlfriend—money, savings, furniture, all gone. Of course, she'd vanished, too. A similar thing had happened to Lo Wei. He returned to Hong Kong after being away on a film to find his house and accounts emptied by a girlfriend. She'd quietly transferred everything to her name. Before she left, she wrote a check for $500,000 and tossed it at him, the ultimate humiliation. He cursed her, tore up the check, and flung it back in her face. She laughed and walked away. When he told me this story, he sobbed bitterly. "How can women be so wicked?" he asked.

Many of my friends felt the same way about women in general, and some of them put a bug in my ear about Joan. They suggested she got pregnant on purpose, and that it'd been her plan all along. I'd never been suspicious of her motives throughout our relationship, but my friends kept saying that I should be. I was young, and I admit, I began to wonder.

Although I frittered away my own money like crazy, I never gave Joan access to my bank accounts and made sure that, if we were to divorce, she wouldn't receive a dime. I sent her a fixed sum every month to cover an apartment, a car, and spending money for her and Jaycee. I'm embarrassed and ashamed to say this now, but I was constantly thinking of ways to keep my money away from her. I was the wicked one, not her, and also stupid.

If I'd thought about it for a minute, I would have realized that Joan Lin had been a famous actress for ten years, with plenty of her own money. Why would she want any of mine? She wanted to be with me because she truly loved me. But I couldn't help being influenced by the stories my friends were telling me. More rational thoughts were crowded out of my mind. Maybe something similar goes on when women get together to moan about their boyfriends and husbands, and end up concluding that all men are terrible?

No matter how ridiculously I behaved early on or for years afterwards, Joan never did anything to deserve a moment's doubt. She was always patient and supportive, and a wonderful mother. We were often apart because of my work schedule, but she managed our household responsibly and never interfered in my career. We stuck together in a less-than-conventional marriage, but then again, I didn't live a conventional life.

In 1999, I made a serious mistake.

When the news broke about an affair I'd had that resulted in a child, the media frenzy was like a bomb going off. I wanted to phone Joan but didn't know what to say. I wouldn't be able to explain this. It wasn't a mistake I could fix just by saying, "I'm sorry."

I thought, *We'll just split up*. I'd screwed up royally, so we'd have to get a divorce.

I'd thought about my freedom many times over the years, but Joan had never given me any reason to split. Once I realized that I'd done something to justify breaking up, my whole body relaxed, because I thought it was a way out of having to explain myself to her. If she started questioning me or said anything along the lines of "How could you?" I'd just say, "I want a divorce!" and hang up. Perfect.

I called her.

"Hello?" she said when she answered. Her voice was very calm.

"Hello. Have you seen the papers?" I asked.

"I have," she replied, and then nothing.

Her silence confused me. I thought she'd yell at me. I *wanted* her to yell at me. Why wasn't she yelling? How dare she not yell!

I had to go on, stammering, "I . . . don't know . . . how to explain . . ."

"You don't need to explain," she said. "I don't want you to hurt her, and I don't want her to hurt us. If you need me or our son to show up and stand by your side, we'll do that. I know you must be feeling awful now. Don't worry about me, I'm fine. You go deal with this."

I started crying before she'd finished speaking. I did not deserve this woman. I was too emotional and tongue-tied to say more, so I just hung up.

I put down the phone and looked up to see a second Jackie Chan standing in front of me. I said to my double, "You're a real bastard. All these years, you were so careful to close yourself off from her, and she's completely open with you."

At that moment, my heart did a 180. I'd behaved abominably, and I'd let her down badly. I had to turn this around.

I went home a couple of days later. Joan opened the door, saw me, and said flatly, "Hi." Then she went back to the kitchen, where she was in the middle of cooking a meal. She asked what I wanted to eat, but I couldn't answer, so I just stood there, not knowing what to say.

After a while, I went back to the living room and sat down. I waited some more, but she kept finding things to do and wouldn't talk to me. My son came home, looked at me, and said, "Hi," then shrugged off his schoolbag and went upstairs. I hadn't seen him for a long time, but he didn't hug me or say anything else. The house felt so big, and I was all alone in the living room.

I went into the kitchen and told Joan to come out for a minute; then I called my son downstairs, and we all sat down together. She hadn't spoken a single word since that clipped "Hi" when I came in.

I said, "Let's have a family meeting for the first time in all these years."

They waited for me to continue. "I've made an unforgivable mistake, and I don't know how I can explain it, so I won't," I said. "Thank you for your understanding and forgiveness. I know you're under a lot of pressure now and will be for a while. I want to apologize to you both."

After I'd said my piece, Joan started crying. Jaycee glared at me and patted his mom on the back. I didn't dare ask for their forgiveness again, so I just muttered, "Okay, meeting over," stood up, and said, "Now let's have dinner."

That short meeting was the one and only time the three of us talked about the subject (although I was the only one doing any talking). It was never mentioned again.

The next day, I went to my lawyer's office to have my will changed. I wanted to leave everything I had to Joan. After so many years together, I finally tried to understand the world she lived in. When I started to empathize with her, I came to respect her more and more. She is a strong woman, stronger than I am in many ways.

For seventeen years of marriage, I'd lived in my own world, wandering around the globe with my stunt team. We'd set off a big explosion one day, thrilled we all survived, and then we'd move on to another scene. It was nonstop. Joan never came to the set unless I asked her to. I didn't want her to see me performing all those risky stunts.

In 1986, after a stunt gone horribly wrong, I almost died. Joan found out what happened only a week later. She phoned to ask why I hadn't called her from the hospital, and I laid into her. "Don't bother me," I said. "I had to go through surgery whether you knew about it or not. If you'd known, could you guarantee the surgery would have been successful? No, right? So why would I want to worry you? I'm a grown man. I'll die if I die, recover if I recover." She started sobbing on the phone, which annoyed me, too. "What are you crying for?" I snapped. "Should I call you every day and report that I got a scratch on my hand, or I broke my leg, or that work is hard? Is that what you want? That's how a kid talks to his mom. I'm not going to treat you like that." I was cruel to her that day.

Another time, I asked my son what he wanted to be when he grew up. He looked at his mom and said, "I want to make movies."

I'd hoped he'd want to study hard and get into a good college, and said as much. He said, "I don't want to study."

"What are you going to become if you don't want to study?" I said. "Even if you make movies, you still have to go to college."

"Okay, I'll go to college first and then make movies."

Later that night, I heard Joan crying in the bathroom. "What did I do wrong this time?" I asked.

She replied, "Didn't you hear what your son said this morning?"

"What did he say?" I'd already forgotten.

"That he wants to make movies!"

I said, "But that's good!"

She sobbed even louder than before. "The movie business has already taken away my husband. I don't want to lose my son, too."

We'd made a rule for our marriage early on that we would never sulk privately about little things, but just say outright whatever was bothering us. When I wasn't away filming, we had a once-a-week standing date to do just that. She'd tell me what she didn't like about me, and I could do the same to her. We'd sit on our balcony and she'd say, "This week, such-and-such happened. You should have done such-and-such," and so on. Then it'd be my turn—and I couldn't find a single thing to criticize her about. Then it would be the same the next week. Blurting out her private pain that night surprised me. It wasn't during our usual night to complain. And she'd never said a word before about resenting me. I reminded myself that she'd given up her career to become a mom and had been a devoted one. She seemed happy with her choice, but now I had to wonder.

I thought, *Maybe she'd like to resurrect her career.*

I asked her about it many times, but she always said, "I'm retired. I have no interest in appearing in a film ever again."

Finally, I convinced her to show her face in the movies again, thirty years after she left the business. I spent a whole year begging her to shoot this one scene in 2012's *Chinese Zodiac*, but she refused. Finally, I asked her to come to my workshop to look at some rushes. When she saw the footage of me getting injured, her heart ached for me, and I took advantage of that moment to tell her how hard it had been to make this film, the years of preproduction, the false starts, how much money I'd put into it, that this might be the last time I was going to do dangerous stunts. She was so moved that she reluctantly agreed to appear in it.

To make her more comfortable, I moved my entire crew from Beijing to my studio in Hong Kong. On the day of the shoot, she wasn't called until afternoon. I told my camera operator to film our rehearsal, just in case she changed her mind.

When she showed up, I said, "Come on, let's run through it." She walked around the room once, and I said, "Okay, that's a wrap!" Joan insisted on only showing her back, but when she came over to me, I gave her a hug and a kiss so she was forced to turn toward the camera. That's why we get that brief glimpse of her face. It comes at the very end of the movie, and it's worth the wait.

I've said in interviews that I've done well by a lot of people, but not my own family. That I haven't been a good father or a good husband, but I did my duty to my son and his mother. I used to spend most of my time flying around the world. Even when I was in Hong Kong, my schedule would be so full, I didn't see much of my family at all. If you asked me now if I regret this, I'd say yes.

But maybe it was better this way. If you haven't lived through this yourself, you wouldn't know how being apart kept us together. If I'd been at home with her every day, we might have separated long ago. When I was young, people looked down on me. As a young adult, I lived in poverty. When I finally found success, I was driven to give the world one good film after another, to show everyone what I was worth. I was selfish and didn't know how to empathize with others. I was also too easily influenced. Yet Joan set me free to make my own way. I respect her a lot and am grateful to her for sacrificing so much for me.

Over the years, I've seen many loving couples get divorced,

while Joan and I weathered every storm. We are often happier than the average couple. I wouldn't say our marriage has been perfect, but we've stuck together and come to cherish each other more and more with every year, after thirty-five years. We'll always be family. How could I have any regrets about our long, sometimes rocky history together now that we've ended up here?

Behind the Scenes by Zhu Mo

At a dinner with Joan, Jackie, and some friends not long ago, everyone was talking about the various techniques for staying young.

Joan said, "I like being the age I am. That's why I don't wear makeup, get injections or facials, or have cosmetic surgery. If you eat more vegetables, get enough sleep, and stay in a good mood, you'll look just fine naturally."

Other people said they wanted to put their stem cells in storage to be used in future rejuvenating surgeries. Jackie joked, "I'll give that a go."

"What for?" Joan replied. "Just age naturally."

Then they started talking about who would die first. Joan said, "I'm afraid that when I'm gone, there'll be no one to take care of you."

Jackie said, "Ha! I'll be happier with you gone."

Joan laughed and said, "You say that now, but just see how you get on without me. You'll be so lonely, poor thing."

I sat there listening to this couple who'd been married several decades joking with each other, and understood their emotional connection. Other people might imagine what their life together is like, but I've seen it with my own eyes. Jackie bolts down a meal, and Joan wipes the sweat off his brow with a dishcloth. Joan walks in the door with her arms full, and Jackie rushes over to take the heavy objects from her. Jackie hits the ball good and hard, and Joan yells exuberantly "Bravo!" with the expression of a girl who's just fallen in love.

I think fate might have kept these two apart to deepen their relationship. It's why now, at this moment, they're so utterly beautiful together.

chapter eighteen

SO WHAT IF I DIE?

By 1985, Golden Harvest had a well-established American branch, and suggested that we give it another go in America. This time round, they tried to respond to the demands of the market by casting me as a tough guy in the mold of Clint Eastwood.

I was against this. It was the American version of trying to turn me into Bruce Lee. A cold-blooded killer type did NOT suit me, nor did I enjoy playing such roles. I had no problem taking on a tough-guy persona, but only if that trait came out in self-defense or to protect friends and family.

Unfortunately, I didn't have any say in this role or the film. Whether I liked it or not, I was going to star in *The Protector*.

Danny Aiello and I played a pair of New York cops who are sent to Hong Kong in pursuit of an international drug kingpin. To escape us, the drug dealer kidnaps the daughter of his former colleague to use as a bargaining chip against the police. The script contained standard Hollywood action-film elements—foul language, nudity, and violence. I didn't condone director James Glickenhaus's style or methods, and working on this project was a tense, unpleasant experience. Audiences weren't excited about it, either. This movie flopped.

Back in Hong Kong, I sought out my writer friend Edward Tang, to talk about making a cop movie in my own way, partly to show that American director how it's done. We called it *Police Story*. (From 1985 to 2013, I made a series of six *Police Story* movies, including *Super Cop* with Michelle Yeoh.)

I already had a concept about the action sequences: My idea was to use glass in as many of them as possible. My fellow stunt artists would come to refer to *Police Story* as *Glass Story*. So many extremely dangerous stunts in this film! In one of them, my character, Officer Chan Ka-Kui, gets into an epic fight at a shopping mall. Spotting the target on the ground floor while he's several stories above, he decides to jump down from where he is to prevent the suspect from getting away. I would have to leap from a high perch, slide down a pole festooned with Christmas lights, and crash through a glass barrier onto the marble ground floor. The distance of my fall was thirty yards. Millions of people have watched this scene in the film, but few understand the harsh conditions of making it.

To start with, we couldn't shoot until after the mall closed for the night. When the last person left the building, we rushed to set up our equipment, which took a while. We had to plan to break it all down and clean up before the mall opened for business the next day. This meant I wouldn't have a chance to try again if I failed. Everything had to succeed on the first take. I was simultaneously working on another film—*Heart of Dragon*, directed by Sammo Hung. After the nighttime mall shoot, I had to rush to Sammo's set first thing in the morning.

Preparation work took up most of our limited time. First, we had to remove the mall's large hanging lights, replace them with three metal poles, and wrap steel wires around them. The wires couldn't be soldered on or I'd never be able to rip them off as I slid down. We used superglue instead. Next, the wires were hung with sugar glass fragments, colored lights, electric cables, and, finally, an explosive rig. At the base of the pole, we laid out another six hundred pounds of sugar glass, then a little wooden hut beneath that was filled with ten thousand pieces of candy. The candies were supposed to break my fall.

While waiting for them to set up, I dozed off.

Once dozens of yards of steel wire were in place, someone woke me to start shooting. I decided to give it a try from a lower height. The first time I leaped, I found out that the wire refused to snap off the pole after the first two strands. I had my hands tightly around the pole, but when the steel wire wouldn't break, I lost my grip and went into free fall. While we were trying this out, it started to get light outside. To prevent light from coming in, the crew sprayed the mall's glass roof with black paint, but then a sudden squall washed away the still-wet paint, and they had to rush to find some black cloth instead. The main set piece of the metal pole still wasn't ready, and meanwhile all sorts of new problems were cropping up.

The lighting director came over and said, "Jackie, the production team's batteries can't power all the lights. We'll have to use the mall's main supply."

I said, "What if it shorts? I'll be electrocuted."

The solution? Have a guy stand by the socket, ready to pull the plug if that happened, which didn't leave me with much confidence.

The props department director came over and said, "Jackie, we had to glue the steel wires firmly in place, so when you jump, make sure you pull them hard, otherwise you'll never slide all the way down."

Many camera operators had been standing by for quite some time, especially the one up on the ceiling, who'd been clutching his equipment for two or three hours now. His clothes were drenched with sweat, the workers below grumbled about water dripping down on them.

I'd been filming those two movies, day and night, for some time, and hadn't had anywhere near enough sleep. Urgent problems from every department kept coming at me, issues that had to be solved, that needed me to make a decision. We were quickly running out of time. I could barely think.

Another innovation we used on this film (I believe it's still a record): We had fifteen different cameras rolling simultaneously to capture this stunt at different speeds and from different angles. This meant fifteen cameramen and twenty or thirty assistants—an extravagance, even today. The high-speed camera caused a concern: If I delayed even a little before I jumped, it'd run out of film too soon. My jumping-off point in this scene wasn't a platform but an ordinary staircase railing, rounded and slippery. I had to step up onto it and then leap right away, no hesitation. From the balcony launch point, I had to make a standing broad jump of eight feet, then slide down eighty feet of metal pole through a muddle of steel wire, colored lights, sugar glass, and explosives, and land on a glass hut on a marble floor. And I had to do it successfully in one take. Failure was not an option.

I looked at the several hundred crew members and extras below, and my costars Maggie Cheung and Brigitte Lin. They were all looking up at me. I said to myself, *You can do this!*

One of my stunt guys came up and said, "Everything's ready."

I said, "Okay. When I shake my head, that's the signal to start rolling."

Finally, I got up on the railing. I rolled my shoulder a bit . . . and heard the sound of fifteen cameras starting to roll at once! *No! That wasn't the signal!* I wanted to shout. *I didn't shake my head yet!* But it was too late. The hundreds of people on set were eerily silent just then. Nothing could be heard but the whir of the cameras.

I thought, *Well, so what if I die?*

Then I jumped and shouted, "I die!" loudly.

My body shot through the air.

I gripped the pole with my hands and legs. As I slid down, light-bulbs flashed and shattered, and glass shards flew everywhere, catching light like sparks. My hands felt hot, then painful, then numb. All eighty feet, the whole way down, I screamed

"AHHHH!!!" until I crashed through six hundred pounds of sugar glass, smashing it into powder, then onto the hut full of candy. Success!

The scene wasn't over yet.

We were capturing this entire sequence in a single take. After my jump, I went straight into a fight with the bad guys. I hit the ground, popped up onto my feet instantly, grabbed one of the martial artists on my stunt team, and started whacking him, ding-dong-ding-dong, until the guy said, "Jackie, please stop."

As soon as I let go, he fell to the ground. That's when I realized I'd lost my mind—it was as if I'd gone mad. I let out a wild roar with all my might.

Then I noticed that Brigitte Lin and Maggie Cheung were crying. So was my manager, the tea lady, the makeup artist, and the women from wardrobe. I asked, "What's there to cry about?" The tension, stress, and emotion of the shoot must have gotten to them.

Only then did I notice that my hands were lacerated and bloody with fragments of broken glass. I got them patched up quickly, and right away I headed to my car and told the driver to take me to Sammo Hung's studio. As soon as we started moving, I fell asleep.

Moments later, my driver roused me and said, "We're here."

I reached for the door handle and saw that my hands weren't just cut and swollen; they were shaking. I had no strength at all. I couldn't even open the car door.

When you literally can't lift a hand, that's when you know you are seriously stressed-out. Since making it big, I'd been writing checks my body couldn't cash. I was on the verge of collapse. That one action sequence, about ten seconds on film, left me with second-degree burns on my hands, a bloody face, and fragments of sugar glass all over my body.

When I think of this now, I still feel proud of myself. Many of my stunts were a once-in-a-lifetime experience, all of them recorded for an eternity on film.

When I was at the drama academy, all the boys had to shave their heads. We spent many years as little baldies. When I graduated, I decided to grow it out, deliberately going against my past or making up for any sense of regret I had about it. My hair got so long, people thought I was a dangerous man, up to no good. In Taiwan and South Korea, I was questioned by the police. Young men in those countries have to do military service, which means buzz-cut hair. Not realizing I was from Hong Kong, the local cops pulled me in for interrogation based on the length of my hair alone.

I got some tips about how to style it properly and brought my blow dryer with me everywhere I went. I used it with great seriousness, enjoying the sensation. When we were filming abroad, my co-stars never brought their own hair dryers because they knew I'd have mine. After they washed their hair, they'd come to my room, and I'd give them a blowout. Liza Wang, Brigitte Lin, Feng Hsu, Charlie Chin, Sammo Hung—I've done all their hair. I also do Joan's and Jaycee's hair sometimes.

The only time I cut my hair was for my first trip to Hollywood in 1980, when I styled it like a Prohibition-era gangster. But it never felt right and I grew it out immediately when I returned to Hong Kong. I thought of my long hair as my "image." (Actually, it was just me being a slob.)

After a stunt accident in 1986, long hair was my mandate. My godfather, Leonard Ho, had been so terrified after my injury, he forbade me from ever cutting my hair short again.

It was, and remains, the most serious of my injuries. The movie was called *Armour of God*. Stanley Kwan was the assistant director, Andrew Lau was a camera operator, and Peter Chan was the production assistant.

The film was about a count who hopes to gather the "armour of god," five biblical treasures that can defeat demons, which have been scattered for eight hundred years. He discovers that three of them have been seized from Africa by the fortune hunter Asian Hawk (me), and the other two are in the hands of a terrorist gang. A tale of hunt and rescue ensues. I directed as well as played the lead. I was thirty-two.

We started shooting in Yugoslavia, a country that no longer exists. The art director on this film, Yee Chung-Man, wanted me to try a new look: short hair. I agreed to it; it was time for a change. We were filming in harsh conditions, and there wasn't a professional hairstylist on set, so Yee Chung-Man cut it himself. When he was done, I looked in the mirror and thought I looked hideous, like a dog had been gnawing at my head. Fortunately, a few days after we started shooting, I took a quick work trip to Japan, and while there I asked a professional hairdresser to tidy it up. When I got back to the set, Yee Chung-Man thought something looked off and got out his scissors to fix it. In any case, my hair ended up taking a lot of time.

We were shooting a scene that wasn't particularly complicated, at least not for me. I was being chased by a couple of guys and had to leap up a tree. After all the action films I'd made, this was just a regular sequence. I did a couple of takes. Eric Tsang, my collaborator, thought we got the shot and could move on. I disagreed. I hadn't been energetic enough as I dropped to the ground after my leap. I insisted on one more take.

No one tried to talk me out of it, so we rolled. On this third take, things went awry. The tree wasn't particularly tall or strong. As I jumped on the branch, it snapped. I went plummeting. As I fell, I instinctively clutched at the trunk and branches, but they broke off in my hands. Just before hitting the ground, I reached out to break my fall as usual—I'd done it thousands of times—but my head hit a rock by the base of the tree. Looking back, we were negligent about so many aspects of this. We should have researched the type of tree, tested whether the branches could hold me, and made sure the ground around it was clear.

My dad was on set that day. He'd hardly ever been to my workplace before, and I don't know how he happened to be at the scene of the accident. The production team quickly ushered him away so he wouldn't get too much of a shock from seeing me lying on the ground, not moving.

I had a sharp pain in my lower back. I sensed that I was surrounded by people. I had no sense of time passing. I tried to sit up, but everyone held me down and told me to keep still. Obediently, I stayed down. I started to feel hot all over. The back of my head had been swelling since the fall. My colleagues noticed a large amount of blood spurting out of my ear—a real geyser—yet I had no visible injuries. They were terrified that I was about to die.

It was nine in the morning. The production team had to get me down the mountain, then to the hospital, in a Jeep. I remember lying in the vehicle while someone sat next to me and hit me hard, saying, "Don't go to sleep, don't go to sleep, Jackie!"

I said, "Stop hitting me!" I already hurt everywhere.

We got to a little hospital, and as soon as I got inside, they stuck me with a needle. As I've said, I hate injections, but at that moment I didn't have the energy to put up a fight. After jabbing me quite a few times, the doctors at the little hospital sent me to a larger hospital. Another doctor examined me and said that if I didn't have brain surgery right away, I was in grave danger. The medical staff were not experts in the field, but they would try it. Ideally, I'd be operated on by the best brain surgeon in the world, a Swiss man, but I couldn't wait for them to find him and get him there.

Through all this, my ear was still bleeding. Then blood poured out of my nostrils. I felt a gurgle of it rise in my throat, too. When that happened, I started to feel scared. I was bleeding from every orifice, like people do when they're about to die. Blood was coming out of my nose and ears and mouth. Was that every orifice? I rubbed my eyes, making sure to use the palest part of my hand. Nothing. Well, at least I wasn't bleeding from them.

Eric Tsang arrived at the hospital, took in the situation, realized how dire it was, and called Raymond Chow, the big boss of Golden

ABOVE: Wearing a traditional Chinese outfit to attend the Academy Awards.

ABOVE: With Chris Tucker, Tom Hanks, and Michelle Yeoh.

LEFT: Hanging onto a flagpole in *Project A*.

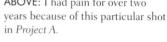

ABOVE: I had pain for over two years because of this particular shot in *Project A*.

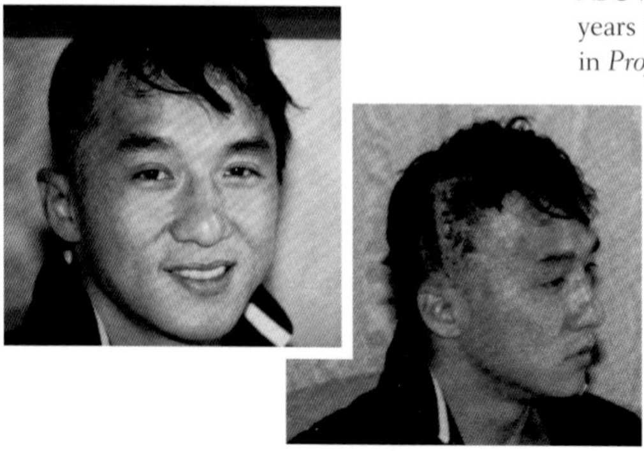

LEFT: These two photos were taken after surgery while I was filming *Armour of God*.

LEFT: My new pets in *Armour of God*.

RIGHT: Master Yu Jim-Yuen sent me an autographed photo personalized with my name at the China Drama Academy: Yuen Lau.

LEFT: A scene from *Who Am I?* I still don't know where I got the guts to jump.

LEFT: My parents didn't have much money, but we lived in Victoria Peak, which used to be the embassy district of Hong Kong. Lots of kids there were bullied by young Jackie.

ABOVE: I always dreamed of being a cowboy.

RIGHT: Will Smith's son Jaden learned from me not to waste any water.

ABOVE: I was only a junior stuntman in Bruce Lee's *Enter The Dragon*.

ABOVE: They told me I was the only Chinese actor to have both a star on the Walk of Fame and prints at the Chinese Theatre.

LEFT: Filming *Battle Creek Brawl.*

RIGHT: In *Battle Creek Brawl,* I climbed up the wire without any safety belt or wire. Everyone freaked out.

ABOVE: This is a scene from *The Protector.* The guy was so scared even with the wire to protect him. I was the one without any protection.

ABOVE: Filming *Cannonball Run*.

ABOVE: In *Drunken Master*, I was both an actor and one of the stunt coordinators. In *Drunken Master 2* (aka *The Legend of the Drunken Master*), I was the director, the screenwriter, an actor, and the stunt director.

ABOVE: Cycling with my panda kids.

ABOVE AND BELOW: Charity work makes me very happy.

ABOVE: With family.

LEFT: With Michelle Yeoh.

ABOVE: Joan, Jaycee, and me at Jaycee's graduation commencement. He nearly forgot to bring his cap and gown.

ABOVE: Jaycee's first encounter with snow.

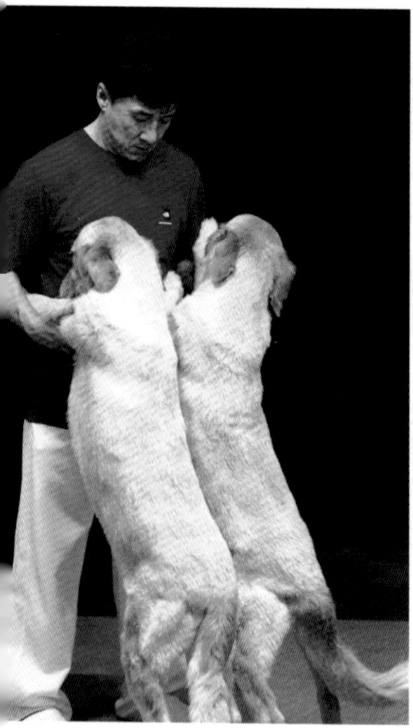

ABOVE: My beloved JJ and Jones.

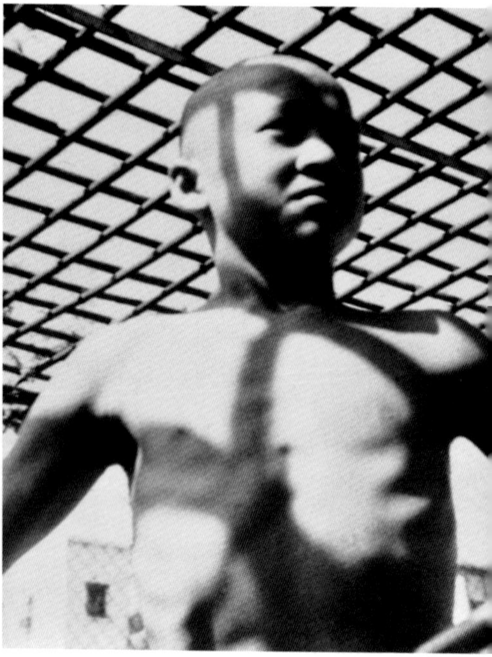

ABOVE: I felt good when I began to learn some martial arts.

RIGHT: I am the second one from the right.

LEFT: I am the first one from the left.

RIGHT: The main gate of my school (I am the one on the righthand side).

LEFT: The 50th Anniversary of the China Drama Academy.

RIGHT: Hanging up there with one hand and no protection. The sign was about twenty-three feet high and everyone thought I was crazy.

ABOVE: At James Cameron's office.

ABOVE: Remember this pose?

LEFT: With Barack Obama.

ABOVE: Another two Guinness World Records.

ABOVE: With my parents.

ABOVE: In *1911*.

I learned more as a stunt coordinator than as an actor in *New Fists of Fury*.

LEFT: Filming *Chinese Zodiac* at Domaine de Chantilly (France).

RIGHT: Filming *The Young Master*.

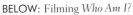

BELOW: Filming *Who Am I?*

ABOVE AND BELOW: Interacting with fans.

Harvest, in Hong Kong. It wasn't easy to make phone calls back then, and international numbers didn't get connected right away. There were delays and bad connections. But Eric got the point across. Mr. Chow said he would get in touch with the Swiss brain surgeon, and then the call cut out. During his next call, Mr. Chow reported that the surgeon was in the middle of a world lecture tour and no one knew exactly where he was. Then the call cut out again.

By now, the hospital doctor was getting anxious. He kept saying, "What on earth are you waiting for? You have to make a decision!" I'd arrived in the morning, and now it was night. Someone suggested getting a private jet to take me to France for the surgery, but the doctor said, "The patient is in no state to withstand the stress of a journey. He'll bleed even faster."

Everyone froze, paralyzed by indecision, terrified that I wouldn't survive surgery or live long enough to get to the operating table.

I didn't really understand what was going on until our fight director on the film, Fung Hark-On, explained it to me. "Jackie, a bit of bone broke off in your head. You need surgery to get that fragment out," he said. "They need to put in a whatever-you-call-it, which they'll take out again in a few years."

If this news had been delivered to me in a calm voice, it would have been no big deal. But Hark-On was weeping and choking on his tears the whole time. He was the mainstay of my stunt team at the time, a real hard man, so I knew things were serious if he was crying like that.

The doctor came and spewed a big heap of words, most of which I didn't understand, apart from "operation."

When he was done, I said, "Who can I trust right now? Only you. So, yes, I'll have the operation."

The doctor and his team proceeded to cut off my clothes and then wheel me into the operating room. It must have been after eight at night. I gazed blearily at the ceiling. The OR had nine lightbulbs. I sensed an old man was asking me how I felt. The voice drifted farther and farther from me. He said, "All right, get some sleep." That was the last thing I remember. I have no idea how long the surgery lasted.

When I came to, I heard a bell by the bed and opened my eyes to see four nurses staring at me. I tried to get up, but they pushed my head back down, and I fell asleep again. The next time I woke, someone was whistling. It was my costar in the movie, the singer and actor Alan Tam, sitting next to me, whistling our tune from the soundtrack, "Friend of Mine."

I opened my eyes and saw everyone waving at me from behind two panes of glass. Relieved that I wasn't dead, I went back to sleep. When I woke up for the third time, I was in a different room. Alan Tam and Eric Tsang were both standing there. Seeing me conscious, they said, "You bastard, do you know how lucky you are? The Swiss surgeon did your operation! He just happened to be speaking at a Yugoslavian university and agreed to take you on as a patient."

The doctor arrived just as I was brought into the OR. For him to appear just in the nick of time like that was nothing short of a miracle.

Not long after I'd fully regained consciousness, I told the nurses I was hungry and asked for some food. They were shocked and said they'd never come across anyone like me. My skull had collapsed around my left ear, and bits of shattered bone had moved around inside my head. After a major operation like that, most people have a severe adverse reaction, nausea or loss of appetite. No one wakes up hungry. Well, my appetite was perfectly fine. They brought me some food and I scarfed it down without the slightest bit of trouble.

Seven days after the operation, I was back on set. The challenge was to come up with ways to film only half my face. I didn't want to wait six months for my hair to grow out and hide the scar; it would be an impossible delay for the hundred-odd people in the production team. After a few days, though, we realized strategic blocking wasn't working, and everyone went back to Hong Kong. We did finish the film a year later, and it was a blockbuster.

I have a small depression in my head to this day, a spongy spot with no bone beneath. In one ear, high-pitched sounds hurt and low ones are inaudible. Souvenirs of the accident.

Now, how does this story get back to my magic long hair?

My godfather, Leonard Ho, said that my mistake was cutting my hair in the first place. He said that I wasn't allowed to do it again. Not only that, he set another rule: "Jackie Chan can't play people who die."

So if I got a script and my character died at the end, I'd have to turn it down. At the time, I was desperate to play the historical role of Xiang Yu, a warlord during the Qin dynasty, the tyrant of the Western Chu. But since Xiang Yu dies, my godfather would never let me do it.

Look, I knew my long hair wasn't the source of my strength, like Samson's, and that cutting it wouldn't mean I'd have another accident. I'm not particularly superstitious. But Mr. Ho laid down the law, and out of deep respect for my godfather, I didn't break either of those promises for another ten years.

chapter nineteen

WILD THINGS

Some fans might remember that, when I walked the red carpet at the 2016 Academy Awards, I carried two stuffed pandas with me. They were custom-made and I call them both Lazy. I take them around the world to be photographed with celebrities and landmarks to raise awareness for endangered Chinese pandas on behalf of UNICEF.

I've always been an animal person and have had many pets in my life. Some ordinary, like cats and dogs, and some exotic pets, too. I once bought a lion cub from a friend for $10,000. I thought it was adorable and unusual, and happily brought it to the office. I fed it milk and took care of it. One day, I was cradling it and playfully pinching its cheeks, and it batted me with its little paw, probably just to say, "Stop fooling around." Its claws just grazed my face, but one whole side of my jaw was suddenly covered in blood.

Just a tiny thing, no bigger than a small dog, could do major damage. When it was fully grown at three years old, would it kill me? I phoned the guy who'd sold me the cub and said, "Take it back. I'm scared." So he came over and collected the lion, but I never got my $10,000 back.

Another friend gave me a hawk that I let fly around the studio. It would land on my shoulder and perch until I shook it off. I kept a sloth for a while. It had enormous, adorable eyes. Jaycee loved it!

We had two huge Saint Bernards. I'd get up early in the morning and make them six eggs, mixed with a large carton of milk. They'd wait patiently for their breakfast, and when I put the food down, it would disappear in a single gulp. Those dogs cost me $3,000 a month on food. They weighed three hundred pounds combined. I was quite skinny when I had them and I couldn't walk them alone. I needed my assistant to help. If I was holding both leashes when one of them stopped to pee, I handed the other leash to the assistant and he slipped it around his wrist. Then I heard someone screaming. It was him, clinging to a telephone pole as the dog strained to run. He couldn't pull the dog back, and he didn't dare to let go of the pole or he'd get dragged along the ground. I almost died laughing.

These days, I have three dogs and two cats at home, and another five cats at the office.

The two dogs are golden retrievers. They're brothers, JJ and Jones. Once, JJ ran away when someone left the gate open. We searched high and low for two weeks, but there was no sign of him. My friend suggested we check Hong Kong's Society for the Prevention of Cruelty to Animals, an organization that cares for stray and abandoned animals, puts them up for adoption, and, if no home can be found, humanely destroys them. We called them up and asked if they had had any golden retrievers lately and gave them JJ's microchip info. They checked and came back with a "Nope." I was devastated. It was my last hope of seeing JJ again. My friend saw how upset I was and offered to go to the shelter and take a look for himself the next day, checking every dog there if necessary.

As soon as he walked in, he saw JJ and said, "That's the dog I'm looking for!"

The worker said, "It can't be. The address on the license doesn't match the microchip."

We sorted it out. I'd moved houses, but the microchip implanted in JJ was still linked to my previous address. That's why it didn't match.

My friend quickly brought JJ home. The SPCA does good work, but JJ was rattled by his experience there. He looked dirty, skinny, and frightened. I think maybe he was bullied by other dogs, the poor thing. He's recovered his health, but to this day, JJ gets scared over every little thing, even our cats. If one of the cats gets in his way, he stops in his tracks. If I call him and there's a cat between us, he'll take a huge detour to avoid it. If the cat is by one of my legs, he'll circle the entire room to get to my other side. Jaycee used to have a tiny dog that liked to ride on JJ's back. JJ hated that!

Whenever I'm in Hong Kong, I take JJ and Jones for a drive, which they love. I bought a special vehicle for them, a jeep with a trailer they can ride in. I take them to the office with me, and Jones is so lively, he'll bark at anything—the wind, people on the street. If we're in a tunnel or on a bridge, he lies down for a rest. Jones stays at my heel at the office, keeping me company, but JJ likes to wander around by himself. Whenever they see me at the door putting on my shoes, they'll rush over and do not let me leave. They know that once I'm gone, I might not be back for a while.

My two house cats are Dingding and Dangdang. Dingding is well behaved; Dangdang is mischievous and likes to fight with other cats. Of my five office cats, Blackie is my favorite. When I first met the other four, they all ran away. But Blackie just stood there and stared at me. I thought, *That little cat has balls.*

When my pets get sick and die, I cry with deep sorrow for them. If you haven't lived with and cared for an animal, it's hard to understand just how much they mean to you. I grieve terribly for each one, but I'll always get another, knowing that I'll cry over him one day, too.

On movie sets, however, I haven't always gotten along so well with animals.

Before my brain injury on *Armour of God*, I made an enemy of a leopard. We'd been shooting a scene in which Alan Tam and I entered the count's ancient mansion, and we needed to emphasize how luxurious it was. My idea was that as soon as we stepped into the hall, we'd be stunned by what appeared to be a wall of animals. On closer examination, they'd turn out to be hunting trophies. We'd walk through the room, exclaiming, "Wow, that's a gorgeous lamp," "These floor tiles are beautiful!" etc. Then we'd see a leopard-skin pelt and gush, "What a beautiful rug!" And at that moment, the "rug" would stand up, startling us both.

The production team got an animal handler to bring a leopard on set. At first, the animal appeared well trained and docile. It followed its trainer's instructions. I even gave its face a good scratch and rubbed its belly. I was convinced we could work with this animal, and told the production team to get ready to film.

We were rolling. The leopard's owner hid to one side holding its chain and bid the leopard to lie flat on the mark. I said my lines: "Wow, the lamp's gorgeous, the tiles are beautiful, and that rug is stunning . . ."

The leopard was supposed to leap up when I said "stunning," but it remained motionless on the floor. The trainer tugged the chain, to no avail. The second take went the same way. I asked the trainer to tug harder to make it stand up. "Would that work?" He assured me that it would, and we tried again.

If we were making this film today, I'd get someone in a green-screen suit to lift the beast up, and we'd deal with the editing in postproduction. But we didn't have the technology back then and had to use more basic methods, like yanking a chain.

But this leopard refused to budge on the third and fourth takes. I was starting to get anxious. Film was expensive. I went back to the trainer for another chat about what to do.

The leopard abruptly stood up. Seeing it on its feet, I yelled, "That's right! That's what I want!" I was pointing at the animal while shouting. Big mistake. In a heartbeat, it lunged at me! It tried to bite off my finger, but I managed to jump back just in time. It was terrifying!

Everyone knows that leopards are fast, and this one moved as quick as blinking. No sooner had the words left my lips than it came at me, mouth wide open, stunning everyone there. Fortunately, the owner was still holding the chain and was able to calm it down. I wanted to go over and help, but seeing how fiercely it was glaring at me, I decided not to.

After that, it was impossible to go on with the scene. Whenever I called "Action!" the leopard tried to attack me, no matter how far away I was. We had to forget about this idea, but it would have been a shame to waste the money we'd already paid for the leopard and its handler. I wasn't about to give up on it so easily, but I had to come up with a new concept.

I decided that Alan Tam and I would walk along a corridor, when suddenly a leopard would stroll by, giving us a shock. Showing that the count kept a leopard as a pet would demonstrate how luxurious his lifestyle was. We found a corridor with an opening to one side where we could hide the beast until it was time for him to pop into the shot. I got the handler to lead it by the chain into the opening and keep it there.

I remember the corridor was not very wide but fairly long. As the cameras rolled, Alan and I began walking and saying our lines: "Wow, the lamp is so gorgeous, the tiles are amazing . . ." Once again, it got dangerous. As soon as we got close to the leopard, it darted out, hitting the opposite wall, leaving claw marks in it—and shredding our nerves, too. Alan and I were supposed to walk straight down the corridor, but on every single take, it rushed out too early and launched yet another vicious attack on me.

In the end, we asked the owner to hold it as tightly as possible, but even then we didn't dare walk too close. We hugged the opposite wall. We just about got through the scene that way.

That's how I learned that you must never, ever frighten a wild animal.

As the saying goes, boats and horses are dangerous. I've had to shoot several horseback scenes, and I'm always very careful here. When I first started riding, I thought it would be fine once I got used to it. When I dismounted, my trainer asked, "Are you still frightened now?"

I said, "No."

"Wrong. Every time you ride a horse, it should be like the first time, and you should always stay alert rather than getting complacent."

To this day, every time I get on a horse, I make sure that the horse and my riding equipment are all fine, just as pilots have to double-check all their equipment before taking off. When I was in

Japan, I noticed that bus drivers would check their rear and side mirrors thoroughly at every stop, using hand gestures to remind themselves. I thought that was commendable.

For *Who Am I?*, we shot many scenes in South Africa. One day after work, I was in my car when I looked out the window at someone walking alongside, and thought, *Why is he so tall?* When I stuck my head out, I saw he was riding a rhinoceros. Naturally, my first thought was, *A rhino would be great in this scene!* I told the driver to stop the car. I got out and asked the man if I could ride a rhino, too. I told the crew to put their equipment in front of me and have all the villagers step to one side so I could get a shot of me on the rhino. At first, it felt good to be sitting on its back. The rhinoceros was good-natured and didn't mind if I stroked it or grabbed its ears.

When everyone else had gone and we were ready to start filming again, someone handed me a long spear. We hadn't rehearsed with this, but holding that spear looked very striking. However, when the rhino caught sight of the spear, it bolted like a startled horse. My reflexes were fast enough that I managed to jump off in time. When it saw me on the ground, it turned around and charged at me. Spotting a nearby tree, I sprinted for it and ducked behind it, darting left and right until the locals pulled the rhino away. That was close!

As soon as it was safe, I rushed over to the crew and asked if they'd gotten the shot they needed. They were so worried about me being chased by a rhino that they forgot to roll the camera. I was furious!

My worst experience with animals was when I was filming *Chinese Zodiac*. I had to face off with two feral dogs in an ancient fort. I was bitten quite a few times. That wasn't so bad. But for many days afterwards, I needed rabies shots.

You know how I feel about needles.

I'd rather break a leg.

Behind the Scenes with Zhu Mo

I was working for Jackie during the publicity of *Chinese Zodiac*. At Cannes, we arranged some interviews with the Chinese media. The publicist gave us a small room, which we'd have to make do with. Big Brother came down promptly at 2:00 p.m., and when he saw the room, he immediately led the journalists up to his own room, and quickly set up five folding chairs on the balcony—one for himself, three for his female costars, one for the reporter. Big Brother asked us to remind the press to direct their questions to all four actors, not just him. Anna Yao, Zhang Lanxin, and Laura Weissbecker were all relative newcomers but shouldn't be neglected just because of that. He took very good care of them during these interviews, making sure they all had a chance to sit next to him, so no one felt left out.

After a few rounds of interviews, his assistant reminded him to have some food. He'd been carrying out interviews with the foreign press all morning and hadn't even had lunch yet. Big Brother said there was no need to take a break. His assistant brought in his lunch anyway: vegetable soup and a sandwich. He continued fielding questions as he ate, and didn't get through the food until the interviews were over.

The next reporter had a recorder, but couldn't find anywhere to put it, and finally set it on the floor. Big Brother stood up and fetched a small table, put the recorder on it, and sat down again. The whole thing was over in ten seconds. The reporter was stunned for a moment, then realized what had just happened, and not knowing what to say, just smiled at Big Brother.

I'd seen all sorts of actors over the past few years of this job. Certainly, some were humble, and others took care of younger performers, but rarely have I seen all these good qualities embodied in a single person.

Later that day, we hosted everyone at a banquet hall with an open-air terrace. Someone had forgotten to draw the curtains across the French windows, and during the dinner, many foreign fans stood outside, mesmerized. As the crowd grew, they started chanting, "Jackie Chan!" Big Brother immediately went out onto the terrace to say hi to everyone, as hordes of women cried out loudly, "Jackie Chan, I love you!"

I was standing behind him, looking at this Chinese megastar's back and the fans' camera flashes in front. It was unreal, a moment I'll never forget.

chapter twenty

FATHERHOOD, PART I

All told, I think I've done all right by my son, now a thirty-five-year-old man. Along the way, when Jaycee was doing well, I taught him sternly. When he was in trouble, when he did something wrong and deserved to be punished, if he accepted the blame and made amends, I've stood by him and lovingly supported him. We got through hard times together.

For much of his life, we weren't together. As a child, he got to see me only in the small hours of the morning. He went to high school and college in the US and does things in a very American way. I was always happy to spend time with him, but he seemed so unenthusiastic around me. I wished someone could train him to stand and sit properly, to stop fidgeting so much when he spoke, but if I tried, he'd stop talking to me.

Jaycee has always been afraid of me. He gets frightened whenever he hears me give him an order. I can't say I blame him.

When he was two and a half, I threw him.

I've always thought little children should be disciplined. Parents punish their kids to prevent them from going down the wrong road. I made some mistakes when I was young, and I wouldn't want the next generation to repeat them. I'd rather they lead better lives. If all you do is talk, children won't listen to you, and by the time they get to a certain age and realize they're in trouble, it'll be too late.

People from my generation, like Yuen Biao or Sammo Hung, would never let a single grain of rice fall onto the table. At the drama academy, if we spilled any, our master would slap us. Things are different now. If you slap your child, he might sue you. If we had that option, we'd all have sued our master! But we didn't. We had no one to issue a complaint to back then. He had ultimate power, and we trembled whenever we saw him.

What happened that day with Jaycee: Joan and I were having an argument. We reached a stalemate, so I walked out, slammed the door, and went to see Leonard Ho. He counseled me for a long time and finally said, "What are you doing? There's no need for this. Just go back home, and you can both apologize." Obediently, I went home.

When I got there, Joan was on the sofa, laughing and chatting with a female friend. That made me angry. I'd been gone only a little while, and she'd invited someone over and they were yukking it up? Just as I was about to say something to her, Jaycee ran in, his hands pointed at me like guns, shouting "Bang! Bang!" like he was shooting me to avenge his mother. Then he snatched the keys out of my hand and threw them on the floor. When I bent down to pick them up, he kicked my hand away! I was furious.

I picked him up with one hand and flung him across the room, and he crashed into the sofa.

With the amount of force I used, if he'd hit the back or armrests, it could have been quite serious. But I'd judged his landing well, and he came down right in the middle of the cushions.

Joan was terrified. She ran over to her son and said, "Tell your dad you're sorry!" He refused. "Quick! Tell him!" She kept repeating this as her friend stared at us, frozen.

I glared at Jaycee. He was embarrassing me by refusing to apologize. Another stalemate, this time with my son. I just walked away.

I regretted my actions immediately afterwards, but I didn't want to lose face by backing down. Joan waited until I was calm and said, "He's just a child. Why did you do that?" I'd been asking myself the same thing. *What on earth are you doing?*

I told Joan, "I'm sorry. I swear I'll never throw him again."

Joan interceded with Jaycee, telling him, "He'll never do that again. Your dad made a promise."

I take my promises seriously, and I'm a man of my word. I never threw him again or hit him.

As a toddler, Jaycee refused to eat, so a meal could drag on for hours.

One mealtime, he refused to touch his food, insisting he needed the bathroom. I'd put some rice in his mouth, and he'd say, "I need to pee." Then he'd disappear into the bathroom for a long time. When his mom asked him to open up for the next spoonful, his mouth was still full of rice. Before we could get more food into him, he'd say he needed the bathroom again, and would disappear for ten minutes again.

I took him back to the bathroom and said, "You said you wanted to pee? So pee!"

We faced off, and he had to admit that he didn't really need to go.

"That's what I thought," I said. "Go eat your food, and none of this bathroom stuff! Don't disobey me! I'm a big hooligan. You know what that means?"

He lowered his eyes and said, "You're a big hooligan, and I'm a little hooligan."

I was raised to respect my elders and do whatever my master said. Jaycee didn't like to listen to me.

Leonard Ho had given me an antique cupboard worth a few hundred thousand, which was a lot of money at the time. Jaycee, then five, was at home when it was delivered and seemed fascinated by it. The cupboard was an unusual design, with very distinctive glass panels. If it got damaged, I'd never be able to replace it. I worried that he'd break it, so I came up with a plan.

After the delivery guys left, Jaycee was still staring at the cupboard. Joan was there, too. I pointed at it and said, "Remember, no one can touch."

A while later, he was still in the room when his mom walked over and touched the cupboard. Immediately, I hit her with a rolled-up newspaper and yelled forcefully at her, "Don't touch it!!"

She pretended to jump in fear and then ran away.

After that, Jaycee always gave the cupboard a wide berth. Excellent. I happily filled my godfather's gift with little antiques and tchotchkes. And still Jaycee stayed far from it. I was pleased. My plan worked!

Time passed. One night, Jaycee did something wrong—I forget what—and I sent him to his room. After we went to bed, I heard him come out and walk into the room with the cupboard. I opened my door a crack to watch him. My light was out, so he couldn't see me, but I could see him just fine.

He turned toward my door, frowning and squinting. Then he looked at the cupboard, then back at my door, then at the cupboard. Suddenly, he dashed across the room and smacked the cupboard a few times. *Bang, bang, bang!* He looked at my door. No movement. Again: *bang, bang, bang!*

I whispered to Joan to come look. We hid in the room, bent over in silent laughter. The cupboard is still in my house, and makes me smile thinking of that night.

At six, Jaycee and I traveled together by plane for the first time. I'd been impressed by how Li Ka-Shing, a famous Hong Kong business magnate, brought up his children so they'd be independent and not rely on their parents for money. I thought I would take a page from his book. We boarded the plane, and I showed him where I'd be sitting.

He said, "Wow, this is so big!"

I said, "That's right, this is the first-class cabin. When you have your own money, you can sit up front with me."

I took him in back to show him his seat in economy. "You have no money now, so you sit here."

He said, "Oh."

I returned to my seat and got comfortable, putting on my headphones and eye mask. I felt something small squeezing into my seat with me.

It was Jaycee, of course. I said, "What are you doing here? You can't sit up here."

He said, "The stewardess told me to come here."

I asked the flight attendant, and she said, "It's fine. There was an empty seat next to you, so I brought him over." My son got a free upgrade!

On every trip after that, I always bought him an economy-class ticket. Maybe because he was cute, or maybe because people knew he was my son, he often got an upgrade. He once said to me, smugly, "You see? I got another upgrade. I don't need money."

I replied, "It's different for you. You have me as a dad, but other people don't. They have to fight their own battles. When you get to sit in first class because of your own hard work, then that's success."

He still buys economy-class tickets from time to time. If he gets an upgrade, great. If not, he'll sit in coach, and that's fine by him, too.

At seven, Jaycee called me one day, and I answered the phone to hear him sobbing. Urgently, I said, "What's wrong?"

"I broke your parrot!" He could barely speak, he was crying so hard. He'd been playing with a ball in the house, and it smashed a glass statue of some parrots.

I said, "Are you hurt? Are you all right?"

"I'm fine, but I . . . broke the . . . the . . ."

"Don't cry—it's all right. Just clean it up and make sure you don't hurt yourself. I'll buy a new one," I said.

When I got home, I asked Joan right away, "Is the boy okay? He was so upset!"

She giggled.

I said, "What's so funny?"

She said, "You know what your son did? When I told him to call you to confess his crime, he picked up the receiver, turned to me, and asked, 'Mom, should I cry?' I said, 'Yes!' As soon as you picked up, he burst into tears."

Damn, it was all fake! The kid could act!

Jaycee came to one of my movie sets for the first time when he was nine. The movie was *Crime Story*. People saw him and said, "The young master's here!" This was his first time seeing so many people at once. He was a little shy and didn't say much.

It was a cold day, and I was filming an underwater scene. I

asked the stunt team to take care of him and jumped into the tank.

He watched as I struggled in the water, looking tormented. After the first take, I came out of the tank, and we swapped the camera angles. When everything was set up, I jumped in again.

The water was actually warm, not icy, but when the wind blew, I still felt cold. Whenever I got out of the water, they'd wrap a towel around me, and I'd stand there shivering, my teeth chattering. Knowing that Jaycee was watching, I made it look worse than it actually was, shaking so hard that my jaw and entire body were rattling. I could have held myself still if I'd wanted. The team had two big lights focused on me to warm me up. Water vapor was coming off my body like smoke.

We continued filming. I looked for Jaycee among the spectators, but he wasn't there. I assumed he'd gone looking for food or something, and I went off to prepare for the next scene.

We wrapped for the day. On the way home, I said, "You see how hard Daddy works? I bet you didn't know that before."

Joan chimed in and said, "Your dad really suffers on set, doesn't he?"

Jaycee said, "Yes. I had to run to the bathroom to cry halfway through."

At ten, whenever he called me, Jaycee's first question was always "Where are you?" His emphasis made it sound accusatory, as in "Where are you *now*?"

Once, I told him I was filming in Australia's snow hills. "Wow, snow hills!" he said wistfully. "I've never seen snow in my life." We talked about something else; then we hung up.

His words echoed in my head as I stood there in the studio, and I felt a twinge of sadness. I'd always been off making movies and hadn't spent much time with my child.

I phoned back, and his mom answered. I said, "Buy a couple of tickets and bring Jaycee to Australia tomorrow."

She said, "You're crazy. We can't do that. He has school."

I said, "This might be the only vacation I ever take with him. It won't matter if he misses a day of school, and he can make it up later. But if I miss this time, I don't know when I'll be free again. I can do it now, so bring him tomorrow."

They arrived the next day. When they got to the studio, I hoped he'd run and hug me, but he lay down on the snow and stayed there a long time. When he got up, I taught him how to ski and ride a snowmobile. He was a fast learner and took to it all quickly. In the photos of that day, Jaycee looks happy, but Joan looks ecstatic. I said to her, "See? It was a good idea after all."

Throughout his childhood, Jaycee complained that I never picked him up after school. One day, I finally had some free time and went to meet him, but he never showed. Later, I found out he was now in middle school. I'd been waiting at the elementary school gate.

We laughed about that one, actually.

chapter twenty-one

ONE MORE SHOT

In 1991, I was in my Hong Kong office, when my assistant came in to tell me that Sylvester Stallone had invited me to his movie premiere in America. I said, "You're joking." No way this could be true.

We made some calls to confirm the invitation, and I was floored. Stallone was a megastar and my idol, and he wanted me at his premiere? He even had his assistant travel to Hong Kong with two plane tickets so we could fly back together. I was very moved, though I felt sorry for the assistant, who had to board another plane after only thirty hours off of one.

On the flight, I wondered why he'd invited me, but couldn't come up with any answers. I wondered what I should do if I got there and something felt off, like if he didn't know who I was. With my bad English, I wouldn't be able to explain myself. I'd have to just run away!

There was a car waiting at the airport. His driver brought me straight to Stallone's house so I could have a look around, see his collections, his paintings, his gym. I even did some exercises in his gym, in disbelief that I was using Sylvester Stallone's equipment. After a while, his assistant came in, glanced at his watch, and said, "Let's go to the studio."

I felt a little uneasy. Stallone hadn't been at the airport or at his home. What was going on? When we got to the studio, he was in the middle of shooting a scene. When he saw me, he seemed to know who I was.

Soon after, he called, "Cut! Okay, lunchtime!" Then he came straight over to me and gave me a big hug.

He was shooting *Demolition Man*. When his costar Wesley Snipes saw me, he also came over and wrapped his arms around me. Stallone pulled me out of Snipes's reach, as if to say, "This is *my* friend, I'm the only one allowed to hug him." It was sweet. Then he grabbed my hand and pulled me in front of the entire production crew, and yelled, "Hey, everyone, it's Jackie Chan!"

They applauded thunderously. Honestly, I didn't understand how they knew me. I hadn't hit it big in America yet. Stallone led me to a big tent full of actors and stuntpeople. Everyone jumped to their feet and bowed to me! I was shocked. Many of the stuntpeople came over to shake my hand.

It turned out Stallone wanted to meet me on set and had dragged out the morning's filming so I'd arrive just in time to see them shoot the final scene. He brought me to his makeup trailer and fired up the VCR in there, already loaded with a videotape of one of my movies! He opened up a cabinet, and it was crammed full with my videos!

He said, "When we run out of ideas, we watch one of your films. You've taught us so much, and we really admire you. Thank you for coming." My English was terrible, so we had to speak through an interpreter. All I could say for myself was "Thank you so much, I'm so happy. You are my idol."

Only then did I learn that many American stunt teams were using my movies as instructional videos. I felt very proud of myself.

The next day, I went to the premiere of Sylvester Stallone's new film. It was my first time on an American red carpet. I hardly knew anyone, so I walked as fast as I could, not wanting to hold anyone up or to get in the stars' way when they were being interviewed. In that feverish atmosphere, with fans and lights everywhere, I said to myself, *One day, I'll walk the red carpet here for my own movie. And I'll have a star on the Hollywood Walk of Fame.*

As I've mentioned, I tried twice to break into American movies in the '80s and failed both times. My burgeoning friendship with Stallone—now twenty-five years strong—gave me the inspiration to try one more time. I was forty years old in 1994, and figured it was now or never. My colleagues were encouraging me to make inroads in the global marketplace, and Hollywood was undoubtedly the fastest way to do that.

This time, I was going to choose the project myself and not get railroaded into anything. Although I wasn't famous with audiences here, movie industry people knew me and tried to get me to work on their projects. Michael Douglas wanted me to play a Japanese killer in *Black Rain*. Sylvester Stallone wanted me to play a master criminal opposite Sandra Bullock, and then play a drug dealer in his next film. I turned down all these offers because those roles weren't right for me. Instead, I conceived of my own story, *Rumble in the Bronx*, written with Edward Tang. The story was about a cop from Hong Kong who comes to New York to visit family and gets involved in a turf war with a biker gang to protect a local shopkeeper. I tapped Stanley Tong to direct.

It was a Hong Kong production, but we always had one foot in the international market from the start. The bulk of the plot took place in New York (we filmed in Canada), and many of the actors were Americans. A lot of the dialogue was in English. Raymond Chow and Leonard Ho had high hopes that this one would finally open the golden door to the West for us.

New Line Cinema, our American distributor, put some real energy into publicity, and once again I had to face the American media. Things were very different for me this time. Journalists welcomed me with warmth, putting me on magazine covers and on talk shows. At the premiere, cameras flashed nonstop as I walked down the red carpet, and people screamed my name. Four years after I'd made my wish at Stallone's premiere, I was living it. It all felt so *right*; I knew the movie would be a hit.

Rumble in the Bronx made $9.8 million USD in its opening

weekend. It was the first Hong Kong film, dubbed in English, to break into the American rankings. My next three Hong Kong films—*Thunderbolt*, *Police Story 4: First Strike*, and *Mr. Nice Guy*—were all released in the US and did very well.

And just like that, I was big in America after fifteen years of trying. Why did these movies work when the others flopped? They were true Jackie Chan films, using all my key elements (although I'm not sure the Bronx qualifies as an exotic setting).

As they say, the third time was the charm. Now that I'd come to America, I was determined to stick around for a while.

In 1998, I appeared in *Rush Hour* with Chris Tucker, and the movie smashed records. *Rush Hour* 2 and *Rush Hour* 3 came out in 2001 and 2007. Although these films weren't my favorite genre, they performed amazingly well at the American and European box offices. As an added benefit, I was able to expose a pair of young actresses, Zhang Ziyi and Zhang Jingchu, to American audiences by casting them in the series.

In 2002, when *The Tuxedo* debuted, it took in $15 million USD its first weekend, the number two film in the country that week. Also that year, I got a star on the Hollywood Walk of Fame, in a very prominent location, realizing my second Stallone-premiere red carpet wish.

From then on, virtually all my movies were shown in every major market around the world. *Shanghai Noon* and the sequel, *Shanghai Knights*, *Around the World in 80 Days*, *The Forbidden Kingdom*, *The Spy Next Door*, and *The Karate Kid* were all American productions and hit movies.

When I think back on those years, what comes to mind is not the screaming fans and applause but the moments backstage that no one else would understand.

When I brought the Jackie Chan Stunt Team to America, people looked down on us. Our English wasn't good enough, and on our previous trips, we'd left the impression that we didn't follow the rules. That was mainly due to the differences between the Asian and American work styles. For instance, Western film studios believe in specialization, so everyone has a specific job that is clearly defined. One person lays the wires. One sets up the cameras. One focuses on the lights. You're not supposed to touch anyone else's turf. But in Hong Kong productions, everyone does everything. If you see something that needs fixing on set, you just pitch in. Efficiency is all that matters.

On my American movies, I wanted everything done fast, like back home. On Chinese film sets, when the director calls for something, you respond immediately, "Coming, coming, coming!" In America, they *slowly* get what you asked for and *slowly* bring it over. They even talk *slowly*. When we first started out, the difference in pace made the Americans think we were slapdash. We saw them as inefficient. After working together day after day, we slowly adapted to their style. Once we eased up a bit, we all started getting along better and building a relationship. Especially after they saw what the stunt team was capable of, the Americans were so impressed, they bowed to us in admiration. We won them over with sheer talent. Nowadays, you just have to mention the Jackie Chan Stunt Team abroad, and everyone gives a thumbs-up. To a person, my guys are honorary members of the stuntperson unions of every country.

I started out as a martial artist, and I've seen many primitive working conditions on set. When shooting a film, martial artists fall and hurt themselves coming out of a stunt, but they don't complain. They go straight on to the next one. That's normal to us, but unthinkable to Westerners.

When we first got to town, I wanted to put on a good show for the Americans so they'd see what we were made of. We were filming *Shanghai Noon*, and I choreographed a one-and-a-half somersault in midair, landing facedown. When I asked the camera crew to pull back, they said they couldn't or the crash mat would be in the shot.

I said, "We're not using the mat."

I nominated Wu Gang from the stunt team to do this, without protective gear. I knew he would be absolutely fine, and sure enough, he completed the stunt, protecting his head and face with great skill. The whole set erupted in loud applause.

I glanced at the monitor and said, deadpan, "Not good enough. Another take!"

Everyone was stunned. "That was great!" they said. "Why do you want him to do it again? It's dangerous."

I ignored them and whispered to Wu Gang in Chinese, "Is that okay?"

"No problem, Jackie."

He did it again. I kept my face expressionless. "No. Go again."

On his third attempt, I said, "Okay, that's fine."

Wu Gang's hands, wrists, and kneecaps were swollen and

bleeding, and my heart ached for him. But we'd been through such vigorous training as kids that these little injuries were nothing to us. To the Americans, however, we seemed superhuman, capable of achieving the impossible and withstanding any pain. I knew that after these three somersaults, no one would think twice about my stunt team again.

Sure enough, from that moment, we got nothing but respect from the US production team. As foretold by Stallone years ago, action producers all over Hollywood started telling their prospective stuntmen, "I want it done the Jackie Chan way!"

Going to Hollywood has been a mystical experience. It's hurt me viciously but also brought me the highest honors. It's given me a lot of praise but also deep insecurity. Hollywood movies are so influential, they make me anxious for the future of Chinese cinema.

There was a time when my colleagues were all talking about "the death of Hong Kong movies." I've seen the unprofessional, ugly side of the industry, and know the reasons why it could die.

Once, Sammo Hung made a film with four big stars, but it didn't have much of a run. All the fight scenes were clearly performed by stunt doubles, always keeping their faces hidden. Who wants to pay to see that?

A former star I worked with would go out drinking every night. Too hungover to work, she'd only be able to drag herself to the studio at 6:00 p.m. I was afraid to embarrass her, so I just said, "If you're not feeling well, don't come in. I'm a little under the weather myself." So she ended up sleeping all day, then going to a bar again that evening. Who wants to deal with that?

Some directors sign the contract and collect their fee, then get someone else to handle the actual shoot while they line up their next big paycheck. I've encountered this type of switcheroo on my own set. I saw a stranger in the director's chair and asked, "Who are you?"

"I'm the assistant director."

"Where's the director?"

"Over there."

I found him in his trailer writing the screenplay for his next film. If these are the people in our industry, how could it not die?

When I've been frustrated or disappointed in other people's work, I tell them, "Get out of here. I'll do it." This always delighted them. They knew the job would be done well by me, I'd save them the trouble of doing it themselves, and often they'd get all the credit. When one film was released after I'd taken over the direction anonymously, people asked me what I thought of the director, and I'd just say, "No comment." Later on, word spread around the industry that I had a habit of sidelining directors. People called me a tyrant on set, but I didn't care.

While we were making *Shinjuku Incident,* the director, Derek Yee, said to me, "Jackie, I know you like to shove directors aside and take the reins, but if you do that, I won't like it."

I replied, "Relax, I won't say a word the whole time. I won't even make a gesture. You're completely in charge here."

Chin Ka-Lok was the fight director on this film. Back when I was a fight director myself, he was just a kid. When he got on set and saw me, he started trembling. Yet I didn't change a single one of his moves; he was that good. I knew Derek Yee loved movies. He once sold his house to get a film made and could spend several years on a screenplay. I had a lot of admiration for both of them, so I respected them completely on set.

When I'm making a film, I've never thought, *Why should I jump off this building? Why should I jump off this bridge?* Even if I break an arm or a leg, I won't regret having done the jump. That's who I am. I take full responsibility for every one of my films, and I take everything I do seriously. It wasn't easy for me to get from where I started, doing odd jobs on set or playing a corpse as a teenager, to having my own empire with people actually listening to what I say. So I hate it when people aren't serious about their work.

Sometimes, I want to shout at lazy, uninspired filmmakers, "What kind of movies are you making? You're cheating the public!" Too many people just muddle through, promising all sorts of things that never materialize. They talk like anything is possible, but as it turns out, nothing is possible for them. People like this make me so angry. I really hope the market will get rid of them soon and the next generation of true innovators will rise up to take their place.

Ten years ago, a bunch of Chinese filmmakers were doing well in Hollywood—John Woo, Michelle Yeoh, Chow Yun-Fat, Jet Li, Ringo Lam, Yuen Woo-Ping, Tsui Hark, and Sammo Hung. I lost many members of my stunt team to the call of the West.

Hollywood learned from us, then became better than us, and now they don't need us anymore. If we were to go head-to-head with the Hollywood stuntpeople these days, do you think the Chinese would win? No way. These days, many of their fighters and stuntpeople have mastered kung fu. Whether it's Shao Lin or Wing Chun, they've learned all our moves. They can do somersaults, too. They can do martial arts, gymnastics, street dancing, parkour, the whole lot. When my stunt team saw evidence of this, their mouths gaped open.

Hollywood filmmakers not only learn from China, they tell Chinese stories, too. We've made so many movies about Hua Mulan, and none of them did well. Then Disney's *Mulan* became a monster hit, and now everyone in the world knows there was once a woman named Hua Mulan. The world has gone mad for the *Kung Fu Panda* films. Kung fu and pandas are both Chinese icons. There's a reason so many people all over the world are learning English. When someone is better than us at something, we ought to admit it.

When James Cameron invited me to visit the set of *Avatar*, I felt like I was back in kindergarten. I had to sign a nondisclosure agreement first, and thought, *You think I've never been on a movie set before?* Then I went in. I didn't see a single actor there, just blue backdrops everywhere and forty people working on computers. When they saw me, they all stood up and bowed. They started explaining how everything worked, and I barely understood a word, but it seemed they wanted me to be a great master, so I just played the part. I couldn't ask "What?" or "Why?" a hundred times, so I just said, "Yes, yes, okay."

They showed me a small camera that projected images of people right in front of you, like a hologram. I tried it out for myself while they controlled the camera from above. The experience can only be described as crazy. I could shoot someone's face, neck, arms, but there was actually nothing there. Another camera had four lenses, like nothing I'd seen before. When I looked up, there were tons of cameras hanging from the ceiling. I didn't count them, but there must have been several hundred. When would you ever see so many cameras in China? I could only take so much and started to make my excuses to leave. James Cameron came over to me and said, "I grew up watching your movies." I was so overwhelmed, I could only humbly thank him and go. My stunt team is the most professional in the Chinese-speaking world, and we have top-notch facilities, but I was stupefied by James Cameron's operation.

Our equipment is wires, wheels, buckles, and string. I insist on using only the very best to keep everyone safe. Times have changed. I don't let my team take risks and suffer like we used to back in the day. But, compared to American practices, we'd still be considered reckless.

When people do wire work in America, safety comes first, second, and third. When I watched a performer jump off a roof, first he jumped onto a ladder and fell to the ground. Then he did a backflip. This sequence of events required a lot of technical skill from the wire operator. He had to be very precise with the angles and make sure the wire didn't jam with all this back-and-forth movement. I watched them smoothly handling the rising and letting go, rising and letting go. Later on, I found out that these movements had already been modeled so the operator didn't need to rely on brute force. He could simply follow the calculations, push a button, and the machine did the rest. On my sets, we still had a few dozen people hoisting the wires. The contrast was huge. I asked how much this piece of equipment cost—not much, around $20,000 USD. But if I brought one back to China, no one would know how to use it. I'm only able to implement improvements that I've cobbled together myself.

After so many years in the business, I go into these studios and feel like an idiot. I wish China could get up to speed with the great equipment and techniques available. I hope our young people train abroad, bring back other people's knowledge, and make it their own. I wish China would *collaborate* more with Hollywood, to learn their skills, and that America could help us train our stuntpeople.

Chinese cinema has many great stories left to tell. I really hope some of our young film students have the passion and curiosity to strive for innovation and originality rather than treating moviemaking as homework to be handed in to their teachers. If you can get a group together that includes a screenwriter, a director, a cinematographer, a designer, and an editor, if you have dedication and inspiration, you can make something wonderful together. We have to learn to work together like the Americans. When I'm in the US discussing a script, the conference room will have several dozen people in it, everyone gathered together, tossing out suggestions. It always leads to great ideas.

I emphasize technology for students and *other* filmmakers, because if I were to produce a film that was full of special effects, I don't think my audience would be interested. We'll have to wait and see. My fans have gotten used to watching me perform my own stunts. In this way, I've hamstrung myself. But what can I do? I started a precedent in the world of action films; I have no choice but to continue. For me, it's a question of innovation, of coming up with new, real stunts. I want to surprise the audience with each film. For decades now, people have kept saying that Jackie Chan is getting old and can't hack it anymore, and I don't bother defending myself. I just use my movies as proof that they're wrong. I can't change the fact that I'm aging, but I'm still just as able to soar through a wind tunnel or leap into a volcano as any younger performer.

After all these years, I'm still just trying to make a good movie.

In recent years, my fan base has been renewed. There are people who've followed my films right from the beginning, but others have only just started watching. Some love my Hong Kong productions; others prefer my Hollywood work. I call them my "classic" and "new" audiences, and feel responsible to both. I hope to do my best to give people what they want and show them different sides of myself. I'm fortunate that I can make movies based on personal interest, not just to make money. I'm even financing my own films, which allows me to take another kind of risk. I put in as much money and ability as I am able, working away at it every day, carefully putting movies together bit by bit, and finally coming up with something I feel happy sharing with my audiences. This is how I'm carrying out my silent competition with Hollywood.

To this day, I look in the mirror and say, *You lucky bastard.* If there is a God, I'd like to thank him, and hope he grants other people just as much good fortune as me. Right now, that's my greatest wish.

I'll end my Hollywood chapter with a little story about the first time I met one of the greatest America directors of all time: Steven Spielberg. I was nervous to be in the presence of such a famous director and had no idea what I would say. But then he walked straight over to me and exclaimed warmly, "Wow, Jackie Chan." Then he asked for my autograph for his son. We naturally fell silent as I signed, and I felt the moment was a little awkward. My brain whirred as I frantically tried to think of a conversation topic. When I was done, I asked him about the special effects for *E.T.* and *Jurassic Park*.

"How did you make it look so real, people and dinosaurs side by side?"

He said, "Oh, that's simple, I just keep pushing buttons—button, button, button. What about your films? How did you do all those dangerous stunts, jumping off rooftops and over cliffs?"

I said, "Oh, that's even simpler. It's just rolling, action, jump, cut, hospital!"

chapter twenty-two

MY FLASHBACK HIGHLIGHT REEL

I started in the movies more than fifty years ago at the age of six and a half. I've now acted in or directed about two hundred films. If you add in my work as a child performer, and the ones in which I was a martial artist or fight director, I've contributed to over two hundred.

I'm not out of ideas or stories yet! I've been trying to make *Firefighting Heroes* for three decades now, but for one reason or another it hasn't happened. My Xiang Yu biopic never happened either. *Little Big Soldier* took twenty years to make it into production. It's probably because I have very high standards.

No matter what, I like films that bring people joy, the kind that send you out of the theater with a smile on your face. Modern society is frustrating enough; there's no need for more negativity in the cinema. If everyone who watches a Jackie Chan film feels good and laughs and receives the positive messages I want to pass on, that's good enough for me.

I've made more movies and have more stories about them than I can share in this book or fifty books. Suffice it to say, some stories stand out in my memory about the joy—and pain—of making movies . . .

Project A: Part II

Maggie Cheung is one of those actors who throws caution to the wind. Our first collaboration was 1987's *Project A: Part II*. Maggie starred along with Rosamund Kwan and Carina Lau. One scene had me, Maggie, and Rosamund being chased across the rooftops. We ended up hanging off the edge. Maggie and I would be running slightly behind Rosamund, and we'd watch her jump off the roof.

I explained the setup to Rosamund, and when I got to the part about her jumping, she said, "No way."

I said, "It'll be a great image if you take this leap."

She looked over the roof's edge. Her eyes widened; then she swore at me and called me crazy. "Do you take me for one of your stunt guys?" Then she stormed off, leaving me standing there looking like an idiot.

I turned to Maggie and said, "Come here, look, this will be a great scene. And it's so simple. I'll get someone to demonstrate. See how taut that canopy is? It's all prepared; it will be just like skateboarding." Maggie nodded, only half believing me.

We were on a three-story building. First she tried a jump from the first story onto a cardboard box. "Okay, this is fine," she said.

"But you can't just jump off the first floor and then have a stand-in jump off the roof. That's bad for continuity, and audiences will know it's fake. We should do the whole thing in a single take. If you jump from the second floor to the first, it won't be very far, and you have the box to catch you below that. It will be fine."

She gritted her teeth and said, "All right, I'll give it a go."

I was delighted to hear that and called for everyone to set up quickly. I saw that Rosamund was watching us from the makeup trailer, and I thought, *I'll make sure this scene is amazing and Maggie will outshine you. You should have listened to me!*

I went up to the roof and called "Action!" Maggie screwed up her courage, jumped, and landed with a couple of loud thuds. She ended up on the cardboard box. I said, "Great! Can we go again?"

She answered slowly, "I guess so."

She did it again. I said, "Well done! Do you feel confident now? Yes? Then let's try again. We'll just get rid of the cardboard box. There'll be nothing for you to land on, but I'll catch you and protect you. How about it?"

She stared at me and, a moment later, burst into tears.

I looked at her in horror and hastily said, "All right, all right, no more jumping, no more jumping." I had to comfort her for a long time, she was so upset. She really had been very brave so far and trusted me. I wasn't completely certain either, but I would never have hurt either of them; I just wanted them to look good in this film. The stunts I gave them were safe, and when I ran through all the possible scenarios, it didn't seem like anything could go wrong. I wouldn't have asked them to jump otherwise. I would have happily injured myself to catch her when she fell.

Ironically, later on, when I was making a music video for one of my songs, I wasn't happy with what I was seeing on film. Maggie came in to costar, and our collaboration resulted in one of the best music videos of all time. The name of the song? "It Was You Who Gave Me a Piece of Sky."

Miracles

While filming 1989's *Miracles*, I spent an entire week on a single shot. I wanted to show Gua Ah-Leh's character's living environment. I envisioned a tracking shot starting on the street and ascending a four-story building. We'd see a rickshaw, people sharing a meal on the first two floors, pigeons fluttering amid drying laundry, all the way up to Gua Ah-Leh's room on the fourth floor, into a close-up on her face—all that, in a single swoop. We had limited resources to construct the set. Still, we wanted the best possible results, so we had to start from scratch. We rented an entire street and set up there.

Every frame had to meet all my requirements. The extras on set are usually members of my stunt team—the rickshaw pullers, street hawkers, passersby, and so on. They understand what I need better than regular extras. As soon as I called "Rolling," flames leaped beneath the woks, and the camera moved up to the second floor, where there were two people eating just as a pigeon flew into the frame and perched there; then we kept moving up and went around the room before coming to a close-up on a photograph. It took seven days of filming before I was happy with this shot.

Many of the scenes in *Miracles* were filmed without a break. During the scene of Anita Mui being photographed, we needed someone to walk in and put up a drape. One of the editors said, "Jackie, let me do it, you won't see my face, and I'd like to be in a movie."

I said, "All right."

He had to put up that drape repeatedly for twenty-six hours in a row because we filmed over an entire day and night. At the end of his scene, he said to me, "I never want to be in another film in my life."

Armour of God II: Operation Condor

The main locations for this 1991 film were Spain and Morocco. All the Morocco scenes took place in the Sahara. We'd be up at four in the morning, head out to the desert at 5:45, and shoot until noon. We had to stop there. The desert sun was at its highest then, and all the equipment became too hot to touch. If we'd continued shooting, the film itself would have melted.

To a Hong Kong film crew used to rushing through a shoot, sitting in the shade all afternoon felt like a giant waste of time. None of us could get comfortable.

We were there more than a month. Following local practice, the crew took one day off per week. I found this rest day difficult to bear. The hotel was surrounded by desert on all sides, with nothing to do and nowhere to go. The outdoor swimming pool was gritty with sand. No entertainment facilities at all. I talked to the producer to ask if the local crew would be willing to give up their rest day for double wages.

The producer made my request to the crew sitting by the pool, drinking and talking. They replied, "A rest day is a rest day. We're not going to work."

A week later, once again, I found the rest day unbearable, and after fidgeting in my room, I went to talk to the crew myself. "Look, if we finish this shoot early, then you'll all get to go home sooner. Plus, we'll pay you double. You'll earn more money."

They said, "What would we want with more money?"

I was dumbstruck. "Well, I don't know what you'd do with it . . ."

"That's right! We earn enough already! We wouldn't know what to do with more. And now it's time to rest, so we're going to rest."

I couldn't argue with that.

The Legend of the Drunken Master

I was filming *The Legend of the Drunken Master* in Shanghai in 1993, and had a martial artist named Ah Kan on set. He had a vicious expression and was covered in tattoos. You'd find him terrifying to look at, but he was a good person. One day, I had a sudden craving for soup dumplings, so I asked him to phone and help me order some, and to make sure they were delivered hot. It took over half an hour for the takeout girl to arrive, and the dumplings were cold. I was very annoyed. When I realized there was no vinegar in the bag, I lost it completely and screamed, "Where's my vinegar? I want clear vinegar!"

Ah Kan ran after the delivery girl, shouting, "Fuck! Give me a fuck! I need a clear fuck!"

She must have been terrified! It turns out, in Cantonese, the words for "vinegar" and "fuck" are very similar. Ah Kan was stressed-out, and his Cantonese was bad, which was why this ridiculous situation happened. You can imagine it, a big guy covered in tattoos, looking like a thug, running after this poor girl yelling, "Give me a fuck!!!"

Which reminds me of another embarrassing thing that happened to Ah Kan, also during the filming of *The Legend of the Drunken Master*. There was a scene where I had to drop off the roof of a train. I needed the mainland Chinese martial artists to arrange the landing mats. Some had to be vertical, some horizontal. In Cantonese, I asked Ah Kan to have them lay the mats horizontally. Unfortunately, the Cantonese words for "horizontal" and "hole" sound almost alike, so he ended up telling them, "Hurry up, put holes in these mats!" At the time, Hong Kong film studios had a lot of power when we filmed in the mainland, especially when it came to fight direction. We were considered the experts. Although the crew found this order very peculiar, they did as they were told, thinking perhaps the idea was to punch holes in the mats so they could be strung together.

When I showed up, everyone was busily punching holes in my landing mats. I asked, "What's going on here?" They relayed Ah Kan's instructions, and I didn't know whether to laugh or get angry!

Who Am I?

We shot this 1998 movie near Johannesburg. Well, not too near. From the city, it was a twelve-hour drive to our camp, then another hour to the actual location. We were shooting in the wilderness by a small village. Once we were set up, we herded all the chickens and goats we could find onto our set, and invited locals from the village to be part of the scene. By the time we finished, many of the chickens and goats had gone missing. The locals told us they had been eaten by leopards. That sounded terrifying, so I made sure my bodyguards were always nearby.

Most of Africa is desert, and the conditions where we were filming weren't great. If anyone had to use the bathroom, it would take at least half an hour. I wanted aerial shots from a helicopter, so there couldn't be tire tracks anywhere around there. All our vehicles had to be parked some distance away, and everyone walked to the location (footprints were okay). In these circumstances, finding a toilet presented some difficulties. It didn't matter so much with the locals, since, once they had their makeup on, they were pretty much interchangeable, so one person more or less in the scene didn't really matter. It was different for me, though. If I needed to take a shit, I'd have to walk all the way to the parked cars, then drive to the nearest bathroom, holding up the entire shoot.

If I needed the toilet at night, I'd go to a grassy patch by the village, carrying a flashlight, with bodyguards holding rifles in front of and behind me. No joke—we were scared I'd get attacked by a leopard. (Remember my bad history with them!) When we got to the spot, the bodyguards gave me a rifle and showed me how to hold the flashlight so the area around me would stay illuminated. Then they waited to one side.

As I took my dump, I saw something swaying around in front of me. Getting scared, I yelled, "What's that?"

"It's just a cow," they said.

It was the worst shit I've ever had in my life. I had a heavy rifle in one hand and was terrified it would accidentally go off. In my other hand, the flashlight. I didn't dare squat fully, in case some scorpion or bug attacked me, so I stood in a half crouch. Then I had to grip the bulky, weighty flashlight in my teeth to use toilet paper while being stared at by a cow. By the time I was done, my legs were numb, my arms and shoulders ached, and my jaw was throbbing. The cow was probably traumatized, too.

The Tuxedo

In Hong Kong, I'm used to being in charge of everything on set, but in the US, on this 2002 movie, my job was only to act, and nothing else. I'd arrive at the location, and the crew would usher me straight to my trailer. If I said, "I'd like to look at the set," they'd just say it wasn't ready yet and that they'd let me know when it was.

So I'd sit in my trailer, and they'd bring me newspapers, magazines, and fruit. Someone or other was constantly popping in to ask if I needed anything, and I'd say, "Thank you, but no."

Finally, someone came in and announced, "Ready to go in five."

I'd open the trailer door five minutes later to find a couple of people from wardrobe waiting outside, asking, "Can we come in?"

I'd usher them in, and they'd fiddle around for a while, but actually there was nothing much to do because my costumes were quite straightforward. Still, they had a job to do, so I let them get on with it. My own assistants were used to helping me with my hair and clothes, but when they tried that here, they were scolded. "That's *my* job," said the wardrobe people.

After they'd done what they needed to do, I left the trailer and went on set, ready to start shooting. It was all very professional. They already had my chair and all my stuff ready for me.

As I've mentioned before, the American style is different from the Chinese. In Hong Kong, if anything needed doing, whoever had a moment would jump on it. There is no division of labor. If a dragon's head needed to be moved, you didn't wait for the props people. My stunt team or I would handle it. In America, if the director wanted something moved, the specific crew would stroll over at their leisure. I never saw them run. According to American labor laws, if someone fell and got hurt because you told them to hurry, you would have to compensate them. So I'd watch the crew take their time, with two people moving something that one person easily could have managed.

At one point in the shoot, I was suspended in midair, and the wind was so strong that the cinematographer had to change his lens. He yelled, "I need a seventy-five lens!"

I watched someone from his team walk . . . *so* . . . *slowly* to deliver the lens. He even stopped on the way to say hi to someone, and they chatted for a minute before he came over. I was in a foreign country and had to respect the way they did things there. But if we were in Hong Kong, I'd have shouted at him, "Hey, three hundred people are waiting for you, and I'm hanging in midair! Move it!"

Chinese Zodiac

This 2012 movie was actually seven years in the making, with many stops and starts.

In one scene, I jumped out of an airplane into a volcano. To get the shot of a volcano, I went to Vanuatu in the South Pacific. As soon as we got there, we heard the volcano boom or rumble every five or ten minutes. There were ashes all over the road. I asked a passerby when the last eruption was, and he said they had a big one ten years ago.

Our hotel was owned by an Australian. There was a restaurant, too, but the whole place accommodated only twenty-eight people, so you can imagine how small it was. After checking in, I thought the room wasn't bad. I put my luggage down and went to join the others in the restaurant. They were already assembled, chatting eagerly about the film. There were a few dozen people in the place, not a single cell phone in sight. They were all talking about work instead, which made me glad. I sat down and took out my cell phone to text that we'd arrived safely. A few dozen voices chorused in my direction, "No signal!" Ah.

Normally, when we got to a hotel, everyone would rush to their separate rooms, where they could take out their laptops or smartphones and get busy. But now we were together because we couldn't use our devices. This made me even more delighted. We'd been talking to one another less and less, which is a problem of contemporary society. Now that there was no signal, we could all have a good chat.

After dinner, I went out for a look around. There was nothing to see on the street, just pitch darkness. When I looked up, I could see the entire Milky Way. I used a flashlight to get back to my room because the corridors were dark, too, with no lamps at all. When I dropped the pen I was holding, I searched the floor for ages with the flashlight, but couldn't find it. Then someone nudged me and said, "Here's your pen."

I turned around but couldn't see anyone until my eyes adjusted and I made out the outline of a hotel staff member. How had he seen me drop the pen? Later on, I learned that the locals have eyesight several times better than ours. They'd been living in this place long enough to have trained themselves to see in the dark. We were there for ten days, and that whole time, I never saw a single person wearing glasses.

You might see the Vanuatu people as poor, but they were very happy. Their main means of transport was their own legs, usually barefoot. Every day, the people I drove past were all walking. The roads weren't always paved, and travel was difficult. It took more than an hour to get from the hotel to the set. Even a Jeep would have had to go slowly, so we weren't much faster than the walkers. By afternoon, more and more people had started arriving on set. They'd all been walking to watch us film. Vanuatu is an island in the sea, so the weather was uncertain. Often, the sun would be blazing, and then suddenly a storm would blow up out of nowhere. We were filming on a large patch of empty ground, and when it rained, the locals didn't try to find shelter but just stood in the rain.

Just by looking at the clouds, they knew when it would rain and when the sun would shine. They had natural intelligence.

Both adults and children always carried knives, not for fighting but to hack at tree branches in their way. Sometimes they bartered the large knives for food or clothes. When they got tired from walking, they'd pick up a coconut from the side of the road, whack it open with their knives, drink the liquid and eat the flesh, then continue walking.

Only 15,000 people lived on the whole island, and everyone knew everyone else. Looking at them, I felt envy. This place truly was paradise on Earth.

I was in my fifties when I made *Chinese Zodiac*, but still I insisted on doing many of the movements myself. At the start of this film, there's a scene in which I'm under a car in a special suit covered in wheels. The car was going fast, and if I'd lost focus for one second and made a move in the wrong direction, I could have lost a hand. My speed had to match the car exactly. It was very risky. You think I wasn't afraid? Of course I was! But after all these years, I've gotten used to working while terrified. As soon as I heard "Rolling, action!" I flung myself under the car. Making movies is a dream and a promise. And I have a responsibility to the audience to take those risks.

We filmed *Chinese Zodiac* all over the world, and wherever we went, we received a warm welcome, a reward for all my years of hard work. Wherever we go, people will say, "Welcome, Jackie Chan!" They believe in me, and I can't let them down. On any location, I take extreme care not to damage it in any way.

We filmed a few scenes in a centuries-old French château and gardens, and I promised at the start that I would be as careful as possible and not leave any mess.

You need a lot of stuff to film in locations like this. For example, tape. There are special kinds of tape for everything, from wallpaper to wood. If you use the wrong type, you'll leave a mark on someone else's property when you rip it off, and then you'll have to pay compensation. As soon as we were granted permission to film at the château, I rushed out and bought all sorts of tape to send to the team.

When we first started filming, the château's management team came to watch us. When they saw my collection of different tapes, they were convinced we cared, and said, "Okay, we trust you." Would this happen if not for my professionalism? When you have experience and standards, and show respect for people and property, you are respected in return.

These days, whether in Hollywood or China, many productions have a limited budget. Most investors won't spend more than tens of millions on a film. When I was in America, I would often ask the filmmakers, "Do you want to stick to your schedule, or do you want to make a good film?" They always said "Make a good film," but then tighten the purse strings anyway.

According to accountants, saving money is good business. I disagree. I'm both the director and the investor in my own movies, and I have no qualms about increasing the budget as long as it makes for a better film. A true Jackie Chan film can go head-to-head with any foreign film anytime and earn just as much recognition and box office success. We can't beat blockbusters like *Black Panther* or *Wonder Woman*, but they can't beat us when it comes to kung fu films or pure action—and no one, but no one, can top my huge collection of sticking tape!

chapter twenty-three

MORE DOLLARS THAN SENSE

When I started out as a martial artist, I earned $5 a day, which later increased to $35. I'd take my tiny amount of money for ten hours of sweat and blood and go gambling. If I won $30, I'd bet $60. If I won $60, I'd bet $100. In the end, I was always the loser, which was painful. I could lose more than $300 in a single go, equivalent to ten days' wages. In despair, I couldn't afford food, let alone anything else. How I envied people with money! They could buy anything they wanted.

And then I became very rich myself. And, man, did I spend it.

I went to fancy boutiques in London. They'd shut the store for me, and I'd emerge with several large boxes of stuff. After all, I had to make this special treatment worth their while, didn't I? Imagine if they'd closed the shop for me and all I bought was a belt.

I'd say to the salespeople, "Those bags on the wall—not this one, not this one, and I'll take the rest. These glasses—not these three, and I'll take the rest. Not this pair of shoes, and I'll take the rest." Back at the hotel, my friends or colleagues would help me sort through my purchases, what to keep and what to gift.

When I was filming *Mr. Nice Guy*, my stunt team and I went shopping in Australia. We passed by a watch boutique, and as soon as the Chinese salesman who was standing in the doorway caught sight of me, he started hollering, "Hey, Jackie! Jackie! Come in and have a look."

I said, "I'm not going to buy anything."

He said, "That's fine, just have a look."

He was so enthusiastic, I thought, *Might as well just look.* He offered me tea or coffee with such warmth, I felt obliged to give him a few minutes. Thirty minutes later, my final bill came up to $580,000. Every member of the stunt team got a $20,000 watch. I was with only three of them at the time, and I thought it would be enough to just get those guys watches, but they asked, "What about the others?" What could I do? I bought watches for everyone! When we got back and handed them out, everyone traded around until they had the style and color they liked best. Seeing them so excited made me happy, too.

When I had spare time while shooting *Thunderbolt*, I hung out with Oliver, the art director. Oliver was a collector. I saw that he had several attractive china teacups in his room, and asked why he'd bought so many. He explained the cultural significance of these antique cups, and also taught me about them. He told me the British use flat saucers now, but they used to be curved because people would pour their tea into their saucers and drink from there. On old cups, the undersides were blank. Later on, they added a dash of red, then a dot of blue, and eventually the words "Made in England." If you come across a china teacup with just a dot or dash, or just the word "England," you know they're old and might be worth something.

This was all fascinating to me. He gave me some items from his collection, and I've been interested ever since. I learned more about the history of teacups and saucers from other experts. I got hooked and I started my own collection. Normal people acquire ten or twenty cups per decade, but I bought 1,200 in just a month. Later, I brought some of these cups into the interior of China, handing them over to craftsmen who made "purple sand" teapots in Yixing to analyze. They were able to make me three or four teapots of purple sand clay in the style of English and German teacups—highly unique.

If I like something, I buy in bulk. While shopping in America, I bought $6,000 worth of flashlights in one go, and everyone looked at me like I was insane. At the time, no one in America had any idea who I was. They probably thought I was just a rich Asian weirdo.

When I became famous worldwide, it gave me pleasure to have designer items—red wine, fancy cars, sunglasses, clothes—custom-made with my name on them. Whenever a craftsman or merchant came out with a limited-edition Jackie Chan item, it always sold out as soon as it hit the market. I'd allow them to make only one batch, and when that was gone, that'd be it. The only thing is, I'd get anxious that the items would be lost to me, so I'd start buying them back from all over the world. I ended up reacquiring many cases of Jackie Chan red wine at several times the asking price. The bat-wing sunglasses I liked wearing were manufactured as a collaboration between two labels. When I wanted to keep making them, the two companies weren't able to reach an agreement and had a falling-out. Since no new glasses were forthcoming, I purchased every pair I could find still on the market. Now I'm the only person who has this style of dark glasses. You can't buy them anywhere else.

Looking back, I guess I behaved like this to make up for past suffering. I wanted to have everything, to buy everything. I could, so I did. But of course I bought far, far too much. I wouldn't purchase just a few pairs of shoes; I'd go scoop up the contents of an entire warehouse. I also went through a phase of buying books, filling every bookcase in my house. When I was renovating the place, I bought three copies of every interior decoration book—one for the shelf, one to read, and one for my designer. This made it easier for us to communicate, even though those foreign books were very expensive.

I've barely read any of the books on my shelves. To be honest, they're mostly for decoration. When I give interviews at home, I ask my colleagues to help rip off the plastic wrapping around some of the books and then stick bookmarks in them to make it look like I'm reading them; otherwise it'd be too obvious to the visiting reporter that I'm only interested in books as décor.

On one occasion, TVB (a channel in China) was throwing their annual banquet. I happened to be in talks with producer Johnnie To, so when he mentioned he was attending the event, I said I'd see him there. I didn't tell anyone I was going, though, to avoid creating a hassle for the organizers. I just snuck in quietly. Spotting Johnnie in his seat, I darted over to him at a half crouch. Cell phones didn't exist back then, so I just squatted there talking to him, and we arranged to meet somewhere else later that evening.

As I stood up to leave, someone from the station caught sight of me and said, "Hey, Jackie, since you're here, why not join in?"

I had no idea what was going on, so I stood up and waved hi to everyone. To my shock, the announcer exclaimed, "Wonderful! Jackie's bid five hundred thousand!"

I did? Wait, what was this $500,000 I'd just bid? That was a huge amount of money in those days. I thought they must be joking. I said good-bye to Johnnie and headed for the exit.

As I was walking out, I heard a voice calling, "Going once, going twice, going three times," and then the crack of a gavel. "Sold to Jackie Chan! Thank you, Jackie."

People applauded, and I nodded, totally embarrassed. I didn't say anything, just walked away haplessly. I told one of the ushers, "Whatever I just bought, send it to my office later." Afterwards, I complained to Johnnie that our five-minute chat cost me $500,000.

The next day, the purchase was delivered and I found out what it was: a large painting of a horse by the famous artist Xu Beihong.

I guess I was meant to have it. Many people have come to my house and seen this painting and told me it's valuable, though I don't know how much it's worth exactly. Some people say millions, some say billions. I once tried to offer it to a charity auction, but someone stopped me. Jaycee said, "Dad, I don't want any of your money, just leave me that painting and that's enough."

I said, "All right."

But wait, he doesn't want my collection of bat-wing sunglasses?

Believe it or not, despite that experience, I started to get into auctions and bidding on antiques. If I couldn't get to a particular auction, I'd send friends to go and bid for me. At one auction, my friend called to report that the next item was a table carved with the *Thousand Character Classic*, in red sandalwood inlaid with yellow boxwood, at a starting price of $500,000. I thought it was too good to be true to find such a precious object for so little and told him to go straight to a million.

He put in his bid, and no one tried to outbid him, and just like that, it was mine. I felt quite pleased with myself and bragged to the people I was with, "I'm so good at this! I just bought a red sandalwood table for only a million!"

I arranged for it to be shipped to my office in Hong Kong, and phoned my assistant, a young woman named Maggie, to tell her to hire movers to make sure it got to my house safely. "No need for movers," she said. "I've done it for you. It's by the window."

"*You* moved it? All by yourself? And you put it by my window?"

And that's how I learned that the table was tiny. A child could easily lift it with one hand. That was why no one tried to outbid me. Is it any wonder why my wife and others always say, "Jackie has more dollars than sense"? A lot more.

chapter twenty-four

COSTARS

I've always liked using newcomers in my films. I don't want the hassle of working with divas. That can get exhausting and make me very unhappy. They're always having scheduling conflicts, so you end up using a body double or reassigning their lines to other actors, though that always comes out looking bad.

Look, I don't really need another big name in my films, so why *not* just use newcomers? They stick with the team all day long, learn new things, and are eager and ready to go into a shot whenever they're needed. It saves a lot of trouble. Newcomers are thrilled by the chance to become known to audiences across the world by appearing in just one of my films. That's a rare opportunity in this industry. Whenever I hire a young ambitious person, it makes me think back to my early days and how I used to wish someone would give me a chance. If people hadn't given me a helping hand, I don't think I would have made it. Now I'm in a position to help others, and I give as much of a leg up as I can to young people who have really impressed me with their talent and attitude.

When I was making *Rush Hour 2*, I wanted to cast a newcomer, and a few people said to me, "What about Zhang Ziyi?"

I introduced her to the director. The Americans agreed to have her as our villain. When we started, her English was terrible, but as we worked together, I saw how smart she was. She picked up the language quickly, and was a fast study in every aspect of filming and choreography. She mastered her moves in no time, and her poses looked pretty good. Foreign audiences liked her, too. I was glad I had taken my friends' suggestion!

When we made *Shinjuku Incident*, Xu Jinglei and Fan Bingbing were able to chat away in fluent Japanese from the start. I felt embarrassed compared to them because I'd studied the language a little and didn't know it nearly as well. When we got to the scene where I had to write some Japanese, I simply couldn't remember *any* of it. They put me to shame with their language skills, which are crucial to a newcomer's success in the world market.

I feel very protective of the newcomers I bring in. While Zhang Jingchu and I were working on *Rush Hour 3*, I noticed that the Hollywood people didn't always treat her well. I did what I could to help her out.

The production team always shot Chris Tucker's and my scenes first. She was a supporting role and had to hang around waiting.

When we had our scenes together, she could have had someone else stand in for the reverse shots, but she always insisted on doing them herself to support us. There was one scene where she had to sit opposite me crying, and even though the camera was only getting her back, as soon as the director called action, she started sobbing.

After he called cut, I said to her, "Miss, you don't need to cry, we won't see your face—save your tears for later." But still she insisted on weeping, hoping to provide a good atmosphere for my acting.

American filmmakers always want to have a long shot, a midshot, and a close-up, and all of them in reverse as well. Zhang Jingchu insisted on doing every one of them, sitting opposite me crying, from morning until night. By the time we wrapped for the day, she must have been exhausted. As soon as the crew heard we were done, everyone seemed to relax, as if they could finally exhale.

When it came time to get Zhang Jingchu's shots, we could have used body doubles rather than sitting there ourselves. The production team assumed this would be the case. Big stars like Chris and me surely wouldn't bother being scene partners for the other actors. But I hung around even though I was done for the day to keep an eye on her. She was new in town, and no matter how much experience she had in China, making her first Hollywood film was surely a frightening, anxious time for her. I'd been down this road before and knew how she must be feeling. I stood in a corner and watched the situation. Everyone on set looked pretty relaxed. The director was leaning casually in his chair when he called "Action!"

In this scene, Zhang Jingchu had to push a door open and walk in with tears in her eyes. From where I was standing, I saw that she was still putting in eye drops when "Action" was called. She got flustered and quickly hid the bottle. There was no one around from wardrobe or makeup to assist her. It seemed unfair.

I burst out onto the set and said, "Cut! She's not ready yet. Why are you in such a hurry?" I told Jingchu she should let us know when she was ready, then turned back to the crew. "Listen, she's ready when I say she's ready."

She got back in position, finished putting in her eye drops, got herself in the zone, and told me, "Jackie, I'm ready."

I turned to the crew. "Okay, we're good to go." They called "Rolling," then "Action," and she walked out. I stood there watching the whole time.

When the director called "Cut," I went over to her right away. "Was that all right? We can do another take." She said okay, so I yelled, "One more time!" I wanted to show everyone that they couldn't bully the newcomer like that. There was going to be another take because I said so.

As they prepared for the next take, changing the cameras over and adjusting the lighting, I went over and wrapped my arms around her, helping her get in the mood. She'd stuck with me all day and had no tears left for her own scene. I waited around until she'd done all her scenes. She hugged me and said, "Jackie, I'm really grateful to you."

I said, "No need for that. We're all in this together. We have to look out for each other."

It's essential that the people I work with have a great attitude. It's more important to me than kung fu technique. When we were looking at actresses for *Chinese Zodiac*, the casting director brought in many audition tapes. After watching the first three, I fixed on Zhang Lanxin. When my casting director and movement team hold auditions, the camera never stops rolling, because it's not just your acting I want to see; I also want to know what you're like the rest of the time. These details matter, but many people ignore them. They shouldn't. When the candidates hear "Let's try again" and they look grumpy, it looks bad. When they hear "Let's try another angle" and they look impatient, it's worse. When I see people like this, no matter how good their martial arts skills, I fast-forward to the next person.

With Zhang Lanxin, it was different. After the first take, she took the initiative and said, very politely, "Sorry, sir, can I try again?" And when she had to turn and kick at the camera, she said, "All right, sir, I'll go again."

That was all I needed to see. I turned to the producer and said, "She's the one."

The producer pointed out that some of the others had better technique.

"It doesn't matter. I don't want any of them. I don't like these kinds of people. Even if their kung fu is better, I only want her," I said.

Behind the Scenes by Zhu Mo

When he was filming *Shanghai Knights*, Jackie wanted to find a fresh face he hadn't worked with before to star opposite him. He said to his assistant director, "I have someone special in mind, a singer who's popular in Southeast Asia, Wong Fei!" The assistant director was a foreigner and didn't know who Wong Fei was. Jackie said, "She's very famous, and she sings well. She's just like the character in the script. Her English name is Faye Wong." The assistant director said, "Faye Wong. Okay, I'll look her up."

A day later, Jackie got a call from the assistant director. "I got Faye Wong."

"Wow, really?"

"Yes. She sounded overjoyed when she heard your name and that you wanted to work with her."

"Excellent."

"She's in Singapore now. She'll be able to come meet you soon."

"Good, good."

The day she arrived, Jackie was in the makeup trailer, when there was a knock at the door. It was the assistant director. "Faye Wong's just got off the plane; she'll be here to see you soon."

When she arrived, the AD knocked again, and Jackie hurried out of his trailer to meet her.

There was a woman standing there. But it was not Faye Wong.

She came over to shake his hand. "Jackie, I'm so glad you like my work," she said. "Thank you for choosing me for this project."

He could only shake her hand and keep smiling.

They spoke for a few minutes, and then he went back into the trailer. Jackie called for the AD and said to him, "That's not Faye Wong! That's not who I wanted."

He looked confused. "Didn't you say Faye Wong? Isn't that her?"

Jackie said, "It really isn't."

It turned out to be a big misunderstanding. The assistant director had hired a Singaporean actress named Fann Wong, whose name sounded similar to "Faye Wong."

Jackie didn't watch much TV at the time, so he hadn't heard of Fann Wong, but he found out later that she was actually quite famous in China and Singapore.

The assistant director was in despair, not knowing how to fix this situation. He kept saying, "What should we do?"

Jackie said, "It's fine, no problem; we'll just have her play the part." Jackie just can't say no to anyone.

Fann Wong gave a great performance in the film. It might be a bit unfair to her to bring up this story now, but it was such a long time ago, and I'm sure she's still grateful to have been able to work with Jackie.

Of all the newcomers I've discovered, Daniel Wu has been the most successful. American audiences know him from the TV series *Into the Badlands*.

I met him at a party, I don't remember where. A friend came over and said, "There's an American guy you should meet. He's a fan of yours who came all the way to Hong Kong to see you." I agreed to the introduction and Daniel Wu came over.

His Chinese wasn't very good then, but I thought he had a good look, and I took his phone number. Back in the office, I gave it to my manager and said, "Here's a young guy who's not bad. Give him a call; you should sign him."

Not long after, we'd cast him in Yonfan's *Bishonen* and he became famous. He'd come to the office every day, find an empty room, and sit there earnestly practicing his Cantonese. He also worked very hard on his Mandarin. He went to language classes, too, and really did his best to master them. I appreciated his dedication and hard work.

We first worked together on *New Police Story*. He made a great villain and got very good reviews. Then we collaborated on *Shinjuku*

Incident and bonded even more. We'd started out as an idol and his fan, but now we were friends. Normally, I treated him like a son, but on set we were more like brothers. After knowing me all these years, he always says what he likes most about me is that I'm not afraid of anything. Actually, he has no idea: I'm scared of plenty of things. Like needles. And angry leopards.

There was a scene in *Shinjuku Incident* where he and I are in a Japanese bathhouse together. In this kind of place, it's normal to get completely naked. It would have been weird if we'd sat there wrapped in towels. I suggested that we shoot this scene naked, filmed from behind. He seemed a bit uncomfortable, so I said, "I'm here, too; what are you scared of?"

So we shot the scene nude, and when we were doing publicity for it, he told everyone that I made him take his clothes off.

After we wrapped on *Shinjuku Incident*, he told me that the hardest thing about making a film with me was treating me as an equal. He'd always seen me as his idol, and it was hard to lose that. But over time, many conversations, and hanging out every day, he slowly got used to me as a regular person. But then, when we went out together and I got mobbed as soon as I stepped out of my car, he'd see me as a megastar again and turn back into a fan.

In one of our movies, Daniel got beaten up very badly in a scene. I've seen countless scenes like this during filming, but on this day, I don't know why, my heart ached for him. I couldn't stop thinking, *If my brother were such a nice person, and he got beaten half to death for no reason, what would I do?* Seeing him covered in wounds and bandages, I started sobbing and couldn't make myself calm down. When we were done filming, I couldn't speak for an entire day. For the first time, I understood what other actors talk about when they say they went too far into a role and needed time to get themselves out of it.

Looking back, I've actually been quite good at spotting handsome men—handsome and hardworking. I'm being scrutinized all the time, and if I only ever chose new pretty girls to work with, it would cause a scandal. But it's no problem if young male stars start following me around.

I hope all the young people I've hired become stars in the firmament, not shooting stars. Flashes in the pan are all over Asia, famous today, nowhere to be seen next month. My generation is still standing because we have the goods. If you don't have the goods, it doesn't matter how handsome or pretty you are, you'll get overtaken in no time. If you have what it takes, you'll keep your place in the spotlight.

The film world is very small, and everyone knows what sort of person you are. When I'm casting a film, I'll have the name of every character on the wall, and a short row of actors' head shots beneath them. When I mention so-and-so and hear someone saying, "Ummmmm" behind me, I'll turn and look at their expressions. If their lips are pursed, I'll understand and pull that picture off the wall. It's that simple. That actor's picture gets torn in two, and they're out of the running. In work and in life, no matter how smart, talented, or beautiful you are, you also have to be a good person. We have to treat one another well and really mean it. Everyone can tell if you're doing it out of genuine concern for them or if you're just faking.

After being left by my parents at the drama academy, I had no one. When I became famous, more and more people flocked around me. I had to work out for myself who were good friends and who were good-time friends. Who I should talk to about scripts, who I should make movies with, who I should just have fun with. I separated them all into categories. People do this consciously and unconsciously. You should always know that you are being sorted, and act accordingly.

To make a good impression, all you have to do is talk to people, look them in the eye, and show them respect and love. At work, I repay with kindness and keep my door open. I'm loyal to my longtime colleagues and have worked with the same team for many years. I give newcomers a chance and take care of them so that they have every opportunity to shine. All those good practices and intentions come back to you.

chapter twenty-five

FATHERHOOD, PART II

One year, Jaycee phoned from the US to say, "Happy Father's Day!"

Why wait for a special day to remember the people important to us? If someone means a lot to you, then every day is Valentine's Day, Christmas, or Mother's Day. I replied, "Don't bother calling me on Father's Day or my birthday, just call me more often!"

Now he hardly ever calls me! Heh.

Growing up, Jaycee liked to challenge me about things big and small. For example, when he came home from school, he'd kick off his shoes and let them go flying; then he'd walk around in his white socks just so they'd turn black.

This drove me nuts. I washed my own socks and knew exactly

how hard it is to keep them clean. I rinse them with soap as soon as I get home, and they stay spotless. But Jaycee never had to wash his own socks. Even if you asked him to do it, he wouldn't know how.

I tried to get him to take care of his things, but he ignored me. Cleaning socks was a small thing, but what about bigger issues, like safe driving? Trying to teach him with instruction or by example failed, so Joan and I applied a sneaky strategy.

When Jaycee was nearby, I'd say to Joan, "Did you hear? So-and-so's son died."

She'd reply, "Oh! How did that happen? He was so young!"

"He drove too fast and got into an accident. His mom cried so much, they had to take her to the hospital."

"Oh, dear. What's the point of driving so fast?" she asked.

"Yeah, and when they found him, his socks were filthy!"

Jaycee listened intently when he thought Joan and I weren't paying attention to him, so we took advantage of that. If I told him outright, "Don't speed!" it never would have worked.

I've always loved tidying up—some might call me a neat freak—and I can't stand seeing a messy room. Jaycee's the opposite. His room is always a disaster zone. If I'm home, I'll sort his stuff out, cleaning up here and there, poking in neglected corners. One day, I went in there to clean it and noticed a box. I opened it up and found a mountain-climbing rope. This was puzzling. Why would Jaycee have such a thing? I thought about it, then went to the window and looked out. Sure enough, there were scuff marks on the brick wall. I lowered the rope, and it just reached the ground. He must have been using it to sneak out at night after he'd told his mom he was going to bed.

So what did I do the next day? I called in Wu Gang from my stunt team and said, "Take a look at this rope. Is it secure?"

He tugged at it. "It's very secure. In fact, Jaycee asked us for it."

What? I said, "You taught him rope climbing? How is he?"

"He's good."

In that case, I could relax. One of his hanging rings didn't look too stable, so I replaced it with one made of titanium alloy, careful to match the color. When I was done, I looked Wu Gang in the eye and said, "Don't tell him that I know; just pretend I didn't say anything." I put the rope back exactly where I found it.

Jaycee never found out. If he ever reads this book, he'll probably get a stab of fear, knowing that I knew his tricks, and then laugh it off.

When he was little, Jaycee never had to worry about having enough food, how to pay his school fees, or if he needed to be driven anywhere. I would arrange it all. I regretted that later. No one should have such a good life from their birth. They'll have no idea what poverty is, and not see the need to work hard for their future. When he was a teenager, I definitely didn't think Jaycee was pushing himself hard enough. I'd work all day, go jogging at night, then get back and see that he'd gone to bed, even though it was only nine-something. I'd grumble, "He's asleep already?"

His mom would reply, "He got home from taking photographs and was completely exhausted."

Exhausted from taking pictures? How?

I'd storm out in a bad mood and go jogging *again*, thinking, *When I was his age . . .* I wished he could follow me around all day to see how much I did. Sometimes I'll have eight meetings in a row, right up until midnight; then I'll go home, do some exercise, and read scripts.

Maybe he needed to be inspired to work hard. After I saw how well Lang Lang and Li Yundi played, I bought Jaycee a piano, but he never touched it. After I saw Wang Leehom, I went out and got Jaycee a violin, but he never picked that up either. After seeing Kobe Bryant, I put in a basketball hoop. Jaycee did enjoy that, and basketball became something he was very good at. I later realized it was wrong of me to demand so much of him based on what I liked instead of trying to find out where his own interests lay. I shouldn't have pushed my ideas onto him. I was too harsh about trying to force him to play those instruments.

When I was away, I'd get reports from his mother that Jaycee was getting very good at basketball, that he could make amazing three-point shots. When I next visited him in Los Angeles, I told him, "A thousand American dollars for every shot you make in ten attempts. If you make ten three-point shots, that's ten thousand. But if you miss one, the whole thing's off."

He liked the sound of that and stood at the three-point line. I tossed the ball to him, and he made the shot. I tossed him the next ball. Pass, tap, basket; pass, tap, basket. Not bad, nine in a row. I deliberately didn't throw the last ball to him for the last shot but rolled it along the ground. He hadn't expected that and had to bend to pick it up. When he stood up again, his position had shifted slightly, and he missed the next shot.

He accused me of cheating.

I said, "Ha-ha, I almost lost ten grand to you!"

A few months later, he tried again. I said, "This time, I'll throw you the ball properly ten times, and if you sink all ten shots, I'll give you ten grand."

He made all ten three-point shots in a row. After the last one, he ignored me and turned to his mom. "Daddy owes me ten thousand!" he said.

His mom got a piece of paper, wrote, "I owe my son ten thousand," and made me sign it.

But he didn't get the money right away! He would have blown right through it. I waited until he was twenty-five to pay up.

When Jaycee moved back to Hong Kong from Los Angeles, I gave him half the house to live in.

Every night, I'd see his light on. I went to see what he was up to, but the place was empty. He'd left every light on, even in the bathroom and closet. When he got home, I asked, "Could you turn off the lights when you go out?"

"Having the lights on makes me feel more alive," he replied.

"You're only saying that because I'm the one who pays the bills. Don't waste energy. If you leave the lights on again, you can pay for them yourself."

The next night, all the lights were blazing again.

I called an electrician to come and split our wiring, so his side of the house had its own meter. "From now on, you can pay your own electric bill," I said.

From then on, he always remembered to turn off all his lights.

When he lived in America, Jaycee met the singer and actress Coco Lee and they became such good friends, he started calling her his godsister.

When he returned to Hong Kong, Coco was in town and he took his godsister out to an Italian restaurant for dinner. A few hours later, Jaycee called me and said, "Daddy, come down to the restaurant. Coco wants to see you."

I said, "You young people are having dinner. What does that have to do with me?"

But he insisted, so I went. Coco had brought a dozen friends with her. I understood what was going on. Jaycee had called me there to pay the bill because he didn't have much money.

I noticed that the novelist Jin Yong and his wife were having dinner at the same restaurant, so I went over to say hello and bowed to him. Jin Yong smiled back. Privately, I told the waiter that I'd pay for Jin Yong's table, too.

The Italians eat at long tables. I sat in the seat closest to the door, while Jaycee was in the chair farthest from me. When we were nearly done, Jin Yong came over and said in Shanghainese, "Little Brother, that was so nice of you, thank you."

I replied, "Not at all, not at all."

When I stood up, Jaycee stood up, too. I told him to come over and say hello to Jin Yong. When he saw me bow respectfully, he did the same.

Jin Yong said, "Is this your son? He's so grown-up." After a bit more small talk, he said good-bye. Jaycee and I walked him all the way to his car.

As we headed back to the restaurant, Jaycee asked, "Who was that?"

I couldn't believe he didn't know the famous, revered novelist! I said, "He's Jin Yong!!"

Jaycee said, "Is he a banker? Does he take care of your money? I guess that's why you were so afraid of him."

I could only just shake my head at that. He didn't understand me at all.

Then again, I didn't understand him either.

Jaycee started to write songs when he was a young teenager, so when he was fifteen, I sent him to Shanghai to study music with Jonathan Lee, a famous Taiwanese musician and producer. This was before the Hong Kong handover, and we didn't know much about mainland China. Many people warned me, "Tell Jaycee to be careful. He's new to the country." I hired a few bodyguards to follow him around to make sure he didn't get kidnapped.

The bodyguards took their duties very seriously and wouldn't let him go anywhere. He wanted to see West Lake, but they said it was too dangerous. Everywhere he wanted to go was too dangerous. He was just cooped up at home.

He wrote a song called "Man-Made Walls." The lyrics went like this: "Four man-made walls, they won't let my body nor my soul soar towards freedom. Wherever I want to go, I have to gaze through the windows in these man-made walls. Empty rooms, the seconds tick by slowly. Romance beyond the walls, I can only sigh, wishing everyone else happiness. I set a little bird free, it was clever but heartless and flew off right away. Flowers bloom beyond the walls, but I can't smell their fragrance. Thank you, man-made walls, for not letting me get hurt. Thank you, man-made walls, if I fall in here, the floor's carpeted. I don't want my dreams to be empty imaginings. I don't want my eyes to just stare at these iron bars. I'm not afraid to fall, not afraid to get hurt. I don't want to be special, I want to be ordinary. I need freedom, I want freedom, you need freedom, people need freedom, we all need freedom, freedom to fly."

While he was writing this song, he noticed the landlord had a little bird, and he set the bird free. He told me that the four walls were Joan, Jonathan Lee, the bodyguards, and me.

After hearing this song, I decided to let him have his freedom and fired the bodyguards.

When he was around this same age, I got him a walk-on part in *Shanghai Noon*.

He was on his summer vacation and came to the studio every day. Everything seemed exciting to start out with, and he'd do this and that with the stunt team, putting the landing mats in place, moving equipment, watching me rehearse. This made me happy.

He hung out with the stunt team in the evenings, too. I wanted them to teach him how to box. A few days later, I walked past the gym and didn't hear any boxing noises, but did pick up a smacking sound. I went in and found Jaycee teaching the stunt team basketball. I asked, "What happened to boxing?"

He protested, "This is a sport, too!"

He wasn't interested in kung fu; he only wanted to practice his marksmanship. I secretly filmed him shooting alone in the garden. I still have the tape.

After sticking around the studio for a few days, he vanished. He'd gotten bored, felt sleepy, and gone off to take a nap in a car that was parked some distance off. *Shanghai Noon* was a period film, so there couldn't be tire marks on the ground, which meant all the vehicles had to park far away. He'd walked a long way for his nap.

I had to do a backflip for one scene and hit my head when I came down. It hurt a lot. I thought, *Why isn't my son here to see me getting injured? He ought to see how hard his daddy works.* I grabbed someone and said, "Go get him, tell him I'm injured." Then I clutched my head and pretended to be in agony.

The assistant walked over to the parking area, shook him awake, and said, "Jaycee, Jaycee, your dad's been hurt."

He was startled. "Huh?" He quickly stood up and came back to me, looking anxious. As he walked, I saw his legs start to wobble; then he reached the mattresses, fell down on top of one, and dropped off right away! He passed out on a crash mat!

Now that I think of it, it would have made a great scene. It's a shame we didn't film it.

He was a bit embarrassed to come to the studio the next day, so he hung around outside catching gophers. They were hiding in their holes, so he set up traps at each hole and lured them out. He managed to nab four.

I thought he should let them go. At first he was unwilling. "No way, it wasn't easy to catch them, I'm keeping them."

It was no use me telling him what to do. I'd have to get someone else to frighten him into letting them go.

And so I got my English coach to play along. The coach pretended to be horrified at the sight of the trapped animals and said, "Oh, my God! Did you touch those things? Quick, wash your hands! They're poisonous! Gophers are covered with awful germs. I hope you didn't get bitten; a friend of mine got bitten by a gopher, and they had to chop off his finger."

Jaycee was horrified and let them all go. As they scurried past us, the English coach and I pretended to be terrified of them. "Don't let them touch us!" we squealed.

Jaycee was bored again after letting the gophers go, so he wrote another song, called "Singing as I Walk." Some lyrics: "I walk down the road alone, watching the cars go back and forth. Everyone's busy, going their own way, having their own thoughts, different from me. I walk into the wilderness, but I've forgotten the way. Mommy's busy, Daddy's at work, and I'm in the wilderness, singing as I walk, singing as I walk." The song went on to explain that his mom wasn't really busy, she was playing mahjong, and that I was too busy with work to take care of him. We listened to the song together. Afterwards, his mom gave up mahjong.

He was putting all the thoughts he couldn't otherwise express and the words he wished he could say to us into his songs. If I wanted to get to know my son, I had to learn to listen.

Long ago, before the Hong Kong handover from England to China, I told Jaycee that many Hong Kong households contained different identities. In ours, for instance, I was from Hong Kong, Joan was Taiwanese, my dad was Australian, and Jaycee was American. There wasn't a single country that unified us. He must have thought about it, because the next time he came home to Hong Kong, he announced that he'd given up his American citizenship. He later got a Chinese passport, and I felt relieved that some of what I'd said had sunk in. After all these years, we'd be citizens of the same country, in more ways than one.

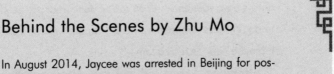

Behind the Scenes by Zhu Mo

In August 2014, Jaycee was arrested in Beijing for possession of marijuana and providing a place for others to use it. He confessed to the charges, and in January 2015, he was sentenced to prison for six months (but with time served he'd be out in just another month). The arrest and sentencing were big news in China and around the world. The media firestorm was tough on the whole family.

In February, when Jaycee came out of prison, Jackie was on a publicity tour for *Dragon Blade* and couldn't be there in person. Jaycee hadn't seen him since the incident, but Jackie recorded a short video so his son could see it as soon as he got out.

On the video, Jackie said to Jaycee, "Son, I haven't seen you in a while. Your dad's the same as always, working away, just like when you were little, and I was always away filming, so I only saw you once in a while. And each time, you were so much taller and more grown-up. It's the same this time. I want to tell you that I'm not angry with you. I made mistakes when I was younger, too. It's fine to make mistakes, as long as you correct yourself afterwards. From now on, you'll have to be a real man, standing strong and alone as you face what's before you. Remember to be humble. If you've done something wrong, you have to admit it. No matter what, your mom and I will always have your back. When you've done what you need to do, I'll have wrapped up here, too, and we can celebrate the New Year as a family."

Jackie and I were working late together on matters related to the People's Congress, and he abruptly asked if I could take a look at something. Of course, I said, "Sure!"

He started playing a video on his laptop, then left the room. It was quite a long video, a compilation of home footage from when Jaycee was three or four, right up to his teens, including many sweet moments, like a very young Jaycee and Jackie taking a bath together and their playing basketball. Out of respect for their privacy, I won't say any more about the contents of this video, only that, seeing them together over more than a decade, I realized that they were no different from any other family. Although Jackie didn't have much time to spend with his child, he hadn't missed any important moments in Jaycee's life.

When the video was almost over, Jackie came back into the room and told me this was a gift he was preparing for his son. The family got together in Taipei for the New Year, and when they watched this video on the first night, all three of them started sobbing.

On the sixth day of the Chinese New Year, Jaycee posted, "Starting anew," on Weibo, which is China's equivalent of Twitter. He included a couple of pictures of Jackie shaving Jaycee's head while Joan stood beside them. Many people were moved by this. Afterwards, Jackie told me about it. "Joan's had long hair all these years because I like her that way. I often tease her by saying I'd divorce her if she ever cut her hair," he said. "I don't know why that is; maybe it's because my mom had long hair. It was so long, it reached the ground.

"When Jaycee went to prison," he continued, "Joan told me she wanted a haircut. She cut it to shoulder length. Jaycee was inside for six months, and during this time Joan didn't take any phone calls, see anyone, or go anywhere. She locked herself up, the same as her son. The night of that Weibo picture, we were all on the couch, watching TV and talking, when Jaycee suddenly said he wanted to shave his head to mark a new beginning. I offered to help, and we did it the next day."

Looking back at this, Jackie said that they were able to turn something bad into something good. During that year, all of Joan's thoughts were with Jaycee, not him. Jackie realized he hadn't paid her enough attention. In the six months that Jaycee was away, Jackie learned how to care for Joan. He sent her photos every day and talked to her about what scripts he was reading, what he was eating, whom he'd met. He talked so she wouldn't feel lonely. Jackie learned not to expect his son to be perfect. He always sees the good in others; he had to learn to see the good in Jaycee, too. He used to go from job to job, but as soon as he could get away, the only thing he wants to do is go see his family in Hong Kong.

Jaycee is starting his life over, and the whole family is having a new beginning, too.

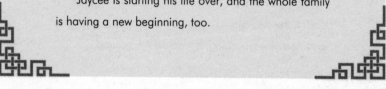

chapter twenty-six

VINTAGE JACKIE

Red wine is an interest I cultivated later in life. In fact, I started drinking red wine at my doctor's suggestion. I didn't like it at first, preferring sweet white wine. While stopping in Singapore on my way to Australia, I got a phone call telling me to get a full physical examination because I was heading to America for a film, and the production team needed the report to get me insured. Every time I made an American film, I had to go for a checkup. At the exam, the doctor said I was fine, but my manager looked like he was in bad shape.

My manager did have all sorts of health problems. He often tossed down entire glasses of whiskey or brandy. The doctor told him that he had to lay off the liquor, but if he absolutely had to have a drink, to stick to small glasses of red wine.

I asked, "Is red wine better?"

The doctor said, "Yes, it is. It helps lower cholesterol."

I remembered that. While visiting my parents in Australia, I got a letter from the American producers that said they didn't accept medical reports from Singapore and wanted me to get another one in Australia, which meant doing all the blood work again, which, I think you know by now, I hated. But I went through with it. After *that* exam, the doctor asked, "What do you usually eat?"

"Everything!"

"But what foods have you eaten regularly for a long time?"

I thought about it and said, "Red bean soup and green bean soup." I hadn't been eating "hamburger-fries-Coke" in decades.

He said, "No wonder your blood platelets and your body are in such good shape. All that bean soup."

I already knew that choosing the right foods is very important for your health. Then I recalled what the previous doctor said about red wine.

"Which type of red wine should I drink?" I asked.

The doctor was no expert there, so I asked knowledgeable people about which red wines were good for your health and satisfying to drink. My ad hoc experts suggested several Australian vintages with complicated names I couldn't remember and immediately forgot. There was one vineyard that used numbers on their labels—28, 407, 707, and so on—that were easy to remember. I started buying those.

If I went into a shop and it carried that brand of wine, I'd grab every bottle. I'd go into every store on a street and empty the shelves. At the next shop, I'd ask, "Do you have this wine? Yes? Bring them all here, I'll take them all." At the third shop, I'd just say, "I'll take everything."

As I moved down the street, I realized that the price was getting higher and higher. Why was that? Later, I found out all these stores were owned by the same person. When he figured out what I was doing, he called ahead to the next store and jacked up the price, until the prices were too high, even for me.

After I'd acquired all the red wine at every place I went to, I opened the doors between the rooms of my hotel suite, turned on the air-conditioning, shut the drapes, and stowed the wine carefully. I had to rush from one Australian city to another for work, and we went out at two in the morning. The whole stunt team got into six jeeps, two of us in each one and cases of wine in the back. The air-conditioning was at full blast, and we sped along for more than ten hours to our next hotel. I'd sent someone ahead to sort out the hotel rooms, so we were able to move the wine straight in and leave it in the center of the room with a fan blowing at it. We kept it there until we were done filming, and every night we'd crack open a few bottles. After we wrapped and I went back to Hong Kong, I set up a wine cellar in my home and put all the wine in there.

One night in Hollywood some time later, I sat down with Sylvester Stallone and a few others, and everyone started talking about cigars, which I knew nothing about, and red wine, which I also knew nothing about but sure had a lot of stored in my cellar! I'd quit smoking cigarettes by then, and never smoked cigars anyway, so I couldn't join in the conversation and just sat there listening quietly. People think it's odd that movie stars don't always sit around and talk about our films. Sometimes we do, but what is there to say? "I liked your movie, that other one wasn't bad, did you like mine?" That could get awkward. And if you don't have anything *else* to talk about, it gets really awkward.

A conversation about alcohol and cigars was a natural for this group. I wanted to hear what they all had to say about red wine, what grapes they liked, whether 1982 was a good year, etc. Everyone had an opinion, but I couldn't contribute and had to just nod and smile stupidly. I quietly decided that being the least informed person in the room—at least about wine—couldn't happen again. I had to know my stuff!

I made a study of it and learned how to choose and smoke cigars, how to sniff and sip red wine. The next time I sat down with this group and the conversation turned to French wines, I was able to say, "There's an Australian red that's very good, it's such-and-such brand." And they were all stunned.

"Tell us more," they said. I went off on the wine's best varietal and described the bouquet, the mouthfeel, the finish. They listened closely, and they all said they were going to try it.

Back then, no one knew about Australian wines; I deliberately made sure I was different from the others. I invited them to sample bottles from my cellar. After that one conversation with this group of heavy hitters, the prices of that Australian brand soared, multiplying again and again. The winemaker was so grateful, he produced a Jackie Chan label of wine, putting his best variety of grape through the same process so the whole vineyard's resources was dedicated to a vintage just for me. I insisted that every label had a warning: "If you drink, don't drive!" At the time, no other type of wine had anything like that.

Responsible drinking had been on my mind for a while. I'd rewatched my old movie *Drunken Master* and was kind of horrified. Why teach people to fight when they were drunk? When I made *The Legend of the Drunken Master* in the early '90s, I changed the message to "Don't drink, and also don't fight." I took that opportunity to correct a mistake from my past.

The Australian vineyard produced only one batch of delicious Jackie Chan wine—22,000 cases, or 132,000 bottles—and it's no longer for sale. When the batch came out, the winemaker asked how many bottles I wanted. He was planning to give me a hundred cases, which sounded like plenty to me. As it turned out, I got through them in the blink of an eye. I found out that six hundred cases had been shipped to Hong Kong, two thousand to Taiwan, three thousand to France. Seeing how fast they were selling, I thought I'd better start collecting them. A bottle cost $800 to start with, but when I began my buying spree, that rose to $1,200, then $1,600. I spent a few million in all. And I'm not going to sell *any* of my bottles, so now I have the only stock in the world. This wine is just now coming into maturity. I often give bottles as gifts.

Early on, I bought a lot of good wine for my dad. One time, I got a call from Australia. A friend of mine was at Dad's home and was calling to say a bottle of very expensive wine I'd given my father had broken. I said, "No problem, I'll get another one."

Dad phoned late that night and said, "Actually the bottle isn't broken. I just couldn't bear to uncork it for your friend."

I had a big laugh about that.

Many years later, my dad passed away, and I went to Australia to deal with his effects. After the funeral, I went back to his home to clear it out and found all the wine I'd bought him over the years, all carefully stored. He hadn't touched a single bottle. It was heartbreaking. I opened a couple of bottles right away, and sat with my manager and the other friends who'd come to mourn with me, drinking and weeping.

Everyone asked, "Are you sure you want to open these?"

I said, "Open them; what's the point of keeping them?"

I'm no longer interested in collecting red wine. I don't buy it anymore because we have so much at home. I give away what I can, or auction the bottles off for charity. Or I share them with friends, which is the true pleasure of drinking wine.

chapter twenty-seven

TAKEN FOR A RIDE

When I was young, a group of us—Sammo Hung, Yuen Biao, Frankie Chan, and Eric Tsang—would go street racing. No one really minded back then, and it wasn't considered illegal. Later on, I went to America to shoot *The Cannonball Run*, in which I drove a Mitsubishi. Afterwards, the company invited me to be their spokesman, a position I still hold today. Whenever I drive a car in a film, it's always a Mitsubishi. We organized a Jackie Chan Cup for professional racers, but that stopped being fun after a few years. I wondered, what *would* be fun? Then I came up with the idea of another Jackie Chan Cup, this one for female celebrities.

It took place in Macau and became popular right away. Many people came to see the Jackie Chan Cup and then left, not sticking around for the professional races, which weren't as interesting to them. I ran the Jackie Chan Cup for quite a few years, but the event venue charged me a high fee every time for renting the grounds and other expenses until I didn't feel like continuing. I was bringing them so much business, and they were charging me a fortune. We moved the event to Zhuhai and Shanghai. In the end we raised only a couple of million, despite all that hard work. It got annoying to keep asking people to give their time and donations, so finally I pulled the plug on the whole thing. Sometime later, Mitsubishi and I jointly organized a Paris–Dakar rally, and I sponsored the Chinese team.

I had a friend who used to work at Mitsubishi. We were quite close, having known each other more than ten years, and were frequent dinner companions. I started hearing from other people that this guy had problems. I didn't pay much attention to gossip, but I would occasionally drop a hint or two that he shouldn't use my name to do anything inappropriate. Eventually, for various reasons, he left Mitsubishi.

I mentioned to him that I had a classic Rolls-Royce I wanted to refurbish, and he offered to take care of that for me. I gave him $500,000 to buy parts. Nothing happened for two years. Whenever I asked about it, he said he was still putting in orders.

I asked Ken Lo, one of my stunt team members, to look into all the stuff that had already been delivered. He opened the boxes and discovered that none of them contained any Rolls-Royce parts.

Starting to get anxious, I told my friend, "I've heard a lot of rumors about you. If you're in any trouble, if you're unhappy about anything, you should come to me. I'll give you money if you need it. We've been friends for more than a decade; let's not let loose talk come between us."

He said, "Don't worry, Jackie. Nothing's going on. How could I possibly cheat you? Those other people are biased against me." And then he asked, "Say, Jackie, weren't you thinking about getting a new Bentley?"

I had, in fact, had a meeting with some reps from Bentley, and they said they wanted to design a special Jackie Chan model.

"What would I want with two Bentleys?" I asked them.

"You could trade in the old one, pay a bit extra, and get a new one," they suggested.

It sounded like a good idea. My Bentley was new, a four-door model. They said I could trade it for a two-door model. We had plenty of four-door cars at home, anyway.

So this friend of mine knew about the proposed swap with Bentley, and I told him that I was leaning toward doing it.

He said, "You should move on that quickly. If you keep driving the one you have, the mileage adds up and it'll be worth less. Why don't I see if I can off-load it for you, and when the new car's ready, you can get it right away."

I said, "Okay," and handed over the keys. I signed a document authorizing him to act on my behalf. Sometime later, he told me he'd negotiated the sale back to Bentley for $2.5 million Hong Kong dollars and arranged transport. I was happy about that; now I'd have to pay only a small amount for the new one.

A little over a year later, my special-order Bentley arrived. They drove it to my house and asked me to pay $3.2 million!

I said, "I already paid two and a half million!"

"Er, nobody's given us anything."

We checked it out and they were right. They didn't have the old Bentley and hadn't received any payment from me or anyone operating in my name or in my friend's name. When I tried to find him, he'd disappeared.

I kept investigating and found out that he'd sold the car to someone for $2.8 million, $300,000 more than he told me. He probably planned to keep that amount for himself from the beginning. But then, when he got his hands on all that cash, in a moment of greed, he decided to run off with all of it.

I'd been cheated out of larger sums than this (I've got more dollars than sense, remember), but I didn't take those swindlers to court. One time, someone cheated me out of $40 million, but when I see him around, we still say hello and have a chat. My colleagues asked me why I never sued him. When I dealt with that guy, I had dollar signs in my eyes and no head for business. I barely knew the guy, but he told me he'd invest my money and earn big profits. I believed him and got scammed. I should have known better.

But this case was different. I considered the Bentley swindler to be like a brother to me. How could he cheat me? He took $3 million from me in total, and I was absolutely furious. I sued him. Even if it cost me a billion dollars, I was going to see justice done. In the end, I bankrupted him.

If people want to pull a scam on me, that's fine. I have more important things to do. I won't stop having faith in people just because of someone like him. So many people have tried to take my money, and not one of them has gotten rich. I've been tricked out of large sums many times, and I'm still not poor. I'm going to go on believing in everyone until they cross me. That's not going to change in this lifetime.

chapter twenty-eight

GIVE

I used to want to buy everything, and now I want to give everything away.

My attitude has changed as I've slowly matured. Now I feel that having so many storage units is a burden and that there are way too many things in my Hong Kong home. You'd be astonished if you saw it. I've set up the Jackie Chan Film Gallery in Shanghai to house all the movie props—forty-seven chests of stuff—that I've accumulated over more than forty years. I even paid to repair the broken items, including bicycles, motorbikes, cars, helmets, and glasses. I plan to find a site for Jackie Chan World, to which I'll donate all my collections, to be displayed for everyone to enjoy.

Jaycee earns enough to support himself. He has said he doesn't want anything except that Xu Beihong painting, which I will keep safe for him. My wife is independently wealthy, so neither she nor our son need anything from me. As long as I have enough to keep my company and household running, and my wife and son don't need to worry about anything, I'm happy.

In fact, I've set aside half my wealth to create a charitable foundation. My will is all prepared, clearly stating who gets what. I've seen many rich families squabble in courts over inheritance disputes, whether they could afford to or not. Our family isn't going to be like that. I'd never want my wife to sue my son, or my foundation to sue my company, so I made sure everything was clearly written down.

I hope that, when I die, my bank balance will be zero.

Giving is my new obsession. It started because, as a celebrity, I was invited to charitable events. A long, long time ago, someone asked me to visit the Duchess of Kent Children's Hospital at Sandy Bay because the kids there wanted to meet me. I didn't want to do it. I was drinking so much each night. How could I possibly get up that early in the morning?

They asked me so many times that I thought, *Okay, let's try it once and see.* I went at night, still wearing my sunglasses, not knowing what I was supposed to do. But when I walked in and the kids saw me, they all rushed over, surrounding me and hugging me, their bodies smelling of medicine. I was a bit frightened to start with, but gradually began to feel sympathy for them. The kids said, "I like you, I love you, can I touch you?" I was moved by their smiles and bravery.

When the attendant introduced me, I wished there was a hole I could crawl into. "Jackie is so busy. He was filming all night last night and hasn't slept yet. That's why he's wearing sunglasses, because his eyes are all swollen. He has to rush off to do more filming in a short while. Let's welcome Jackie Chan." Actually, I hadn't slept because I'd been drinking. It was shameful.

The children applauded vigorously, and the attendant went on: "Jackie's brought presents for you all!" They were delighted.

"What presents?" shouted the kids.

I couldn't answer because I hadn't bought any of them myself. Someone else had taken care of that for me. I felt extremely guilty. Then the kids asked, "When will you come to see us again?"

I replied, "Christmas, I guess." I went home and spent the next week in a funk. Every single day, I thought to myself, *Why am I such a lousy person?*

At Christmas, I brought a big load of stuff with me to the children's hospital. The kids were overjoyed to see me. This time, I knew exactly what was inside each box, and gave them out one by one. They loved it, and only then did the guilt subside. It all changed for me then. I've been so very lucky in my life, despite my beginnings. I had to give more of myself to people who haven't been as fortunate.

I've worked for charity regularly ever since. I started by donating gifts from fans to old folks' homes or orphanages. Then I got cleverer about it. My company at the time had a large, empty outside wall that I decided to decorate with drawings. I posted a message to fans all over the world, asking them to send me their art on the theme of love and peace. A stream of pictures started arriving.

Then I had the idea of asking everyone to help me set up a school. Some of the fans said they didn't have that kind of money. I replied that if they had one dollar, it'd be enough. I offered to match my fans' donations, even if they gave a million dollars. Money arrived from all over the world. Some made beautiful origami creations out of their banknotes. Others had special designs or incorporated the money into their artwork. The money art was all so pretty, I couldn't bear to rip the dollars off, so I ended up giving two dollars for every one of theirs, leaving their original donations intact. Fan art from all over the world went up on my wall, and many people came to see it. Then we had a big storm, and they all got washed away. I didn't want that to happen again, so I started putting the art on an inside wall. You can see this fan art today at Jackie Chan World, in the Jackie Chan Art Film Gallery, and on the walls of my office. I've kept them all these years. And, yes, my fans and I have built many schools together.

These days, I'll wear the same outfit again and again, to multiple award ceremonies and events. It's wasteful not to. Once, I was taking part in a Wang Leehom concert, and everyone said, "Jackie, you're wearing the same clothes as last year."

I said, "There's no point to chasing after material possessions," which was ironic coming from me, considering my history.

When I was helping deliver water in drought-plagued Yunnan, I saw victims who had nothing, no water or food or electricity, let alone cell phones or anything of material value, yet the little kids never stopped smiling. On the way back, I worried what they'd do when the weather turned cold. Soon after, I had dinner with friends.

They kept complaining that the food wasn't tasty and their drinks didn't have enough ice, and how they wanted to get a new car or a new phone, and I was really annoyed.

Some people are forever chasing luxury products, but there's no end to this, and they'll never be satisfied. If we already have more than enough, we shouldn't ask for more. I ought to have taken those complaining dinner companions into the hills so they could see what it's like out there and learn to care for others instead. As for people who have nothing better to do than steal or destroy property, we should do what the English did when they transported criminals to Australia: abandon them on a wild island. They'd have to build their own huts and farm their own food, and exhaust their excess energy on survival instead of hurting others.

The more I get into charity work, the more incredibly valuable experiences I accumulate. The day after the 2010 Yushu earthquake, I filled a plane with supplies and flew over with my staff and stunt team to help. When we got there, we realized we were just adding to the chaos. The army was already on the ground saving lives, but when we arrived, they had to allocate manpower to help distribute what we had brought. Even the commanders took time out to welcome us. The next day, we loaded some injured survivors onto the plane, only to find it was now too heavy to take off. I told my people to get out. They complained that it might be hours until the next flight, and I said, "So what? We can wait. The victims can't." On that mission, I learned not to react with haste when a disaster strikes. Now I wait to see how things develop so I don't add to the problem. It's better not to rush but to bide your time and bring them what they need most at the appropriate time.

Recently, I've started doing international charity work. People have said that there is so much that needs doing in China, why would I go anywhere else? I have personal life experience to justify my actions. The first time I went abroad, all sorts of people helped me—Thai, Japanese, Australian, American, and so on. There are no borders on kindness. They helped me, and I want to help back.

I think of it as a kind of civilian diplomacy. When you're in trouble and a foreigner helps you, how do you feel? I help people all over the world, and everyone knows that I'm Chinese, that it's a Chinese person helping them. I was at the Indonesian tsunami, the Japanese earthquake, and the Korean floods. I am a Hong Kong man doing what I can do, in as many places as I can reach. And I'm touched that my Dragon's Heart Project, which helps poor kids in China, receives donations from children in Vietnam, Cambodia, Laos, Japan, Korea, Germany, Russia, and many other countries. We all need to help one another.

One time, I was invited to East Timor on a peacekeeping mission. Two of their tribes were at war with each other. I asked, "Is there any use in me going?"

The people who invited me answered, "Well, if you don't come, we'll never find out." Six months after my visit, their prime minister wrote to tell me that the fighting was over. I don't want to say that was *my* doing, but at least I can say I was part of the effort.

Of course, even giving brings little setbacks along the way. On Valentine's Day, my Japanese fans used to send me mountains of chocolates. I could never finish that much candy, so it just melted. I urged them to stop mailing me stuff and to give the money they saved to charity. Instead, they started mailing *me* cash. When the yen started coming in, I sent it to a Japanese charitable foundation along with $5 million Hong Kong dollars of my own money, with the *Yomiuri Shimbun* newspaper as our trustee. At the press conference, I said, "First of all, I'd like to thank my Japanese fans for supporting my charitable activities. Now that I have a Japanese foundation, I hope to help more Japanese people, so please tell me what you need."

A Japanese reporter stood up and said to me, "In Japan, we don't have poor people."

That annoyed me, but I dealt with his comment politely. Afterwards, I used my money to help Japanese orphans stranded in China. Apart from fans in Hong Kong and Japan, those from America and Europe have also helped me set up foundations elsewhere in the world. I have a group of wealthy friends in Beijing who I always hold out my begging bowl to whenever I find a charity worth supporting. No matter what I donate to, they'll donate, too.

There are also times when I feel helpless. In the media, celebrity gossip always takes up much more space than anything about charity. When stars are involved in a scandal—and as you know, my family has been involved in some big ones—everyone wants an interview to talk about that. But when I want to talk about my charity work, they think it's boring or that I'm doing it just for show. Each time I organize a charity event or launch a new foundation, we have to beg people to care about those in need. I really wish the media would spend more energy on concern for others, on poor, remote areas, on regions with unfavorable living environments. We need to pay attention to these people, and once we've understood their circumstances, we must help them. Andy Lau's marriage has nothing to do with you. What do you care if Daniel Wu's wife has a kid? But if you possibly can, donate some money to children enduring terrible illnesses.

Money isn't important, but doing and leaving something good behind in the world is.

Behind the Scenes by Zhu Mo

When Jaycee came back from America many years ago, he asked his father for two things: a new computer and a new car. This was not long after the Southeast Asian tsunami. Jackie didn't say a word, just dispatched his son directly to the Thai disaster zone so he could see exactly what people there had suffered through. When he got back to Hong Kong, Jaycee said, "Dad, don't buy me anything; the people there don't even have water to drink. I'm going to donate all my money to them."

Jackie told me, "You see how charity can be a form of education, too. Without me needing to lecture him, he was able to understand this for himself."

Jackie has been a global goodwill ambassador for UNICEF for eight years. Other people who've held this position include the late Princess Diana, Angelina Jolie, and the soccer star Lionel Messi. Jackie is still the only Chinese goodwill ambassador to date. During his tenure, he's visited schools for trafficked children and centers for children with AIDS in Myanmar, orphanages and an old folks' home in Thailand. Wherever he went, he listened to the children's painful stories and did whatever he could to make their lives a little easier by bringing water and supplies, doing interviews to support the centers, and entertaining the residents.

He's been doing charity work for more than thirty years, with no sign of slowing down. The Jackie Chan Charitable Foundation is the only one in the world that doesn't divert any of its donations to administrative costs. "Charity has taught me how to be a human being and how to look at the world," Jackie told me. "These days, I have no interests other than making movies. When I'm not filming, there are many things I can no longer do. I can't go out for a meal, or take a stroll, or go shopping. Charity work allows me to travel to many places around the world and meet different people. I do charity work to make myself happy, because seeing other people get help and find joy brings joy to me, too. By doing this, I've made my life much fuller."

chapter twenty-nine

THE KARATE KID'S DAD

Sometimes, when I meet Hollywood stars for the first time, they already seem so familiar to me. It's interesting. Maybe it's because I've seen their films. This happened with Sylvester Stallone and Steven Spielberg—and with Will Smith.

I was in America when I got a message from my manager that Will Smith wanted to talk to me about a collaboration.

"Really?" I asked, surprised.

I only half believed whatever my manager told me. People talk a big game; they say things and make promises that never pan out. In the movie business, nothing counts unless it's on camera. Even if you're in costume, your makeup is done, and everything is all set up, they could still cancel filming at any moment.

Sometime later, I was in Japan and found out Will Smith was there, too, doing publicity for a movie—I think it was *I Am Legend*. We happened to be in Nobu at the same time for dinner. I was in a private room, and a waiter told me that Will Smith was at the restaurant in the main room. I found him at his table, and we gave each other a big hug right away.

He said, "I want to work with you."

I said, "All right, all right." I'd heard these words too many times. Everyone says they want to work with me, and I always say, "Sure, great!" and never hear about it again.

Not long after that, he actually did send me a formal invitation to star in *The Karate Kid*, which he was producing, opposite his son, Jaden.

Four months before production started, I asked Wu Gang, a fight director who'd been with my stunt team for more than a decade, to go to America and help me train Jaden Smith. Wu Gang understood what I wanted and knew all the techniques I do, more or less. By going ahead of me, he got to improve his English, and Jaden got an immersion in kung fu. Will Smith wasn't too comfortable with this arrangement at first, but then I showed up and worked with Jaden on and off for more than two months to teach him and to try to bond with him as much as possible.

I got on very well with Jaden. I knew right away that he'd been brought up well and understood that he should respect his teacher and practice hard. If he needed a break in the middle of training, he'd ask, "Master, can I go to the bathroom?" He always called me "Master," which was very respectful of him. He'd seen many of my movies and seemed to admire me. Gradually, his dad relaxed about my teaching his eleven-year-old son some complicated kung fu, and stopped coming to our sessions to keep an eye on him.

All the way through preproduction and filming, I saw nothing but determination and self-awareness from this extraordinary kid. His twelfth birthday came during our shoot, and I gave him a picture of me when I was young and muscle-bound, saying I hoped he'd soon have an eight-pack like I did back then. Sure enough, not long after we wrapped, he'd trained so much that he, too, had an impressive eight-pack.

During the publicity tour for *The Karate Kid*, we were all on a plane one day, when Will said, "Let me tell you about a script, Jackie. The idea's already developed, and I want you to be in it. Here's the story . . ."

Wow, just hearing him talk, I almost burst into tears. There wasn't a single kick or punch in this film, just people talking. It was called *The Greatest Gift*. The script is still being written. Will is going to produce and might act in it, too. This will be a big challenge for me, but I'm looking forward to it.

And I bet it will actually happen. Like me, Will Smith is a man of his word.

chapter thirty

SING

One of the reasons I have a singing career at all—which many Americans don't even know about—is Jonathan Lee. Thanks to him, I got to sing for charity many times on behalf of Rock Records. Later, he produced and helped me put out an album in 1992 called *First Time*. We sold over a million CDs and topped the charts. Then we worked on a second album and slowly became friends. He demanded very high standards from my music, and so I called him "the demon producer."

I spent three years making the first record. This would have been unimaginable with any other singer. No one else would record one part in Taiwan, another in Australia, another in Hong Kong and America, all over the world, just a few lines each time. But I was just so busy that I could squeeze out only small chunks of time and slowly work on bringing it together.

They had me sing a couple of songs on *First Time* in Hokkien, because I had a lot of fans in Southeast Asia and was doing well in Taiwan. It seemed like a good idea. I needed to please my fan base. Later, though, I realized they'd been laughing at me all along. Apparently, I spoke Hokkien with a Shandong accent, with Peking opera inflections, so I sounded like a child who'd just learned to talk. The album sold very well all over, so I guess everyone in Taiwan was making fun of me, too.

One day, I was recording a Hokkien song and closed the curtains so I could concentrate better. All by myself in the booth, I finished the whole song, then heard nothing but silence. Normally, Jonathan and the others would be busily talking about what I needed to improve, where we should start the next take, and so on. That day, nothing. I went into the booth and found them all laughing so hard that they were rolling on the floor. I didn't know what to think. Was my Hokkien really *that* ridiculous?

While recording the second album, Jonathan had picked really difficult songs for me. The syncopated beat on one song was just too hard for me to grasp. Others were pitched so high that it felt like torture getting through them.

After one session, I thought that our collaboration really wasn't working, and said to Jonathan, "Write more songs like 'Understanding My Heart.' I can remember that one, and I can perform it onstage. I don't want to record any more songs like this one."

He replied, "You can't keep singing tunes like 'Understanding

My Heart' or 'Every Day of My Life.' I want to help you upgrade."

I said, "I don't want to upgrade; I need to downgrade. I want to sing ordinary songs. Write me a song that anyone can sing. All the ones you're giving me are so difficult. I make films for regular people, not art house films that only a few people ever watch. You keep giving me weird 'hey-yo-hey-hey-hey-yo-hey' rhythms and high notes, and I just want to sing easy tunes."

I talked for about forty-five minutes, and everyone listened very patiently. When I stopped ranting, Jonathan said, "Are you done complaining?"

"Yes."

"Good, now get back in the booth."

"Okay."

Whenever I've sung "A Lofty Goal in My Heart" from then on, I make sure Jonathan comes with me, even if I am giving a concert far away, like Las Vegas. He stands offstage during the song, and when we get to the "hey-yo-hey-hey-hey-yo-hey" section, he stands by to give me the beat, and I'll watch the waving of his hands to make sure I stick with the rhythm. Once he is assured that I'm on top of it, he'll vanish into the wings. He just needs to get me started with that hand signal, and then I'm okay.

We recorded "No Way" in America. I got to the recording studio each day to sing, day after day. After a month of this, Jonathan said, "All right, we'll start recording today."

Huh? "What have I been doing for the past month?"

"Rehearsing!" he said.

It took another whole month to get this song on tape. Other

people record songs in phrases or sections, but he wouldn't let me do it that way. I had to sing it from beginning to end each time. It was crazy. I threw a tantrum and said, "You sing it for me, then!"

So he came into the booth and sang the song once, really well. Then he sang it again differently, sounding great. And again, same thing. He syncopated it, slowing down the beat, all to his own rhythm, the show-off.

Then he used all sorts of languages when he told me to try it again: English, Cantonese, Hokkien, Mandarin. Each time he'd say, "That sounded great, but let's try it again."

Then there was the day I drew the curtains in the booth. I was in a bad mood and didn't want to see his face. I was in there, singing on my own, and halfway through I heard him say, "Let's stop there for today."

"Why?"

"There's too much hatred in your voice; we can't use any of this," he said.

Despite my anger, I had to laugh at that. I'd been singing through my anger, using too much force and gritting my teeth.

He said, "Ask yourself whether you have hatred in you."

"No way!" But I did that day.

Why was I so upset? Singing wasn't my main profession. I just wanted to do well and please him, but I was frustrated. Any artistic endeavor has a way of forcing you to explore new sides of yourself, which can be annoying in the moment but is worthwhile in the end.

I wouldn't call myself a singer, though I sound better than many of them (wink). I never set out to be one, but I've ended up with quite a few albums and songs, some that have been big hits, like "Understanding My Heart," "Every Day of My Life," "True Hero," and "The Myth."

I consider myself very lucky to have had the chance to work on all these songs, and it's all thanks to Jonathan Lee that I go around the world singing. If you think my singing isn't bad, then you ought to thank him, too. He's my teacher as well as my friend, my brother, my demon producer.

chapter thirty-one

THE REAL KUNG FU STAR

Since Michelle Yeoh was a child, she's always been athletic, and has a natural talent for languages, speaking excellent Cantonese and Mandarin.

When she was young, she became Miss Malaysia and entered the world of entertainment. She was a ballet dancer by training, but suffered an injury when she was twenty-three. After recovering, she started learning kung fu from Sammo Hung and myself, practicing nine hours a day. We were training anyway, and made Michelle and Maggie Cheung join in. Michelle's ballet skills gave her a leg up when she learned kung fu, and she was great at it.

I asked her to be my costar in 1992's *Police Story 3: Super Cop* as a showcase for her kung fu skills. Plus, I thought we'd have great chemistry as police officers with very different personalities, which would make an exciting movie. Michelle had (almost) as many action scenes as I did in that film, and insisted on not using a stunt double in the sequence where her motorcycle hurtles toward a moving train. That took a lot of effort and courage, and I admired her for doing that. *Super Cop* was the first film of mine with a female lead as a fighter and not just an onlooker. Later on, Michelle did well in Hollywood, and had the best fighting skills of all the Bond girls. *Crouching Tiger, Hidden Dragon* made her even more famous. I'm very proud of her.

Once, when we were both in Hong Kong, she said to me, "Jackie, let's get some friends together and go skiing." She loved all sports.

I said, "No skiing."

"Why?"

"I don't want to do these dangerous sports. I already have to do risky stunts all day. I hardly ever get a break, so why would I want to do something like that? Besides, wouldn't it be terrible if I died skiing, skating, or mountain climbing? If I have to go like that, I'd want it to be recorded on film, so people would know what I was doing. When I do risky stunts in my films, at least I know it's all on camera, so if anything goes wrong, people can watch the footage and see how brave I was."

She was a bit nonplussed by that. I said, "Go, if you want. Just be careful."

The next time I saw her, she showed up for dinner on crutches. She'd snapped a tendon while skiing. I said, "You see? That wasn't worth it."

"You were right, Jackie," she said.

Tendon injuries take a long time to heal, and she had to lie low for a whole year. No one knew about her injury, and she had to keep it a secret. If the media found out, the headlines would have been very embarrassing: "Action Star Michelle Yeoh Has a Skiing Injury." So instead she hid away and didn't make any movies for a while.

Over the years, I've had to try all sorts of sporting activities in my films, and skiing is the most accident-prone. When we were filming in Australia, skiers would turn up at the hospital each day with all kinds of injuries. When I noticed this, I told my crew that if anyone went skiing on their day off and got hurt, I'd send them straight back to Hong Kong.

When it comes to filming dangerous stunts, like the ones Michelle and I did on *Super Cop*, I feel the fear, then do it anyway. What sort of person would voluntarily jump off a building, out of a plane, or into the sea? I'll try anything. Not many people can match me in my willingness to go for it. Michelle Yeoh is one of them.

chapter thirty-two

MY THREE FATHERS

After the China Drama Academy closed, our master Yu Jim-Yuen settled in America. In 1988, he returned to Hong Kong for a birthday celebration, and my classmates and I all showed up. Gathered together, we realized that he'd trained an entire generation of action performers in the Hong Kong and Asian film industries. Along with people like Yuen Woo-Ping, who'd left the school before I arrived, the Yuen brand had infiltrated all the major studios and a large number of cast and crew lists. This alone would count as a great achievement. However we might have felt about his methods, his training produced successful artists.

In September 1997, my master passed away. When I heard the news, I got an instant flashback to the moment I was brought to him at seven. I didn't know at the time that I was in for a long ten years of suffering. Of course, I also had no idea that those ten years were necessary for me to become Jackie Chan.

As I've often said, Chan Chi-Peng is the father of Chan Kong-Sang, but Yu Jim-Yuen was Jackie Chan's father.

Former members of the Yuen schoolroom, including the already famous Lucky Seven, came from around the world to Los Angeles so they could attend our master's funeral. I took a break from filming *Who Am I?* in the Netherlands and hurried to California. My production company Golden Harvest lost millions of Hong Kong dollars due to my absence, but my bosses knew very well there was no way they'd be able to stop me.

Although I went through the devil's own training every day of those ten years at the academy, including frequent punishments that left me bleeding and in tears—and though all of us silently cursed our master as we lay in bed each night—as we got older, we understood that these experiences hadn't just brought us suffering; they'd also taught us many valuable lessons. Apart from developing bodies that would allow us to break into movies and perform our own stunts, we also had determination, courage, spirit, and discipline running in our blood. All these things would help us get past one difficulty after another in life until we reached our current lofty positions.

When I returned to the filming location in the Netherlands, we created original and beautiful scenes that would later be described as "martial art." People often talk about a scene with a fight on a high-rise roof terrace, a plunge from a helicopter into the primeval jungle, and a plummet down the side of a glass skyscraper. The skyscraper scene was filmed at a twenty-one-story building in Rotterdam. I had to jump off the roof and slide down the sloping side of the building, stop just short of the ground, then climb into the building.

I was forty-three at the time, which would normally be considered too old to take on such a dangerous sequence and face a drop of seventy yards. This wasn't like in *Police Story*, where I at least had a pole to slide down. There was nothing at all.

I thought, *I'll do it in honor of my master.*

Before we started filming, the stunt team fastened themselves to ropes and slowly rappelled down from the roof, feeling the sloped surface carefully to check for protruding nails or other sharp objects. They scoured the whole surface, making sure it was safe. Now we were ready to roll. The action team made their preparations, including the most important task of putting landing mats on the floor. When I looked down from the roof, those mats looked no larger than half the size of my palm. My heart leaped wildly, and my temples throbbed like drums. Below me the entire production crew was jostling for room with local fire trucks, police cars, and ambulances. The local government had sealed the bridges and roads in anticipation. Also milling down there was a large, enthusiastic crowd of onlookers.

They were all waiting to see my jump—any moment now, I would plunge down as fast as a speeding car. A crew member came over to ask if I was ready, and I nodded. Then I heard, from the ground, a few shouted commands: "Camera." "Rolling." "*Action!*"

I threw myself into the wind.

Later on, I asked myself if that leap was truly necessary. And the answer: Yes, it was. For my master. For our honor. And for my audiences all over the world. They longed to come into the movie theater and, for two hours in the dark, watch a true hero on the silver screen. And of course, I also did it so I could live up to the name of "Jackie Chan."

That same year, I lost my godfather, Leonard Ho. Ten years earlier, he'd made me swear never to cut my hair short again, and never to play a character who died. With him gone, I let go of those promises. My characters in *Shinjuku Incident* and *Little Big Soldier* both died. And in Ding Sheng's *Police Story 2013*, I played an officer in a special police unit, which meant I needed cropped hair to be credible; otherwise I would have stood out as the only person on the force with long hair. And so I got a crew cut, my first since the brain operation in Yugoslavia. Had he lived, Leonard would have understood that times were changing, and my roles (and hairstyle) had to keep up.

Leonard taught me a lot about regular life. I remember him telling me, "If you're buying an apartment, first make sure the fire engine can get near the building, then check that the firemen's ladders can reach you, and stay away from the higher floors."

I still heed his advice. My apartment in Singapore is on the fourth floor. This way, if anything happens, I can jump out the window and grab hold of a nearby tree or railing.

Leonard was always there for me, especially in times of disappointment and struggle, to comfort and guide. I was sometimes too stubborn to listen. When my earliest ventures in America were unsuccessful, I felt defeated and returned to Hong Kong hoping to wipe the slate clean. Instead, my godfather suggested that I take a break, hang out with friends, and enjoy life a little. I didn't want to take his advice, and he said, "I hope one day you understand that life isn't only about work, but there are more important things to care about. And if you neglect them, you might find one day that you've left it too late." My thinking at the time was that anything might disappear at any time, and only the work that was recorded on film would last forever. My career was everything to me. I didn't take in what he was saying.

As I've gotten older, though, I've started understanding what he meant more and more. Recently, I've started putting more energy into maintaining my relationships with my family and friends, and I've started to treasure my life outside of work. Fortunately, it's not yet too late. For this lesson and so many others, Leonard's wise voice will always be in my head.

I didn't realize how little I knew about my father until he was very old and I was old enough to appreciate just how chaotic his life had been before he met my mother and had me.

When my dad retired and moved back to Hong Kong from Australia, I noticed he was sending money from the company to mainland China. He also went there in person, but he didn't tell me why, and I didn't ask. I've never liked prying into people's lives.

One day, a letter arrived at the company addressed to him as "my dear father." I was confused. I certainly hadn't written to him. I brought the letter to Dad and said, "Who is this from? There's a photo inside. Who's that in the photo?"

He didn't answer directly, just muttered, "Why so many questions?" I thought it was fine if he didn't want to tell me. I didn't really care. Back then, plenty of people in Hong Kong had multiple wives, and I thought it must be something like that.

Then I started hearing rumors that my surname wasn't Chan, and that it was actually Fong (or Fang in Mandarin). I thought, *No way. How could that be?* At the first opportunity, I asked my dad, and he shrugged it off: "I could talk all day and only dent the story. I'll explain it all to you when we have more time." This made me even more curious. What on earth could this be about?

Finally, the day came. Dad and I were driving along a road in Hong Kong, when he said, "Son, I'm getting old, and I'm afraid I'll fall asleep one day and never wake up, and then you'll never know your true history." Hearing him talk like this, I knew it must be a very complicated story. If that was the case, I'd better get the whole thing on tape so there'd be a permanent record.

I happened to be having dinner with the Hong Kong Film Directors' Guild that evening. During the meal, I looked around the room and tried to decide whom I should ask. Out of all the directors there, the most suitable for the job was Mabel Cheung. I approached her and asked if she'd be interested in turning my father's life story into a documentary. She got excited at the prospect and seemed very enthusiastic, so we made an agreement on the spot.

The filming process didn't go as smoothly as I'd hoped, though. Every day, the cameras would be ready, the lighting would be set up, and we'd be ready to roll, but we were always at the mercy of my dad's mood. Some days, he'd grumble impatiently, "What are we taping this for?" and storm off, and we'd have to wait to see if he came back. Then there were times when he'd abruptly turn to me and say, "So, let me tell you . . ." and we'd have to start rolling before we were prepared to. Other times, he'd talk and talk, then suddenly stop.

I asked, "Dad, is there more?"

He snapped, "Don't bother me when I'm fishing," get up, leave, and disappear for days.

While we were trying to shoot this, I had to take long breaks from the project to rush around all over the world making movies. In fits and starts, it took us three years to complete the documentary. We shot on film, so you can imagine how much it cost!

Traces of a Dragon came out in 2003 and told the pretty harrowing story of my parents' lives. Here is the very condensed version:

My dad was born in Shandong in 1915 and lived in Anhui and Jiangsu. He trained in Hung Gar martial arts between the ages of sixteen and nineteen. At twenty, he enlisted in the Nationalist Army at Nanjing as an orderly, and later went into military intelligence.

When the Japanese army invaded China, my dad was transferred to Anhui. There, he married his first wife, and had two sons named Fang Shide and Fang Shisheng. Not long after that, his wife died of cancer. When the Communist Revolution started, his military background made it unsafe for him to remain there, so he had to leave his two young sons and resume his life of wandering. My two older brothers were eight when they were abandoned by him, poor things. They later tried to find him, but couldn't.

My mother's father died before she was born. My grandmother adored her and raised her as a son. My grandma ran a grocery store and made a good living. My mother grew up to marry a businessman, the owner of a shoe shop. When the Japanese invaded, he got caught in the crossfire and died. My grandma urged my mom to sell his shop and escape. Still dressed in mourning, my mom left her two daughters behind and went to Shanghai on her own. She became a servant at a foreigner's house and a street peddler, and started to learn English.

Meanwhile, my dad was still on the run. He came to Shanghai and found work as a "dock fighter," a.k.a. a guard or hired muscle. My dad was out patrolling his area, and he caught my mom dealing opium. He felt sorry for a recent widow who'd had to resort to doing this kind of work, and so he let her go. Later, he found out she was actually notorious in Shanghai, and had quite the underground reputation. She was known as "Third Sister," and would often be seen smoking and gambling.

Fate threw the two of them together more and more, and they got to know each other. Once, my dad happened to notice my mom had a whole stack of pawn tickets, so he helped redeem all her stuff. Moved by his kindness, my mom resolved to give up gambling. Their lives settled down, and my mom moved her daughters to Shanghai.

In 1949, many Nationalists fled to Taiwan to escape the Communists. My dad changed his name from Fang Daolong to Chen

Zhiping (or Chan Chi-Peng in Cantonese) and escaped to Hong Kong. Two years later, my mom snuck into Hong Kong via Macau, leaving her daughters behind with relatives. The boat she was on was so overcrowded that five people died from suffocation. Mom almost fainted before she came ashore, but she managed to hang on. In Hong Kong, my dad got a job through a friend at one of the consulates on Victoria Peak. He'd never stepped into a kitchen before and didn't know how to do housework, so he started as a gardener while he learned to cook. Later, my mom got a job there, too.

These two lost souls got married in Hong Kong, and in 1954 they had me.

Now that I think of it, my mom's main characteristic was always frugality. I watched her tear up my dad's torn underpants to patch his other underpants. She never threw any clothes away, no matter how tattered they got, but would use them to patch other clothes. The seats of my father's boxers were networks of patches.

When I was in my teens, my mom was still wearing the same clothes she'd worn when I was a little kid. She saved all the tips from her job, adding them to her meager savings. In Australia, she'd often show me a box and tell me that inside was a bracelet worth a few hundred American dollars. One day, she asked me, "Son, could you lend me one hundred thirty dollars?" I asked why. She said, "If you let me have one hundred thirty dollars, I'll have enough to make up one thousand American dollars." She opened the box and showed me. It was full of two-, five-, and ten-dollar bills. Her tips from more than ten years of being a servant added up to $870. I felt so sad, I gave her $10,000 right away.

My mom passed away on February 28, 2002, before the documentary was released. One of her long-lost daughters came to care for her during her illness. I got to know both my half sisters. My father died almost six years to the day later, on February 26, 2008. In August 2013, I traveled to Anhui to meet my half brothers for the first time, along with many other people from that branch of my family, and it was very moving.

I wasn't with either of my parents when they died. During the final stages of my mom's illness, her private doctor told me, "There's no hope for a recovery. All she can do now is hang on for as long as she can."

I talked to Mom on the phone and was sorry to tell her that I had to go, that my movie wasn't finished yet, and that I was needed on set. I don't know if she heard, but she definitely understood. If I could have sat by her side every day, holding her hand and talking to her until she woke up, then I would have, but that was impossible.

I was in Thailand filming *The Medallion* at the time. I'd just set up a shot when someone said, "Jackie, you have a call from home."

It was the hospital. My mother was gone. I hung up and immediately shouted, "Move the camera over there, and let's keep rolling." No one on set knew what had happened.

After we were done with that scene, I found a Jeep at the studio, opened the door, got in, and started crying. I sat there weeping for a very long time.

My dad's last days were in Hong Kong. I visited him in the hospital every day, and watched helplessly as he got weaker and weaker. While he could still speak, I teased him, "Dad, when you're gone, I won't make offerings to you." Making offerings to your ancestors is a common practice in China.

He replied, "Fine, don't make offerings; it won't do any good."

Jaycee was with me. I turned to him and said, "And when I'm gone, you don't need to make offerings to me either. If you want to show how devoted you are, do it now. Don't wait until I'm gone."

Sometimes I ask myself if I should have been at my mom's side during her last days, looking after her, spending every waking minute with her until she was gone, and taking care of all the arrangements afterwards. Isn't that what it means to be a good son? But I don't feel guilt. I was a very good son. When my parents were alive, I treated them very well, and spent as much time with them as I could. They enjoyed everything there was to enjoy while they were on earth. I was able to help them do that.

Many people repeat the saying "The son wants to care for his parents, but they are already gone." You have to be good to your elders while they're still alive. Don't wait until it's too late and then do the rituals, like burning paper money, for them. Do you think that money *really* gets to them? It's all fake, just something we do to comfort ourselves or for others to see. Even now, I can't remember my parents' birthdays because I behaved as if every day was their birthday.

My parents' story is ordinary and extraordinary. I imagine that there were many similar tales of hardship during those turbulent years. I'm very lucky to have been their child, and I know they were proud of me, too.

chapter thirty-three

NATIONAL TREASURE

China used to measure time in twelve two-hour units. In the eighteenth century, the Qianlong emperor came up with a device that would squirt water once every two hours. He worked with artisans from both East and West and designed twelve bronze heads, one for each year of the Chinese zodiac—rat, ox, tiger, rabbit, dragon, snake, horse, sheep, monkey, rooster, dog, and pig—to decorate his fountain/clock at his grand summer palace, known now as the Old Summer Palace, part of the Imperial City sprawl in Beijing.

In the mid-nineteenth century, the palace was looted and destroyed by British and French troops, and the twelve heads were taken. Many have never been seen again. But some have surfaced and, in 2000, came to auction. The tiger head went for more than

$10 million, and its price continued skyrocketing afterwards. I tried to win some of the animal heads at auction, but I didn't get them. The prices were just too high. I asked a friend to keep an eye on the horse head for me. My spending limit was $30 million, but the bidding started at $60 million and it sold for $68 million.

I had dinner with some people from China Poly Group, and they told me, "Jackie, you should make a film about this. It would be such good subject matter!"

Over the years, I've been to Angkor Wat in Cambodia, where I've seen many half-destroyed Buddha statues, perfectly good bodhisattvas, with half their faces gone. I've been to Egypt and seen some of its treasures. When I saw a pharaoh's beard on display in another country, I asked the custodian, "Why hasn't this been returned to its country of origin?"

The answer was cute. "This is the world's heritage. It belongs to everybody," he said.

I wanted to say, "If it belongs to everybody, what's it doing on display here? Why not send it back?"

And then I got the idea for a film that combined the story of the twelve animal heads and the concept of national treasures being taken from their countries of origin and the effort of art activists to retrieve them. The movie became a self-financed passion project, seven years in the making, called *Chinese Zodiac*.

The first thing we needed to make the movie? The heads themselves. I didn't want to use shoddy replicas. That would be disrespectful to the audience, to the history, and to myself. I spent my own money to make some bronze heads for the movie and commissioned several more afterwards, spending up to $6 million in total. Whether you're making one head or a hundred, you first need to cast a mold. Making the mold was the most expensive part of the process. My team had to learn the techniques, pouring silica gel, creating a wax impression, and so on. There were many steps. We made more than forty heads in our first batch, but only six were usable.

I listened as the artisans discussed the process, but it all got too technical for me. Apparently, you can take only two wax impressions before the silica mold breaks. Then you need a new mold. But if it doesn't harden well enough when you pour the molten bronze in, it won't fill both nostril holes and, when you open it up, a piece will be missing. You can't just tack on the piece; you have to start from scratch.

We spent three years on this and ended up with only two sets. One was used for the film. I donated the other set, piece by piece, to various organizations, including the Olympic stadium, the Old Summer Palace, and the Military Science Museum. I might make a set for France and a set for the United Kingdom to remind them that these cultural artifacts belong to China.

When we started filming, the locations were known for seven of the twelve heads plundered from the Old Summer Palace. Another location was suspected, and the whereabouts of the other four were completely unknown. It's unlikely those four will ever turn up. Whoever has them is probably afraid to try to sell them now in the glare of the media, so the heads will stay locked away, hidden from the world. Or they might have been buried or destroyed during the course of history.

While making *Chinese Zodiac*, I couldn't help thinking about using the power of cinema to convince the current "owners" of the original bronze heads to return them to China. If someone stepped forward to return these heads to where they belong, even a single one, I'd consider my mission complete.

If you look back on my lifetime of work, the theme of plundered national treasures pops up again and again. More than thirty years ago, in *The Young Master*, I told the story of a gang shipping national treasures abroad, only to be foiled by a couple of kids. In *The Legend of the Drunken Master*, a treacherous foreign merchant wants to ship China's heritage overseas, but Wong Fei-Hung stops him. Then came *The Myth*, with that line that attracted a lot of attention: "No one should steal another country's history and display it in their museum, and then claim they're protecting these things. They just want to take these things for themselves. It's shameful." That belief motivated the entire plot of *Chinese Zodiac*.

I've always tried to transmit certain messages through my films. While doing publicity for *The Myth* in 2005, I told the media that if someone from another country saw this film and decided to return one of our cultural artifacts to us, wouldn't that be a very good thing? At the time, many people thought that wish was pie in the sky. They were right. Nothing happened.

I expressed it again while promoting *Chinese Zodiac* in 2012.

Behind the Scenes by Zhu Mo

François Pinault is one of the richest men in France, with a personal fortune of over $70 billion USD. He owns the Gucci luxury goods consortium and is an art collector with over two thousand pieces to his name. He is the biggest shareholder in Christie's auction house.

In April 2013, the Pinault family announced that they would return to China the two heads in their possession, the rabbit and the rat. The heads had been bought at auction in Paris in 2009 for more than 29 million dollars. The family didn't ask to be compensated for the return of the heads, which made a lot of people very happy, none more so than Jackie.

Was there a connection between *Chinese Zodiac* and the Pinault family's returning the heads? We had no idea at first.

In July 2013, one of Jackie's rich Singaporean friends happened to bump into the top executive of Gucci. When he brought up the animal heads, he was told that Mr. Pinault had decided to return them to China because he happened to watch *Chinese Zodiac* on a plane and the film convinced him.

Throughout the years of preparation and shooting the film, Jackie often thought there was a chance it could influence people to return China's lost treasures. It seemed like a beautiful dream, not something that might actually happen one day. And then, miraculously, it did.

Only we knew the truth. No one else put two and two together, and Jackie didn't go around blowing his own trumpet. Having been a publicist for seven years, I knew that if this had happened to any other star, there would have been umpteen articles and interviews about it. But Jackie didn't need the attention. He was just thrilled that his work had helped return national treasures to China.

chapter thirty-four

FOUR HOUSES IN SINGAPORE

Around the same time the zodiac heads were being returned to China, I wrote four posts on Weibo to announce I'd donated four old Chinese buildings to Singapore. This attracted a storm of criticism in China, but I don't regret it. Quite the opposite. Social media is a great way to see how people react, and I sort of expected this donation to be controversial. After all, I was sending examples of our classic architecture to another country. But there's a lot more to the story than that—like how I came to have them in the first place—and it wasn't something I could explain in a sentence or two.

The saga began many years ago. My parents had finally moved back to China, and I sent my assistant to look for a house for them. We saw place after place, but there was always something wrong.

The pathways were too narrow; there was no parking, no indoor bathroom, no air-conditioning, no heating.

Our search expanded to old-fashioned houses in the classic style, and we found some that could be had for next to nothing. But they were all so run-down, they had to be restored before my parents could live in them. I wound up buying one. It had only one intact beam in the whole place. The pillars were rotted through. Anything valuable and charming about it, like the cornices, had been sold off. I bought it anyway, and said that I paid $9,000 for one good beam. I got into old houses and would buy a dozen more—built between 1755 and 1858—for a lot more money, up to $1 million. I had them dismantled and shipped, piece by piece, to a giant warehouse in Shanghai, and hired a team of workers to restore them.

These houses were all in the same condition. The framework was original, but I had to refurbish everything else. For instance, if a statue was missing its head, I'd replace it. If something had been made of camphor wood, the replacement would be, too.

The process of rebuilding them was a nightmare. Every piece had to be washed, soaked, fixed, and laid out and then the whole structure reassembled before I could take a look at it. Each piece of wood had to be immersed in disinfectant for fifteen minutes and agitated the whole time by a worker's gloved hand. It took two years to restore a house completely. Then it would be reassembled for my approval, diagrammed, and taken apart again and mailed to me in Hong Kong. I had nowhere to store these buildings, so the main beams and pillars went into a good warehouse, and all the other bits of wood had to go somewhere more remote. That's how it was for many years, the buildings getting shipped over as each one was finished.

For the next two decades, those buildings sat in that warehouse while I fretted about what to do with them. Over time, they started to decay *again*, which meant more refurbishment. The whole endeavor became a stressful burden on me. I've lost count of how much money it cost me in total. I had to find these homes a home.

The reason I chose Singapore was very simple: I liked their sincerity.

A few years ago, I bought some British-style houses with no investment value in Singapore. A Singaporean government official came to see me and said, "Thank you. I guess you like these old buildings."

I replied, "That's right. Actually, I have some even older ones back in China." I happened to have the documents with me, so I showed the official some pictures and explained how I'd taken on the task of caring for and restoring these old buildings, which had become quite a chore.

She looked through everything and asked if she could try coming up with a solution for my problem. I was open to any suggestions, of course.

She went off with all the information, and less than a week later she got back in touch to say, "We have a piece of land for you. It's at the Singapore University of Technology and Design. You can bring your old buildings here. We'll pay for the shipping, maintenance, and all other costs."

The transfer would be treated as a cultural exchange, which

meant I had a great deal of freedom in how it would be carried out. When I read their detailed proposal, I was moved by how professional and thoughtful it all was, from the restoration and maintenance to the computer scanning, information gathering, and preparation. They truly believed these houses were valuable and sincerely hoped to be entrusted with them, which is why they'd come up with such a thorough plan. It's hard to find such dedication these days.

That was six years ago. At the time, I was in a rather odd state of mind. I could feel myself getting older and was thinking about no longer being around. Such thoughts made me feel desperate to donate and give away everything I had. The Singapore plan had the government's backing, and would place these buildings at a well-known university. The university was so great that, since it opened, Southeast Asian students have been clamoring to get in there and choosing it over colleges in New York. It sounded too good to be true. I had a lot of faith it would go well. I chose four of the buildings to send them right away.

They sent a team over to get them, led by the tourism and culture ministers. You could see they were taking this seriously. The artifact restorers and engineers came to Hong Kong to figure out the best way to deal with these buildings. They'd brought many scholars of ancient Chinese construction, whose knowledge was profound. I tried to understand their discussions, but they went over my head. After close examination, they told us what was missing from here, what was missing from there. In order to fully restore these buildings, we'd need to understand Chinese craftsmanship and find Chinese artisans to do it. We started advertising in China to find the best people for this project.

If you'd asked me if I was reluctant to put all this effort into finding and collecting these buildings, not to mention all the manpower, materials, and money that it cost to restore them and then give them away for no return on the investment to another country, I'd probably have said yes. But when I saw how seriously the Singaporeans treasured these items, carefully taking them apart and packing them for shipment to a piece of land the university had cleared for me, as well as constructing a big warehouse so each piece of wood could be marked, restored again, scanned by computer, dusted with insect powder, and blown dry, I knew my decision was the right one. I subsequently found some stone sculptures in China that I also gave to them to complete the set.

I asked only one thing: that the area on the university grounds would be a Chinese Cultural Exchange Garden, which would also help create an international conversation.

Patriotism isn't just about bringing things back to your country. I wanted to spread Chinese culture constantly so everyone will get to know it, which means some artifacts will need to leave the country. It's fine as long as they aren't one-of-a-kind national treasures like the zodiac animal heads. Those we must definitely bring home.

For another thing, these four buildings also needed to go to—and stay in—Singapore, because I didn't want to go back on my word. I have full confidence that Singapore will take good care of them indefinitely. Look how they maintain their own artifacts, and you'll see that they know what they're doing.

So, after all this, people on the Internet said things like "Jackie Chan claims to love his country, so why not keep these four buildings here?"

I'd actually tried to donate them to Hong Kong, but that didn't work. My home here is basically a tourist destination, and fans come from all over the world to raise a ruckus outside and knock at my door. Why not make a *real* sightseeing spot and put all my collections on display? For instance, the ancient houses could be laid out like a village, and there could be a museum. Everything would be on view.

I'd previously met with two of Hong Kong's chief executives for coffee to talk about this concept. They were worried about what people might say, like "Why haven't we created a memorial like this for Bruce Lee, or Leslie Cheung, or Anita Mui? Why should Jackie Chan get one?"

I understood their concerns. Any move they made might come off badly, so the safest choice would be to do nothing. Hong Kong is a small, densely populated place, and I certainly couldn't just have as much land as I needed for the project. The execs suggested putting the houses in Ocean Park. In that case, I asked if I would be able to visit late at night after the tourists were gone for the day. They said that wouldn't do. It made me sad to think I wouldn't be allowed into the buildings I'd donated. I suggested making one of the buildings into an office for me so I could use it as a base to keep an eye on the houses' condition and fix what needed fixing. They discussed that for a month and then said no. I'd spent a lot of money on these buildings and I wanted some access to them, even after giving them away. Was that too much to ask?

In the end, the Hong Kong officials offered me a piece of parkland, but it was just too small. I turned it down. I thought of taking out a lease on some land myself, but that didn't work out. I don't really understand these things, so no matter how I tried to talk it through with various civil servants, as well as the government, no one would budge.

It was just a shame. I was born in Hong Kong, I became famous in Hong Kong, and yet this city doesn't have one thing named after me, not a thing. Even my props from decades in the movie business are now displayed at the Jackie Chan Film Gallery—in Shanghai.

I *also* tried to arrange a location with organizations in mainland China, but none of the four people I spoke to wanted to do this. They'd talk about monetizing the buildings as commercial properties, or else come up with nice-sounding plans that never materialized. I discovered that they were all property schemes to lure me in. They'd suggest a Jackie Chan Garden or something, but right next to it would be a luxury villa development they wanted to sell. What was the point of that? Wouldn't a plan like that attract just as much criticism as donating the buildings to Singapore? I beat a retreat. After being messed around with for so long, I'd learned to judge for myself. Whenever anyone offered to take the buildings off my hands, I'd first investigate how they managed their own buildings. That became my first criterion for basic trust. Then I'd see if they were more interested in using me or if they were genuinely interested in preserving the houses.

In the end, Singapore fit the bill. The overwhelming winner. I announced on Weibo that I was giving these four buildings to Singapore. And then everyone suddenly sat up and took notice, and many more organizations came forward to talk. The uptick in interest meant I'd gone about this the right way. There are so many old houses in China, and I hoped that various local governments would pay more attention to them and think about how to take better care of them. For instance, they could set up a fund just for this purpose. I travel all over the world, and when I'm in small towns in France, Italy, or Germany, I see buildings many centuries old being taken care of very well. Hardly any original architecture is preserved in small Chinese towns. They've all been destroyed or sold off. When you look at "before" pictures of the buildings I've collected, you can see right away that their pillars and cornices were gone, ripped out and sold off long ago. This project of mine did indeed get the attention of the Chinese government and the public. That made me very happy. I really hope more people learn to cherish our cultural artifacts and realize we need to take good care of the ones we have left so our own people and travelers from other countries can see what small Chinese towns used to look like.

I've been in talks with Beijing about exactly this, and they are moving along. The direction ahead is getting clearer. The commercialization I feared will not happen. We're going to put up some buildings (not those original four—they are already in Singapore) and create a Jackie Chan Peace Garden that will include both environmental and cultural elements. Cultures from all over the world will be represented, and there'll also be lectures, and maybe a clock-striking ceremony to mark the New Year. I hope we can make this garden happen.

When I bought these buildings decades ago, they were standing neglected and exposed to the elements. If I hadn't purchased them, they'd probably be completely ruined by now. I didn't buy them because I thought they were national treasures. At the time, no one was talking about the importance of preserving historic buildings, and honestly, it's only because of my fame that we are paying attention to it now.

The original four buildings are now erected and on display at the Singapore University for Technology and Design, and they look fantastic. If you're in the area, take a look!

As for the debate over whether old houses count as cultural artifacts, the answer is yes. I've spoken to experts from the National Museum, and they say the buildings I've chosen were all once the homes of wealthy folk, and the handiwork in them is rare and exquisite, with uniquely Chinese architectural features. They aren't actually considered antiquities, though, because they're just not old enough.

In total, I bought more than ten of these buildings. Four are in Singapore. The rest will go to Beijing and other parts of China. Their value is now widely acknowledged; one sold at auction for $22 million. I also hope to find a place in Hong Kong for a couple of them. I yearn to leave something of mine in Hong Kong. When my parents were still alive, I was anxiety-ridden about how long it took to restore these homes. I didn't know when they'd ever be able to move into one of them. Then my mom passed away, and my dad followed soon after, so I never got my wish to create a beautiful home that my parents would enjoy in their final years. I'm in my sixties now, and my anxiety about finding my houses a home hasn't let up. If I don't give them away to careful custodians before I die, they'll just end up as so much wooden rubbish. Whenever Jaycee comes by my office and sees me working on them, he has zero interest. He's not the person to continue this work after I'm gone. I don't know who is! So while I still have time, I hope to get them off my hands as soon as possible.

After my decision to send the original four to Singapore and the criticism I got online, my friends were indignant on my behalf. They said to me, "Jackie, you've spent so much of your own money on these things, tens of millions from acquiring them to restoring them, not seeing any return on the investment, and you're still being criticized! Doesn't that upset you?"

It's been a few years since I first posted about this on Weibo. By now, I'm used to it. Even my staff is used to it. As I always say, "You can't please everyone, just strive not to feel guilty about it," "Whatever you do, heaven is watching," and "The innocent know themselves to be innocent." I make sure that in everything I do, I'm not letting down my country or my people. I can only do what I think is right. As long as I haven't gone against my conscience, then I'm happy, and that's how it's been for many years.

At this point in my life, what desires do I have left? Fame? I'm already very famous. Money? I haven't been poor for a long time. I can pack a rucksack and fly off in my own jet whenever I like. I could retire and circle the globe if I wanted to. But I want to stay busy, stay involved. That's what makes me happy. All these years, I've walked through a storm of criticism. I'm grateful to the people who've scolded me and who hate me. It's because of them that I'm constantly examining myself to see if I'm doing the right thing. When I realize that I might be doing the wrong thing, I'm glad to be called out, and I change. I'm also grateful to the people who praise me. Having people in my corner inspires me to work harder, and gives me the energy to try to be better in every way.

chapter thirty-five

FOR THE FANS

If it weren't for Jackie Chan fans, there would be no Jackie Chan! I've met a lot of my fans over the years and have tons of stories about them—crazy, strange, touching, scary, the works.

I'll start with the legendary "tattoo guy." In December 2012, I took the train to Shenyang as part of the publicity tour for *Chinese Zodiac*. As I entered the movie theater to meet the public, I saw him there. This man had been a fan for many years, and the names of many of my films were tattooed on his back. He'd just added *Chinese Zodiac* to the list. He'd brought his child to meet me, and I gave him a padded jacket from my own line.

My most ardent fans have to be Japanese girls, especially early on. They've always been able to find out my itinerary and will buy plane tickets to follow me all over the world. When they learn which hotel I'm staying in, they'll book every room on my floor, three or four girls per room. They've never bothered me, but as soon as I step out into the corridor, all their doors swing open at once.

Sometimes, local friends take me out for a meal after we've wrapped for the day, and much as I'd like to relax, it's a challenge. After work, I need to go back to my room and change, because it would be ridiculous to go out in a tuxedo. The fans often follow me. So when I go back and then leave again, they'll all open their doors and stare, so much that I don't dare step out, knowing they'll show up wherever I go.

I've tried stealth, tiptoeing out and whispering to my friends, "Let's go," but no matter how quiet I am, as soon as I step into the corridor, every other door swings open and they come out. I'll get embarrassed and say, "Oh, I was just coming out to say hello to you all. I'm going to bed now."

After going through this a few times, it began to feel awful. I couldn't go anywhere, couldn't even pop out to get some food. At night, as long as my light was still on, they wouldn't sleep but would keep waiting. I like to stay up late but didn't want to keep them up, so I'd block the crack beneath the door with a hotel towel so they wouldn't be able to see my light and I wouldn't have to worry about going to sleep as late as I liked.

When the light went dark, the girls went to bed. After discovering this tactic, I started waiting for this to happen, then sneaking out with my friends in the dark, late in the night.

By now, many of my early Japanese fans are middle-aged. When

I do publicity in Japan, they still show up with their children—and grandchildren! They really are devoted.

Fans from all over the world come to my office in Hong Kong to stand outside and wait to see me. The office has two doors. If I'm rushing into a meeting, my employees will phone me first and let me know if there are a lot of fans waiting out front, in which case I should come in the back door instead. I always do as they suggest.

Years ago, when travel between the mainland and Hong Kong wasn't so easy, not too many of the waiting fans were from China. One time, I'd just been awarded an honorary doctorate in sociology. Feeling pleased with myself after the ceremony, I returned to the office. I still had a banquet to prepare for, as well as some interviews, so I was in a hurry. As I passed the entrance, I saw a young boy. Though it was cold, he was wearing only a torn, dirty sweater. My car zoomed past him into the compound, but then I kept thinking about him waiting outside, shivering. I sent someone out to talk to him. It turned out he was a devoted fan from the mainland who'd gone through a lot of trouble and expense to get to Hong Kong, all to catch a glimpse of me.

I stopped what I was doing and told my assistant to bring him inside. He walked into my office clutching three thick scrapbooks. He was so cold, his nose wouldn't stop running. I asked someone to pour him a cup of hot tea, and we got him to sit down and warm up. I flipped through the scrapbooks, then stood up and patted him on the shoulder. He started to cry, perhaps overwhelmed by what he'd been through and the excitement of realizing his goal. I had no idea what to do. He just sat there crying! We fetched him some signed photos, some other little souvenirs, and after half an hour he left the building smiling, which was a lot better than shivering and crying!

A German man used to wait outside my office every day clutching a suitcase. When my employees asked him in for a glass of water or offered him a small autographed gift, he ignored them and stayed put. After passing by him several days in a row, I felt sorry for him and sent a message that I would like to see him. He came in trembling all over. I asked why he stood there every day, and he told me he had only one dream, and that was to join my stunt team. He'd come all the way to Hong Kong determined not to return to his country until he'd seen me and gotten his wish.

I turned and asked my assistant to bring him to the set the next day. I was shooting *Crime Story* at the time, and I thought I might as well just bring him onto the team. He asked if he should demonstrate some kung fu, and I said, "No need, you have to learn first."

The next morning, he turned up on set and carried out chores alongside the rest of the team, moving stuff, laying out landing mats, and so on. He did well. Based on past experience with my more intense fans, I knew I shouldn't get too close too quickly—otherwise he might go off the rails—so I didn't say a word to him on set and didn't invite him to join me at mealtimes. He ate with the rest of the stunt team.

Sometime later, my assistant came and told me the German guy wanted to go home because his mom was ill, but he couldn't afford the ticket. I said, "Fine, buy him a ticket." A week later, he was back again. I asked him what was up, and his reason made everyone bend over laughing.

"Everything since I came here and met you, worked in the studio, and went home all feels like a dream," he said. "In the week I was back in Germany, when I told everyone what happened, no one believed me. They all thought I was making it up. It got to the point that I don't believe it myself. Did you really take me in and give me a job? I forgot to take a photo as proof. So I'm back again to take a picture with you to show them."

I took a photo with him, and he went off with it. A few years later, when I was promoting *The Karate Kid* in Germany, I saw him calling my name from the crowd. It was a pleasant surprise. I asked how he was doing, and he said he was a fight director in Germany now. This made me happy. Now that I think of it, his kung fu skills were pretty good.

For a while, a Japanese girl would show up on set every day. She got in the habit of checking my schedule at the Golden Harvest studio in Hong Kong. There was a spot where the next day's schedule would be posted, saying what was filming when, with which actors. We always checked it before leaving for the day, and she learned to do the same.

I'd see her every day at the studio, always leaning against a wall so only half her face was visible. She would stare at me, her eyes following me wherever I went. If I moved, she'd find a different wall to lean against and keep staring. If any other woman spoke to me, she'd glare at her with hatred. After a while, I started to feel sorry for her. It couldn't be easy doing what she did. I told the crew to ask her to join them for meals. I've always liked eating with others. I sat in the private room eating and got the crew to sit outside with her.

Sometimes, when she saw me, she'd greet me with an "*Ohayou*" and a wave of her hand; then she'd swiftly stuff a piece of paper into my hand. These notes were quite normal to start with, just good-luck wishes and so forth, but their contents slowly changed. For instance, she wrote, "I know you can't acknowledge me openly, but that's all right, as long as you keep looking at me, I'll know that the connection between our hearts is still alive." She'd learned Chinese for my sake, and although there were grammatical problems with her writing, I was able to understand what she meant. Her first notes were signed Yumiko, but then she switched to "Mrs. Chan." That was how she introduced herself to other people at the studio: "Hi, I'm Mrs. Chan."

She was in Hong Kong on a regular tourist visa, so she needed to leave Hong Kong from time to time. She'd go to Macau and come right back. Later on, she didn't even bother to do that. When the immigration department tracked her down and asked her to leave, she told them she was my wife. The officials were perplexed by this. *Huh? Jackie Chan's wife?* Even though they didn't quite believe her, they still extended her visa. When she kept doing this, they phoned my company and learned the truth. By the end, she started running out of money and was staying in worse and worse hotels. I knew she couldn't go on like this, and I couldn't bear to let her continue throwing her life away on a delusion.

She really scared us one time. We'd wrapped and were in post-production. When she no longer saw me at the studio, she asked around until she found out where I lived. One night, we were watching the latest cut, and didn't finish until four in the morning. We got out of the car and hurried to the office. As we turned into the corridor, she suddenly popped out of a dark corner and said hi to me. My colleagues and I got quite a fright; it was like something from a horror film. After a few such incidents, everyone was really scared. She was still calling herself Mrs. Chan. We had to call the immigration department and have her sent home. This was very sad, but there was truly no other way. If she'd stayed, who knows what she'd have ended up doing.

I used to have a Christmas party every year for my fans. Hundreds or even thousands of people showed up—four thousand in our biggest year. Guests would come to Hong Kong from all over the world, and I'd have ten or more buses at the airport to pick them up, with "Jackie Chan International Fan Club" written on the side. Hong Kong's not very big, so the whole city knew about it whenever I did something like this, because all the hotels would be full to bursting. If I happened to be filming at the time, I'd have the buses bring my fans to the set, two busloads at a time. Each batch would have to leave before the next could come; otherwise there wouldn't have been room.

At these parties, sixteen members of the stunt team would stand around me as bodyguards and assistants. I'd meet and greet while they distributed souvenirs and took photos. The fans would stand in line and hand over their cameras before coming over. As I shook their hands, the stunt team would take a picture and hand them a gift. With so many people attending, we needed this kind of efficient system. Walk over, shake hands, take a photo, get a gift, leave—next, please. I used to sign autographs, too, but that ended up taking almost an entire day, so now I don't do that.

Once, a girl stepped up and said in English, "May I . . ."

There were a lot of people on line, and I couldn't understand what she'd said, so I just said, "Sure, all right."

She raised her hand and lightly slapped me on the face. I was stunned, and so were my bodyguards. No one had expected this. "Okay," I said. She left, and the next person stepped up.

She came again the next year and stood on line for an autograph. I dropped my pen, and when I bent down to pick it up, she slapped me in the face, hard this time. I stared at her in shock, but she just smiled at me. The stunt team guys were about to grab her, but I said, "It's fine, don't worry." She smiled again and departed. The other girls in the line were sobbing at the sight, but I told them not to worry, and we continued.

When she showed up *again* the following year and slapped me again, I'd had enough. What was wrong with her? After the event, I said to my team, "Keep an eye on her; find out what her deal is." Why would she do this three years in a row? They got the security footage from all three years and searched for her on the tapes. It turned out she'd changed her appearance each time. Different hair, different clothes.

When she came a fourth time, as soon as she stepped off the plane onto the bus, my staff recognized her. At the event, the stunt team all knew who she was and kept their eyes fixed on her. She walked over and smiled, but as soon as she raised her hand, the bodyguards grabbed it and dragged her to one side.

The fan club leader asked her, "Why did you do that?"

The slapper said placidly, "Now I've proved that you remember me, so he'll remember me, too." Everyone stared, eyes wide. What kind of fan was this?

"But now we'll have to ban you from future events."

"That's all right," she said calmly. "I'm happy watching from afar."

When they told me about this, I abruptly remembered that John Lennon was shot dead by a fan and felt a jolt of fear. Compared to that, though, a slap is nothing. But could it escalate?

At future events, I started shaking with my left hand. While the photo was taken, I put my right hand on their backs, and after the click gave them a gentle push to send them on their way so the next one could step up. If they made any sudden moves, I was holding their left hand, and could block with my right. My staff began doing stricter checks, making sure no one had anything dangerous on them.

It's now been years since I've done one of these events. I've also become less alert. I ran into that woman unexpectedly a while ago. I was standing onstage at some event, and she was in the audience. Just before the end, I waved good-bye, and noticed a woman in the audience waving frantically at me. When I went closer to see what she wanted, she stood up and tried to slap me, but my reflexes were quick enough and I jumped out of the way. When I looked closely, I realized it was her. She'd changed her appearance again. After so many years, when I'd almost forgotten about her, she'd appeared again, as determined to smack me as ever.

There was also a woman from the Philippines. She bought a one-way ticket and came to Hong Kong, where she stood outside my office every day. My staff told her I was in America, so she bought a plane ticket there. She thought I was in San Francisco, but I was actually living in LA. Then San Francisco organized a "Jackie Chan Day" with the mayor attending. The event ended with me riding down the street in a convertible. Suddenly, I saw this woman, screaming from across the road.

I'd seen her in Hong Kong before. I thought, *What's she doing here?*

The next day, I had to be in Sacramento for a charity auction. As soon as I got to the hotel lobby, there she was, red lipstick, red dress, red leather shoes, red suitcase. She ran toward me. "I came all the way here just for you," she said.

I replied, "Thank you, thank you."

She followed me everywhere after the event. I stepped into the elevator and she tried to rush in. The security guard said, "I'm sorry, you can't come in."

She pointed at me and said, "I'm with him," but was held back anyway, and so I made my escape upstairs.

Later on, the hotel staff came knocking on my door to say the woman had nowhere to stay and had told them she was my girlfriend. I explained that, no, she wasn't, and could they please find her somewhere else?

I was supposed to leave at six the next morning. Before I could go, the security guard came to me and said, "That woman's still in the lobby."

I felt sorry for her, so I thought I'd go and say hello at least. The guard said, "It would be better if you didn't go to her. The car's parked outside, and we'll get you straight in as soon as you reach the lobby. Our job is to ensure your safety, so I hope you'll do as we suggest." I was going to argue, but this little speech convinced me.

I looked down from my room window. A woman in red was standing on the sidewalk. She noticed my car pull up at the hotel entrance and knew I was about to come down. It felt heartless to ignore her, so I said to the guard, "Maybe I should just speak to her. She's waited all night for me, and what could a woman do to me?"

But they insisted, "No way. If anything goes wrong, it'll be our responsibility."

"All right, forget it, we'll do as you say."

"We'll go down now, you'll get in the first car, and we'll drive away."

There were three cars, parked on either side of the road. I reached the ground floor and walked straight into the one across the road. The girl had been by the entrance, keeping watch on the other car. When mine started, she looked shocked and then ran, full speed, toward me. I'll never forget the sight.

I turned around and watched through the rear window as she sprinted after my car. Before long, she dropped her suitcase. Then she lost her high-heeled shoes. A few steps later, she fell to the ground. It was like a scene from a movie. It hurt my heart to see it play out. I actually felt tears in my eyes. Had it been cruel not to give her a minute?

Soon after, she showed up at my LA home, standing at the

entrance and refusing to leave. My staff had to call the police to get rid of her.

Soon after *that*, I was giving a concert in Las Vegas. She phoned my staff to say she'd planted a bomb at the venue. They called the police, who cleared and sealed the building, then searched the whole place with dogs. They didn't find anything. It was a false alarm, though it still caused us a lot of trouble. She was out of control. From then on, we were on high alert, in case she did something really stupid or dangerous.

I've been through too many of these experiences. My stunt team have a saying: "Eyes always on Jackie." They want to protect me, and I need to pay attention, too, to make sure strangers don't get too close.

Anywhere I go in the world, I always find flowers and cards at my hotel room door. All sorts of things, funny and adorable. These often have weird messages. Some say, "I'll wait for you in Room XX, I don't need anything else from you, but I want to have your baby. Don't worry, I won't tell anyone."

Some say that connections between people are just a matter of fate, and I'm grateful that I've connected with so many fans in this lifetime. I dedicate these words to all my lovable, crazy fans.

kicker

The philosopher Zhuangzi once wrote, "Human existence is like a white horse galloping past a half-open door; you catch a glimpse of it, then it's gone."

I remember, many years ago, I was in an airport in some country or other when an old man stopped me to say, "Jackie, can I have your autograph?"

I was hurrying along with a lot of people, but turned back to say, "Maybe next time."

He smiled at my retreating back and said, "Next time? I may not get to see you again in my life."

I kept walking, but his words stuck in my mind. I'd already gone through the gate, but I came back out and called to him, "Sir, please come back, I'll give you my autograph now."

The world isn't that big, but it's not that small either, and connections between two human beings are always a little mystical. Zhu Mo and I needed three years to write this book—a turbulent time for me—and it's been a revealing experience for me to reflect about my life with her, and to share it with you. Whenever I hesitated, I recalled my stunt team's motto: "We don't ask why, we just do or die."

Now that you've read my book, you know the ultimate truth about me. I'm just an ordinary person, but I've dared to do some extraordinary things.

The question I have to ask myself now is how much longer I can continue to do extraordinary things.

Many years ago, when I went to America to see Jaycee, I exclaimed, "Wow, you're so tall!" It had been a while since I'd last seen him, and he'd suddenly shot up. Every time since then, I've had a strange fear whenever I see him again, and it feels a bit unreal. So I have a son, and he's already this old. When he's not with me, I'm relaxed to be all by myself, and I feel very young. But then I see him, and I become an old dad again. I have to put on a stern face and be all solemn. For thirty-five years, it's been like this. And now I look at him and worry that he's going to marry and have kids, which would make me a grandfather. The horror!

A few nights ago, I couldn't get to sleep. I thought that if I live until I'm eighty, I'll be dead in sixteen years. All of a sudden, I was so scared. I imagined myself lying underground, eaten by bugs, and decided I should get cremated instead. Then I thought that if Jaycee also lived to be eighty, he'd be gone from the world in less than half a century. How cruel. I felt a giant ball of fire growing inside my body, blazing painfully. I jumped out of bed and started doing some exercises, working up a sweat until those thoughts were gone.

I guess this is what happens if you are lucky enough to have a long life.

If I do have only a short time left, I will make good use of it. As far as retirement goes, all along I've wanted to find a good reason and a way to step down gracefully. I have been thinking about when the right moment would be. I don't want audiences to look at me on-screen and think, *He's too old to still be fighting.* I've imagined them shouting from their seats, "Please, stop now! This is pathetic to watch."

There aren't that many action stars from my generation still in the business. Many have moved on to making movies about guns, which are a bit easier to handle at our age, rather than continuing to slug it out like I am.

Is it time for me to stop?

I first started thinking about retirement in my forties. The fighting might have looked slick to audiences, but they couldn't see the pain behind the glamour. Most people wouldn't be able to comprehend the agony I've felt taking a shower at night, or not being able to straighten my back in the morning. I often told myself that I was forcing myself to do things no human should do, but then I forgot all about that when the pain passed. And whenever I stood in a movie theater, watching audiences clap and cheer, all the suffering went to the back of my mind, and I thought only of how I could do even better next time, jump even higher.

I think I'll hold on for another year or two and see how it goes. Maybe my best work is yet to come. For a while now, I've taken on roles that show people that I'm a legitimate actor as well as a martial arts performer, notably in *Gorgeous*, *The Myth*, *Shinjuku Incident*, *The Karate Kid*, *New Police Story*, *Police Story: Lockdown*, and *The Foreigner*. I have evolved to become an actor who can move, not a martial artist who happens to act as well. You have to adapt to changing times—and changing bodies. That's the only way I'll be able to stay in this profession.

What's the best way to go out? Bruce Lee left at a young age, and so became a legend. If I'd jumped *into* the volcano during the filming of *Chinese Zodiac*, it would have been a beautiful exit. Fans all over the world would have wept for me, and everyone would be talking about how Jackie Chan sacrificed his life to cinema. That would have been great, but there was a problem with it: I didn't want to die. I don't want to retire either. Sometimes I wonder if I should just vanish suddenly one day, just pack a bag and fly a plane to somewhere. That might be the way to do it.

But I probably never will. I hope that, when the time is right, I'll know when to stop working. I'll take care of myself. Or I'll keep plugging away and fighting until the very end. Either way, I just hope the audiences won't judge me too harshly.